Dear Lois—

you are exceptional and bright

is even more than I could have hoped for—

Thanks
&
love

Rich

ADVENTURES WITH D. W. GRIFFITH

KARL BROWN

Adventures with

D. W. GRIFFITH

But you the pathways of the sky
  Found first and tasted heavenly springs
Unfettered as the lark that sings
  And knew strange raptures—though we sigh,
"Poor Icarus!"

F. E. COATES

FARRAR, STRAUS AND GIROUX
New York

Library of Congress catalog card number: 72–97001

ISBN 0–374–10093–4

First printing, 1973
Printed in the United States of America
Published simultaneously in Canada by Doubleday Canada Ltd., Toronto
Designed by Gus Niles

CONTENTS

ILLUSTRATIONS

ENDPAPERS: The members of Griffith's stock company inscribed their names on a message of good wishes for Karl Brown, on his departure for Camp Kearny.

A thirty-six page insert of photographs will be found following page 156.

FOREWORD

by KEVIN BROWNLOW

Karl Brown was an eyewitness to the most momentous occasions in the history of the cinema—the making of *The Birth of a Nation* and *Intolerance*. As assistant cameraman to the great G. W. Bitzer, Karl Brown was on the firing line of all the D. W. Griffith pictures from 1913 until *Broken Blossoms* and Griffith's departure for New York.

Following his years with Griffith, Karl Brown joined Famous Players–Lasky and gained a firm place in the history books for his remarkable photography of *The Covered Wagon* (a second volume is in production dealing with Famous Players, James Cruze, Roscoe Arbuckle . . .). He turned director in 1926, and it was his first directorial assignment, *Stark Love,* that led indirectly to the writing of this book.

Stark Love was a documentary-style feature, shot entirely in the mountains of North Carolina, among a people scarcely aware of civilization. The film had been lost in America, but it had been preserved by Myrtil Frida of the Czech Film Archive. He considered it one of the finest silent films ever made.

I shared his enthusiasm and wrote an article for *Film* magazine entitled "How Could We Forget a Film Like This?" The Czech archive eventually presented its original print to the Museum of Modern Art in New York. As a result of my article, the museum called me at the American Film Institute in California; could I find out if Karl Brown was still alive? The people I checked with were uncertain, but the American Society of Cinematographers were of the opinion that he had died in the nineteen thirties.

Karl Brown was someone I had dreamed of meeting ever since I first saw a tinted print of *The Covered Wagon;* his breathtaking photography (so despoiled in grainy dupes) combined qualities of Mathew Brady and Frederic Remington. Having spent months hunting directors and cameramen of the silent era in Hollywood, I was convinced that were Karl Brown alive, someone would have told me. I reported back to the museum that I had no positive news, and soon afterward returned to England.

When the American Film Institute presented *Stark Love* at its Washington theater, archivist David Shepard tried to find out about Karl Brown for himself. He contacted historian George Mitchell, who, as a former army intelligence officer, did the obvious thing. He simply looked him up in the Los Angeles telephone directory. There was one Karl Brown. The number, however, was disconnected. Was it the same Karl Brown? And was he still alive?

Mitchell succeeded in tracing the assistant cameraman on *Stark Love,* Robert Pittack, who confirmed that he had been in touch with Brown four years earlier. Mitchell was hard at work on a film, however, and since he lived some distance from Los Angeles, he had no opportunity to continue the search. When I returned from England, he suggested I take up the hunt.

From that point, in December 1969, I subordinated all other activities to the search for Karl Brown, which was as frustrating and as obsessive as the one in *Citizen Kane*. The ending, however, was considerably more rewarding. It turned out that Karl Brown was living with his wife in North Hollywood. He had retired after fifty years in the motion-picture business, having achieved his aim: "obscurity on a comfortable income."

If I feel little remorse at having shattered this obscurity, it is because he proved such a gold mine of vital information. Every visit with a tape recorder produced astonishing material. It soon became clear, however, that no amount of interviewing would result in the fidelity and precision that Brown could provide himself. If only he could be persuaded to write a book . . . I remembered with gloom his remark that he had abandoned writing and that he used his typewriter only for his checks.

Nevertheless, at the urging of historian Jay Leyda, I mentioned the matter in a letter. As usual, Karl Brown was way ahead of me. His reply was a carefully thought-out list of chapters and their contents. The project was under way almost before I had gathered the courage to bring it up. This pattern continued as the book was written: Brown always seemed to know what was happening before I had told him.

He turned the book out in record time. Each chapter arrived on its own, impeccably typed, and so carefully structured that the term "editing" became a euphemism for a cozy afternoon's read.

"I am keeping away from all cinema research," he wrote, "for the simple reason that I want to keep my memory 'pure,' if that makes sense. I cannot permit this book to be a pastiche of carefully rewritten quotes. What's the thing we used to say about that? 'Steal from one and it's plagiarism; steal from two and it's research; steal from fifty and it's scholarship.'"

Brown asked me to correct whatever howlers there might be with extensive footnotes, but his extraordinary memory provides few opportunities for additions or corrections. He has provided so much new information that most published sources are rendered obsolete.

The book is indisputably authentic. In my opinion, it represents the most exciting, the most vivid, and the most perceptive volume of reminiscence ever published on the cinema. (It is also one of the few that bears no trace of a ghost writer.) Instead of reciting bare facts, Brown has given the events the kind of vitality that Griffith would have admired. His word portraits bring the people to life in such a way that film history will never seem the same again.

The book will have a particular appeal to those setting out to make their own films. For this is a dramatic, and often hilarious, story of a boy trying to cope with a complex technical process and helping to make history. It will have a much wider appeal than the majority of film books, for it is basically about *people*. And above all, like the best films, it is extremely entertaining. Everyone who loves the cinema should be profoundly grateful that when D. W. Griffith was working on his greatest pictures, Karl Brown was there—on our behalf.

I want to acknowledge the help I have received from the Oral History Department of the American Film Institute in my search for Karl Brown. I am also grateful to the following individuals for their help in reading the manuscript and/or the proofs, correcting errors and making suggestions. Some of their points have been incorporated in signed footnotes. These individuals are DeWitt Bodeen, Eileen Bowser, William K. Everson, George Geltzer, Jay Leyda, George Mitchell, George Pratt, David Shepard, Anthony Slide, and David Thaxton.

ADVENTURES WITH D. W. GRIFFITH

$\mathcal{O}\, 1\, \mathcal{O}$

A Rainbow Passes

*Wise people are foolish if they cannot
adapt themselves to foolish people.*

MONTAIGNE

KINEMACOLOR, which had brought me, a kid in short pants, from New York to Hollywood, which had taught me all the closely guarded secrets of color cinematography, was in the year 1913 dying, a forlorn victim of box-office malnutrition.

Why? Because Kinemacolor required the expert care of specially trained technicians to make its glories come to life. It had begun with royalty no less, having recorded in full faithful color the great Durbar staged in India to commemorate the accession of George the Fifth. Every true Briton throughout the empire felt bound to see this picture, if it took his last farthing. It took time—two years at least, because the color could be shown only with a specially designed projector—as the film traveled the world from London to Cape Town and from New York to Sydney.

The profits were so huge that the Kinemacolor Company decided to go into commercial production. In that decision lay the cause of its eventual downfall, for Kinemacolor was expensive. There were not enough theaters equipped with the Kinemacolor projectors, or enough projectors, or enough free grand spectacles to be filmed. What Kinemacolor really needed was another Durbar, but George the Fifth was in remarkably good health.

The one theater in the Los Angeles area equipped to show Kinemacolor pictures was the California, at Ninth and Main. I went there regularly to see our pictures, because my job of developing negative kept me literally in the dark as to what was happening outside on the open stages. Our little one-reel pictures were made to exploit color for color's sake. There was one about a hospital fire, showing lots of flames; another, from a Hawthorne story about a pumpkin that becomes a man, showed up the golden yellow of the carved jack-o'-lantern very well indeed. There was another about British soldiers, featuring the red and gold and white of their uniforms.

The audiences at the California seemed to care nothing about our beautiful colors. What they wanted was raw melodrama and lots of it, and what seemed to stir them most of all was the steady flood of pictures made by a man named D. W. Griffith, formerly of Biograph but now, late in 1913, a free agent making his own way and sweeping all opposition away by the sheer audacity of his conceptions. This fellow Griffith seemed to delight in scorning tradition. He moved back into the caveman days, and showed long-necked reptiles and savage cavemen and a weak little lad who somehow managed to fit a string to a bent stick of wood and with this shoot a sharp stick—*zingg!*—right into the belly of a horrible, club-waving enemy.

Then there was *Judith of Bethulia,* in which the lushly opulent Judith gets another monstrous giant dead drunk, after which she cuts off his head with his own sword. The huge figure of the wine-guzzling Holofernes fascinated me. I had never before seen so much man in one piece. He towered over everyone in the picture. I wondered who he was and where they'd found him. In some circus, I supposed, but when I mentioned this at the studio, everybody laughed at me. This "giant" was Henry Walthall, a small man made to seem huge by the magic of Griffith's cameraman, Billy Bitzer. No, they didn't know how it was done, but only that Bitzer was a wizard who could do anything with a camera. So now I had to find out, any way at all, how this particular trick had been done. I was sixteen, and as curious as a dog's nose about everything, whether it concerned me or not. It was the sort of itch that Kipling poeticized as "Something hidden. Go and find it."

Meanwhile, I was a regular patron of the California out of loyalty to Kinemacolor. One night I bought my ticket and took my place at the end of the line. There was a big, specially featured Biograph picture, *The Battle at Elderbush Gulch,** directed by that same old everlasting D. W. Griffith. His pictures kept cropping up everywhere you looked, there was no avoiding them: if you dodged *The New York Hat* in one movie house, you'd run bang into *Pippa Passes* in another. I disliked this fellow Griffith for the way he hogged all the audiences. Then I saw something that made me despise him all the more. For the first time in weeks, the California was *not* showing a Kinemacolor. They'd taken it off to make room for this big two-reel special —by Griffith, of course. I seethed.

* Biograph officially released *The Battle at Elderbush Gulch* in the U.S. on March 28, 1914 (it had previously been released in England). In those days films were occasionally pre-released in individual theaters ahead of national distribution. KEVIN BROWNLOW

The waiting line was moving up. When more came out, we went in, to occupy the still-warm seats they had left. There was a short, expectant wait. Then the picture title came on, *The Battle at Elderbush Gulch,* bringing an "Ahhh!" from the audience, which was no different from any other. It swallowed everything that was ladled out—the Brave Pioneers, the Pioneer Women, the children—all the standard items, especially two cute little puppy dogs and a baby. Well, the picture ran its appointed course as truly as a train follows its rails. This being Indian country, there had to be Indians. Now they had gathered all their strength for a mass attack of deadly fury. Arrows, knives, tomahawks, spears, and everything else that was throwable came hurtling in like a hailstorm. Our Little Girl (Mae Marsh) had somehow rescued the cute little puppy dogs and had jumped into a chest and slammed down the lid. She had her share of feminine curiosity, so she'd lift the lid enough to peek out. In would come a tomahawk or an arrow, and down would go the lid, just in the nick of time. The audience laughed every time she did this, more out of relief than anything else.

For there was really no cause for laughter. Indians were charging and crawling and climbing and filtering in from all sides. The defenders fought back as bravely as they could, but the casualties were heavy and their ammunition had run out. But wait! What's that long shot of empty land doing here, cut right into the height of the battle? But it isn't empty, after all, because off in the distance something is moving, coming closer and closer, until finally it becomes the United States Cavalry, sabers flashing, pistols at the ready, pennons flying, and horses pounding hell-for-leather as fast as horses ever ran before.

The audience went into a frenzy of delight. "Come on, come on, come on!" they called. That troop of cavalry hit those Indians with the impact of a huge sea swell bursting over a rock. The carnage was fearful, sabers rising and falling, dropping an Indian at every stroke. Pistols fired with deadly effect each and every time. The defenders rushed out to greet their rescuers, who had arrived just in the nick of time. The cavalrymen continued to slaughter Indians. The Little Girl came out of her chest with her cute little puppy dogs, all safe and sound, while joy reigned everywhere. Regretfully, all too soon, the title came on, THE END.

In the lobby I stopped to look over the list of coming attractions. They were the usual run-of-the-mill Trust pictures; that is, those made by companies that had signed up with the Patents people and had the right to use perforated film, shuttle movements, and loops, like Kalem, Biograph, and all the rest. New companies were showing up all the time, like the Flying A.

The Battle at Elderbush Gulch was being held over. I knew it would be.

They'd probably keep on running that one until the projector wore out, after which they'd install a new projector and start all over again. What really jolted me was the fact that they were advertising an old John Bunny–Flora Finch in the place they usually listed our Kinemacolors. This burned me to a crisp, because it meant that we were through. Done. Washed up. Too bad, but there it was. The handwriting on the wall was all too abundantly clear.

✑ 2 ✑

A Season in Limbo

*There's never a door closes but
what another one opens.*
OLD THEATRICAL SAYING

AND SO Kinemacolor died. The final rites were conducted by old man Wiener, the front-office boss, who sat at a desk in the big, two-story, chalet-type building that had been our laboratory and handed out the final paychecks to all of us waiting in line. Fair to the last, Kinemacolor offered free transportation back to New York to all who wanted it. Nobody wanted it. Hollywood was becoming the Hollywood of pictures, with little studios springing up all over the place. And besides, it was the off-season for the theater in New York, where no shows of any consequence would be opening until well into the end of the year.

So my father and mother and I took our money and went back home. It was a good home, too, the best we'd ever had—six rooms and a service porch; a part-time maid named Ida Belle; a pet dog named Lily, who had come to us out of nowhere and who had adopted us as her very own; a large garden full of flowers and grapevines and fruit trees. No, we'd take our chances in Hollywood.

And the chances were good, too. The gold-rush of ambitious amateurs to Hollywood, hoping for a sudden bonanza of discovery and stardom, was well under way. But experienced people were in very short supply. We had the advantage there, because we were all as well trained as a trio of performing seals in a vaudeville act.

I had been particularly fortunate in having for my teachers the best cameramen that the once affluent Kinemacolor could find anywhere in the world. Gerald MacKenzie, from Inverness; Alfred G. Gosden, from London; Marcel Le Picard, from Paris, and the two Scheurich brothers, August and Victor, from Germany. They gave freely of their knowledge, because who can resist the eagerness of a stripling grateful to sit at the feet of wisdom and willing to accept as gospel their lightest word? But they could not give me

[7]

their experience. That was something I'd have to acquire by myself in the only way possible, which is to make so many mistakes that there are no more mistakes left to make and that the right way is the only way possible.

My father and mother went to work elsewhere, here, there, and wherever a job was to be had. My father was big and fat and carried himself as a personage of the greatest possible importance. He could play anything from a ruffian to a ruler, a sailor to a saint. Long years on the stage had taught him this versatility. My mother was equally talented.

I was not. I had a head full of theories, but who wants to listen to the theories of a sixteen-year-old kid who was just then getting used to wearing long pants? Furthermore, I was faced with what had come to be known as the elevator problem. You can't run an elevator unless you have had experience running an elevator. How, then, do you ever get to become an elevator operator? Or a cameraman? Or a director? Or any job when the first question always was, "Where have you worked? What have you done?" And they sometimes added, after hearing your breathless recital of unmatchable virtues, "If you're as good as all that, why ain't you working?"

No, words would never get me anywhere. I had to have experience, so I dipped into my slender savings and bought a battered old view camera and tripod and accessories in a Main Street pawnshop and went hard at work giving myself the experience that was so essential to any future I might have. It was a poor camera, but I shot pictures of everything within walking distance, developing and printing them myself in my makeshift darkroom in the cramped space of a clothes closet.

Some of them came out quite well. There was one of Franklin Avenue, shooting west from Vermont, that was my pet. Franklin Avenue was a narrow dirt lane completely arched over by pepper trees. If I could only have shot it in color to get those feathery green leaves and all those clusters of red berries, it would have been perfect.

Then fate, or whatever you want to call it, stepped in. Selig was shooting a big epic of the frozen north called *The Spoilers*. My father and mother were both working in the picture. The newspaper cameramen they had hired to make still pictures were unwilling to ruin their clothing by wading in the deep mud that had been contrived to match the mud of Nome, Alaska.

I didn't mind a little mud. On the contrary, I was still kid enough to enjoy mud, the muddier the better. So I went to the Edendale studio of the Selig company, saw Alvin Wyckoff, who was in charge of the photographic department, spoke my piece, and got the job.

It was a glorious experience, wading out in all that lovely mud and bossing everybody around. I didn't care who they were: Bessie Eyton or William

Farnum or Tom Santschi—it made no difference to me. When I called "Still!" they froze in place until I said "Okay" and released them from their immobility.

The fight between Farnum and Santschi could not be stopped for stills or anything else. But I had a fine Goerz lens with a Compur shutter that could shoot at one three-hundredths of a second, so I shot them in action. It worked. The stills were good enough to use, and any little smearing of the action seemed to enhance the fury of that most furious of fights.

But all things must end. *The Spoilers* was eventually finished and I was out of a job again. But this time it was with a difference. I was now experienced, *The Spoilers* was a runaway success, my pictures were in every lobby where it played and in all the trade papers advertising the picture, so the actual proof that I had worked on a really big one was on record for all to see.

For some incomprehensible reason, producers were not clamoring for my services. I gave them a fair chance to come to their senses, and when they continued to ignore their golden opportunity to snap up my talents, I asked around to find out why.

I found out. Nobody wanted anyone to take stills. That was part of their regular cameraman's job. As for *The Spoilers,* I had been hired only because it was a mud picture and they didn't want their regular cameraman to get all muddy just for a few stills. If they ever made another mud picture, they'd get in touch—sorry.

It was a black moment. Then a ray of hope broke through when the news seeped out that the great D. W. Griffith was moving his entire company to Hollywood. He had taken the Kinemacolor lot as his studio, not more than a hundred steps from our front door.

Unknown to Griffith, the greatest living master of suspense, a harrowing suspense situation was being played right in our home. It was: how could we wangle our way into his organization and have steady jobs in our old studio located practically at our doorstep? No carfare; make-up at home; come home for lunch; be within call at any moment, day or night. Perfect. The problem: how to work it?

My father made the rounds, finding out about Griffith's every move. Thanks to this one-man espionage bureau, we knew when Griffith was coming, when he would leave New York, when he would arrive at the Arcade station. Should we meet him at the train? No; too many reporters, too many job hunters. He'd have to come to the studio. We'd trap him there at the only entrance, the flight of steps leading up from Sunset Boulevard.*

* The studio was located at 4500 Sunset Boulevard, at the point where Hollywood Boulevard joins Sunset. Prior to occupancy by Kinemacolor, it was the Revier Laborato-

The great day arrived after a sleepless night. We were gathered, all three of us, at what we considered the most strategic spot—the steps. He'd have to go up that little flight of seven steps from the Sunset Boulevard level to the lot itself. So there we planted ourselves and there we waited.

My plans were all made. I'd get hold of Billy Bitzer, as soon as I found out who he was, and take him on a grand tour of the studio, showing him all the wonderful things we had built. Quite incidentally, as a careless side mention, I'd manage to drop a word or two of the part I had played in bringing all this about. I felt this would be the most dignified way to make the approach. I did not dare hope for anything like immediate acceptance into the bosom of the Griffith family. I would plant the seed, and who knows? Maybe someday . . .

People kept gathering. My father knew most of them, because there wasn't a studio in town, however sketchy, that he didn't visit. It was an article of faith with him to get to know as many people as possible, because he kept telling me over and over again, "It isn't *what* you know, but *who* you know."

The people were from all over the picture world. Everyone who was not actually on a set shooting was there: cameramen, directors, actors, and a swarm of people who hoped to be actors someday—all waiting for the great man to make his entrance.

A high-bodied limousine purred around from the curve of Sunset Boulevard. A uniformed driver was at the wheel. A man and two young ladies and a very young gentleman were seated in back. All eyes followed the car as it pulled to a stop just beyond the steps where we were standing.

The driver got out and opened the door. A tall, spare man got out. He held his hand to help his two young lady guests out. The very young gentleman followed.

"That's Griffith," said my mother softly. "And that's Lillian and Dorothy Gish with him, and Robert Harron."

"Are you sure?" I asked, unable to believe that this slender gentleman could possibly be the giant of the industry. "Why, he can't be more than—than thirty."*

"Why, yes, I'd judge him to be in his thirties. What do you think, Will?"

We looked around. My father was gone. We searched for him with our eyes. There he was, shaking hands with Frank Woods, the company's super-

---

ries. It was a rental studio until about 1943, when it was purchased by Columbia Pictures and thereafter used as a branch studio. Damaged by fire, it was torn down about 1961 to make room for a shopping center. GEORGE J. MITCHELL

* Griffith was born on January 23, 1875. The date is disputed because no birth certificate exists, but this birthdate appears on Griffith's marriage certificate in the Museum of Modern Art's Griffith collection. KEVIN BROWNLOW

visor, and being very, very jovial. Woods advanced toward Griffith, my fa[ther] in tow. Woods was greeted warmly by Griffith. He introduced my fat[her] who took Griffith's proffered hand warmly. There was nothing shy or diffi-dent about my father. He might have been the owner of three railroads and a couple of munitions factories.

"Looks as though we're in," said my mother happily. "Trust Will to be Johnny-on-the-spot when the box is open."

People were crowding in to smile their prettiest on the new arrivals. It was hard enough for me to swallow the fact that these three youngsters with Griffith really were the famous Gish sisters and the Robert Harron we'd all seen in so many Griffith pictures. But what was impossible to believe was that anyone so obviously young, so boyishly slender, so unmarked by the battles of the world, could possibly be the one and only, great, and world-famous D. W. Griffith. He must have started when—well, when he was not so very much older than I was. The miracle was not that he had done so much, but that he had done so much so young.

Another car drew up, this one a big, seven-passenger open touring car. It was crowded with men. The man in the front seat got out. He walked to the place where a sidewalk would be someday, followed by the others, who grouped around him as they looked the place over.

"That's Billy Bitzer," said my mother. "The chubby one with the cloth hat. Go on. Ask him for a job."

I felt suddenly all weak and helpless. "You mean—*now?*"

"Of course. Go on. Hurry up. Get to him before all the rest of the mob does."

"Couldn't we wait until he's—not so—busy?"

"Look, if you don't get to him now, you'll *never* get to him, because the jobs'll all be gone. Do as your father did, walk right up and speak your piece as if you owned the place."

I still hung back. My mother shook my arm and snapped, "Karl!" in a tone that could not be mistaken. I made a quick appraisal. The worst Bitzer could do would be to say no, but if I didn't go, I'd have to live with that woman. I decided to go, but somewhat slowly. I thought that any unseemly rush would be undignified.

I approached the king of cameramen and asked, "Mr. Bitzer?"

He looked around from the men he was talking with. Bitzer was a round man with a round face and a round neck that bulged a little over his collar. He was also a brown man, with brown eyes, a brownish skin, and definitely brown lips, of all things. He looked at me and said, as though annoyed by an unwelcome intrusion, "Yes?"

Well, I did my usual rush act, the same as I had done with Wyckoff. Named all the people I'd worked with, my latest job as still man for Alvin Wyckoff, and then I paused, to give him his turn to talk.

He looked me up and down disapprovingly and said, "So?"

I couldn't think of an apt answer right off the bat. While I was trying to think of one, he spoke rather sharply, in a don't-bother-me-can't-you-see-I'm-busy tone of voice, "Well, out with it. What do you want?"

"Well, I'd sort of like a job." This didn't strike me as being particularly brilliant, but it was out and there was no changing it now.

Bitzer came right to the point. "Look. We've got our own laboratory and we've brought out all our help. I take all the stills. And as for your many qualifications, I think you'd do well to apply elsewhere, because I do all my own photographic work as well. Does that answer you?"

I made one last try. "Couldn't I be your assistant or something? I don't cost much and I work long hours. Ask Al Wyckoff, or Johnny Leezer. Ask anybody!"

He smiled for the first time, shaking his head in advance of the no I was sure was coming. But he did qualify it. "Look, kid. All I require of an assistant is a strong back and a weak mind, and you just don't strike me as being the type. Sorry."

Griffith's voice called, "Billy!"

"Right away, Mr. Griffith." He started to move away. I ran after him, keeping pace as I pleaded, "Please, Mr. Bitzer! I know I'm not wanted, but before you go, will you *please* tell me how you managed to make Hank Walthall look so big in *Judith of Bethulia?*" He stopped now and stared at me. I continued, recklessly, now that the game was lost. "I asked Johnny Leezer and he didn't know and he said I'd have to ask you, so I'm asking you, and if you'll please tell me I won't ever bother you any more, honest I won't." It all came out pretty fast, but I knew he was in a hurry.

His face softened into kindness. "Sure, be glad to. But it'll take a little time. Report for work at nine tomorrow morning and I'll show you what you have to do."

Griffith repeated his call. Bitzer hurried to join him. I stood there, trying to make myself believe that what I'd heard was true. Suddenly I believed, and in that instant I whirled and made a headlong dash toward my mother, so suddenly and so unexpectedly that I all but knocked down a dignified lady who was walking toward the steps.

I apologized, got a sniff for my pains, and I then hurried to tell my mother the miraculous news.

I never got a chance to open my mouth. She was furious. "Do you know who that was you nearly knocked down? Mary Alden, the actress! When will you *ever* learn to look where you're going?"

All the joy seeped out of my life. "I dunno."

"What did Bitzer say?" There was no real interest in her voice. She had been watching and knew a turndown when she saw one.

"He said I wouldn't do. But I was to report for work at nine tomorrow morning anyway."

"He said *what?*"

"That's what he said."

"Then—then you're *in!* Do you realize that? You're *in!*" She was wide-eyed with amazement. I suddenly became wide-eyed with amazement, too, as the realization finally hit home with a jarring, delayed impact.

It was hard to believe, but I was in—actually, honestly, really in. Things like this were forever happening to somebody else. But now, incredibly, it had happened to me. Nothing I could think of to say could possibly do justice to the situation, so I simply murmured, "Well, whadda ya know," and let it go at that.

3

The Great D.W.

Upon what meat doth this our Caesar feed,
That he is grown so great?
SHAKESPEARE, "JULIUS CAESAR"

BITZER had been absolutely correct in his statement that all he required of an assistant was a strong back and a weak mind. The work was not only physically heavy, it was so diverse in its demands that it would take at least three competent workers to do it properly.

Consider this as a daily stint of duty. Arrive an hour before shooting is to begin. Load magazines. Carry all equipment to the first setup. Camera, tripod, magazine cases, accessory case, still camera, still tripod, case of plates, and accessory equipment. Have sideline stick handy, with chalk, chalk line, hammer, and roofing nails ready. Have notebook ready, with extra pencils. Be sure to have the white sheet ready for instant use as a hand-held reflector. Load camera, making doubly sure that the upper and lower loops are exactly right. Check ground glass. Clean with alcohol to be sure there's no trace of oil, which would make it deceptively transparent. Check pressure pad, a satin-covered oblong of brass that held the film flat against the aperture. Check aperture plate for any trace of roughness. Have tests of previous day's work ready and marked by number in their own film can. Check focus of the low-power microscope Bitzer used to balance depth of field of each scene. Be sure the hand magnifier is clean and polished. Wash and dry slate—the common, wood-framed slate used by schoolchildren of that day. Be sure there's plenty of chalk. Check notebook to be sure there are enough empty pages to cover a day's work.

The company arrives. The cast in costume, Griffith groomed and tailored to perfection, as always. Apparently vain of his appearance, a holdover from his acting days. He tells Bitzer the setup. Bitzer moves camera to proper position and begins to light the scene. A diffuser pulled back here, another run forward there. White flats angled to catch the sunlight and throw it in from

[14]

one side of the set. During this, Griffith has taken off his coat and has begun to shadowbox, weaving and bobbing and ducking, dancing forward and back, throwing whole series of left jabs, darting his fist like a rapier as he charges forward at his invisible opponent, his face aglow with the joy of combat. He becomes savage, a killer, throwing whistling rights and deadly left hooks while ducking and blocking a barrage of blows from the Invisible Man.

These one-man exhibition matches startled and fascinated me just at first. I'd have liked nothing better than to have taken a ringside seat to watch them through in comfort, but I was never given the time because lines had to be put down.

This business of putting down the lines was a standard preliminary to the shooting of every scene. I'd take a long white stick, about an inch in diameter and six feet long. I'd hold it up by thumb and forefinger, grasping it lightly at the upper end to let it hang in a true perpendicular. I'd move to where the forward edge of the set ended and then, following Bitzer's hand motions as he looked into the camera, move the stick one way or the other until it was lined up exactly with the side of the frame as seen in the camera. A downward motion of Bitzer's hand. I'd let the stick slide through my grasp until it touched the stage. Then, still holding the stick, I'd bend over and mark the spot where the stick rested with a piece of ordinary school blackboard chalk.

The next step was to move the stick, which was again hanging upright between thumb and forefinger, forward until Bitzer's hand motions indicated that the bottom of the stick was exactly on the bottom of the camera frame line. Then out, out, out, until the stick rested on the bottom corner of the frame line. Mark. Cross to the other side. Find the other corner. Mark. Then back to the other edge of the set. Find it and mark.

Next, drive a broad-headed nail—a roofing nail was ideal—into each mark. Then stretch strong white cord from nail to nail, beginning at the back, progressing to the front and across, and then back to the nail at the other edge of the set. Tie off. Now everyone knew exactly the stage area covered by the camera, which was not only never to be moved but which was sometimes even anchored to the floor with strong lash-line secured by a stage screw. Actors could then walk carelessly down toward the camera, secure in the knowledge that as long as they stayed inside that white cord, their feet would not be cut off and audiences would not wonder how people could walk around without feet. They could move from side to side freely so long as they stayed within the lines. It was especially valued by stage-trained actors, who were used to working in a clearly defined area, wings on the side and the apron in front. Without these guidelines they were constantly moving outside camera range to deliver their most telling effects. Griffith and his lines removed all that danger. It was considered to be a notable advance in the art of picture making.*

All was ready. Griffith abandoned his athletics to take his seat beside the camera in an ordinary kitchen chair. A rehearsal was run through, more of positions than anything else, because the actors had already been rehearsed and they knew the mood and timing of every scene. Shooting was merely a matter of committing to film what had already been worked out in rehearsal. I'd dearly have loved to enjoy the scene, but there was too much to be done. Get rid of the stick and chalk, hammer and nails. Pick up the book, a pad of ruled and columned sheets in which all scenes were to be recorded. Reading from left to right, the columns were to register the date, the scene number, the characters in the scene, a brief hint as to the action, spaces to be checkmarked as to Interior, Exterior, Daylight, Electric, Effect; the camera stop number and the amount of footage.

Because of the pressure of work, everything in the book had to be reduced to initials or contracted words. Character names were abandoned in favor of the real names of the actors involved. These were clear at a glance: LG for Lillian Gish; RH for Robert Harron. Some others were HW, BS, EC, GS, DC, GW—representing Henry Walthall, Blanche Sweet, Elmer Clifton, George Siegmann, Donald Crisp, George Walsh—any one of whom might be working on the set that day. The stop number could be read from a dial on the upper left side of the camera, the footage from another dial on the upper back of the camera.

Since there was no script, the scene numbers were registered in consecutive order of shooting. A scene shot six different times would carry six different numbers. These numbers were chalked on the slate and held before the camera to be photographed on the film. To erase an existing chalked number with a dry rag and to replace it with a clearly legible succeeding number called for hard scrubbing and firm marking, so very firm as to break the chalk, until you learned to hold the crayon close to the tip so as to eliminate leverage. Drop chalk and slate and grab book and pencil. Note bare mechanics of action. A typical entry: "MM ER MRH PS RH XR 35 4.5." Anyone connected with the picture could tell at a glance that the entry meant that Mae Marsh enters from right, meets Robert Harron, plays scene, Robert Harron exits to right, and that the scene ran thirty-five feet and was shot at f. 4.5.

And so the day would go, scene after scene, setup after setup. The simple

---

* This is *not* one of the innovations for which Griffith claimed much credit. (Author)

notation, PS (Plays Scene), could apply to one or two or a roomful of characters. There was no hope of describing just how the scene was played because of six takes of the same scene, no two would be played the same way. Griffith's method of staging was similar to that of a composer writing a theme with variations. The theme was always the same, the variations as many as Griffith could think of at the time. There was no such thing as printing one selected take. Everything was printed. The final selection was made in the projection room, and the final assembly might very well be made up of bits and pieces of three or four out of six or eight takes.

Whenever a still picture was needed, the still camera had to be unpacked from its case, set up, and made ready for Bitzer to use. Once the picture had been taken, the still camera went back into its case, and the tripod was folded and put away. No still camera was ever left standing, because sure as fate someone would pass close enough to hit one of the outspread legs and down would go baby, cradle and all. It took time to unpack and repack the camera for each shot, but it was my time so it didn't count.

The break for lunch meant dismantling and stowing everything away out of sight. Reason: there might be snoops from the Trust prowling around to see what they could see or photograph. One clear picture of a Pathé camera on a Griffith stage would be enough to offer in evidence of patent violation, to secure a cease-and-desist order or even a warrant for seizure of the camera. And besides, the Trust had it in for Griffith with a vengeance. He had been the bright particular star of Biograph, one of the principal members of the Trust organization, and he had walked out on them to form his own independent company. So he was their number-one target.

Lunch itself was a matter of personal convenience. It was no trick at all for me to trot home and find a hot lunch waiting. Most of the working crew brought their own lunches in old-fashioned bright tin dinner buckets. Griffith ate in his own office from a hamper prepared by the Alexandria Hotel, where he lived. There was a small hotel on Fountain Avenue, nearby, where many of our cast lunched regularly.

The day ended when the light became yellow. The cast was given the call for the next day and dismissed. Griffith would go to his office to meet with Frank Woods, Albert Banzhaf (his lawyer), someone named Harry Aitken,* who had something to do with money, and another named J. A. Barry, who seemed to be a manager of sorts. These were not secret, closed-door meetings; they were merely private business meetings. Nobody snooped or listened at doorways. Privacy was privacy, not to be invaded. What they discussed and

* Harry Aitken was president of the Mutual Film Corporation. KEVIN BROWNLOW

what they planned was their business. In fact, I learned very early in the game *never* to listen to secrets of any kind. Then, if the matter ever became public, it could never be traced to me. So I added one extra beatitude to the Biblical list: blessed are the ignorant, for they shall never be called to account.

My job was to lock all equipment securely away, go home to dinner, and then return for the rest of my day's work. All the exposed film of the day had to be "wound out." This meant going into the darkroom with the exposed magazines, dousing the light, and then opening any magazine at random, placing the roll on the spindle of one rewind and then running it carefully onto a second rewind, feeling the edges very carefully for notches. Bitzer notched the film between every setup and sometimes between every scene, if it involved a change of lighting. Bitzer made these notches with scissors, the big sissy! Couldn't even tear film. It was the only thing I could do that he could not, and I prized my poor little single advantage accordingly.

The film* was broken at each notch. I tore off a five-foot length for testing, numbered it 1, and placed it to one side. This test was marked with a figure 1, using a wax pencil. The length of film was placed in its own separate can and secured as a tight roll with an elastic band. The can was closed and taped and marked with a loud, clear figure 1. And so on through the entire day's work, a test strip to each take and a separate can for each roll, however short. By this time the pieces had been all canned and sealed with adhesive tape. The test strips were still in the open. The last step was to tear a small strip of eight inches or so from the test strips and mark them with corresponding numbers. These were pinned together, as were the longer strips. The short pieces were to be developed then and there, for Bitzer's examination in the morning. The longer ones were to be canned and marked "Tests" for Abe Scholtz, our negative developer.

Abe Scholtz. An endlessly fascinating and vaguely repulsive character, not for what he was but for what he had been, through no fault of his own. Abe Scholtz was a pale, bloodless skeleton of a man who had lived through more horrors than I cared to hear about. His companion and sharer of these horrors was Joe Aller, a bright little cricket of a man who seemingly had never had a care in the world. Both were Jews who had lived in Czarist Russia. I happened to hear them talking about certain indignities to which Russian Jews had been subjected in those most evil of old days, things such as having sulphuric acid poured into their ears, and I got away quickly before I could hear any more.

* Film stock at this period was Orthochromatic (except for a Panchromatic film used in the Kinemacolor process but not generally available). Its emulsion speed would today be rated at approximately ASA 25. GEORGE J. MITCHELL

Abe spoke with a thin, high-piping voice, and he had no growth of beard but only a fine, silky trace of down on his cheeks. He never shaved because there was nothing there to shave. I greatly preferred not to know what had caused this transformation in a fully adult man, but I could not keep from making haunting guesses that bordered upon shocking certainty.

If genius be an infinite capacity for taking pains, then Abe Scholtz was unquestionably a genius. He would develop these test strips himself, by hand, watching and remembering the first flashing of each image on each strip. This time of appearance meant much to him, how much I was never expert enough to know. Once developed, fixed and washed, these strips would be placed on the familiar old light box, where a lamp of known intensity would shine through these strips against the even illumination of a sheet of opal glass, which was kept meticulously clean. These he would study with all the concentration of a master of chess deciding a crucial move. No snap judgment of anything, no surrendering of the film to less expert hands. He developed every foot of every scene Griffith ever shot. He would change the developer from strong to weak, from fresh to old, to whatever he felt—not knew but felt—to be the one particular treatment for any given scene. If twenty different scenes required twenty different developers, he would treat these twenty scenes twenty different ways, if it took all day long and into the night. And if, by any possible chance, the finished result fell short of his concept of what a perfect negative should be, he'd attack the problem afresh, with reducers or intensifiers, to finish with twenty negatives of exactly the same ideal quality, all twenty of which could be printed at the same printing-light reading.

Bitzer used to complain, "Damn it, Abe's developing these negatives thinner and thinner every day." Well, they *were* thin; this to the point of ghostliness according to my Kinemacolor training. But thin as they were, everything was there; and Joe Aller, only a degree or two lower on the scale of genius, knew exactly what to do with these negatives. He used the standard metol-hydroquinone-sodas, but with a difference that consisted mostly of heavy on the hydroquinone, don't forget the metabisulphate and administer the bromide with the delicate judgment of a pharmacist turned doctor of medicine.

The result, on the screen, made Bitzer the greatest cameraman in the world, the king of them all. This is to take nothing from Bitzer. For in all truth, all the best, even the most inspired, of cameramen can do is put a latent image on the raw film stock. Bitzer was great in the sense that a great designer or architect can produce great plans. But Scholtz and Aller brought the greatness of his plans into physical, lasting being. Probably this has always been true. We admire the Parthenon without so much as a fleeting thought of the slaves who worked all that marble into being, and we philosophize about the Sphinx without realizing that it was once a shapeless mass of age-defying stone of surpassing hardness that workmen wrought into a heroic symbol of eternal mystery, with no tools but copper chisels and no encouragement but a slave driver's whip.

The same principle was true of us. One man who was the master designer, Griffith, drew all the plans. The rest of us, from the highest to the lowest, gave whatever was in us to the realization of the master plan. I was the lowest, a beast of burden by day and a chore boy by night. The work was cruelly hard, the hours exhaustingly long.

But cruel as was the work and long as were the hours, my little stint of daily duty was as nothing compared with the working hours Griffith himself spent. I had no way of knowing how much of his time and energy were absorbed by meetings concerned with money, costs, expansion, hiring, firing, contracts, deals, profits and losses, matters which only he could decide, because it was his studio, his fortune, his future; and although others might advise, only he could make the final decisions. What I did know was that he was on the set promptly to meet any call. He worked as long as the daylight held. He might go to the Alexandria for a dinner conference, but he was always back in the studio and in the projection room with his two cutters, Jimmy and Rose Smith, to run film over and over and over again, altering, changing, trying this, trying that.

Late as some of my night chores might be, whenever I had finished and had locked up the camera room for the night, the projection room was always going. We had two projectionists, Billy Fildew and George Teague, who divided the work between them. The projection room was open and ready from eight in the morning until twelve, one, or two, or even longer past midnight if Griffith so desired.

For the projection room was really Griffith's cutting room. Here he would sit, hour after hour, studying scenes he had run dozens of times before. They might be good. Very good indeed. But then again, there might be a way to make them even better, if only he could think of it. Over and over, endlessly over and over.

He was constantly musing aloud. "Maybe if we took the last part of the third take and used the first part of the sixth, it would hold together better."

Whispered consultation between Rose and Jimmy. "Get a bad jump—" would be the verdict.

"Then cut away and come back."

"Where to?"

"We have a shot of Crisp approaching the house. Use that. Not much. Enough to cover the jump. Ten frames."

"That'll mean double-cutting."

A shrug. "Who cares, if it works. Try it and see."

His highest objective, as nearly as I could grasp it, was to photograph thought. He could do it, too. I'd seen it. In *Judith of Bethulia* there was a scene in which Judith stands over the sleeping figure of Holofernes, sword in hand. She raises the sword, then falters. Pity and mercy have weakened her to a point of helpless irresolution. Her face softens to something that is almost love. Then she thinks, and as she thinks the screen is filled with the mangled bodies of those, her own people, slain by this same Holofernes. Then her face becomes filled with hate as she summons all her strength to bring that sword whistling down upon the neck of what is no longer a man but a blood-reeking monster.

And then I would trudge on home past darkened houses where everyone was asleep, leaving behind the whirring projection room and the man within it, trying to drive his dreams into a corner where he could capture them and show them to the world.

Thanks to my inborn laziness, I found ways to make my work a little easier, day by day and by slow degrees. Take this business of struggling with all the heavy equipment I had to move from camera room to set, and from set to other sets. There were always men standing around doing nothing in particular—stagehands, carpenters, drivers, and actors—and when it came time to move all those back-breaking cases from one place to another, the simple appeal, "Aw, come on, fellows, gimme a hand, won't you?" brought instant response every time. Not that I put all the burden on these willing helpers. That would not be fair. So I was always careful to do my own full share by leading the way and showing them where to put everything.

For some reason this delighted Griffith. Always in the habit of voicing his thoughts aloud and of addressing his remarks to nobody in particular, he said with an amused tone of dry comment, "I see that our young colleague has acquired for himself a staff."

My next labor-saving device was a line stick armed with chalk at the bottom end. As soon as the sideline was found, a slight movement of the stick marked the spot where the nail was to be driven. This brought another murmur from Griffith: "Ah! It would appear that our youthful comrade-at-arms has distinguished himself, not only by raising three whiskers and a pimple but also by becoming something of an innovator."

This didn't bother me. Griffith was forever voicing whatever thoughts happened to cross his mind. There was a time when one of our assistants, a goggle-eyed, wobbly-gaited, dim-witted idiot-type, went weaving uncertainly across the stage. Griffith followed the unfortunate young man with his eyes and then murmured in a voice of deepest compassion, "Ah! Masturbation is a *dreadful* thing!"

There was one problem that bothered everyone, especially me. The slate. It is impossible to rub all the chalk from a slate with a dry rag or a dry anything. Washing was out of the question: too long to dry, and chalk will not bite into wet slate. Try as I would, there were always traces of previous numbers left on the slate, and after a few takes what was registered on the film was a sort of palimpsest of 3's and 8's over 5's and 2's, indistinguishable even to their maker—me. What poor Rose and Jimmy Smith ever managed to make of them in the cutting room is more than I can ever know. Of course, I got the blame. Not that I was really blameworthy. There was no way of making a clean erasure. But that didn't matter. I was at the bottom of the pecking order, and so ...

I soon became very tired of starting every day with someone yelling at me, "Why the hell can't you make numbers a body can *read?*" So one night I worked late after my regular chores had been done. What had been an ordinary shelf in the camera room had been rebuilt as a carpenter's workbench. There were all sorts of hand tools, including a heavy iron vise. So I cut a piece of plywood to form an oblong of nine-by-twelve inches. On this I fastened three open-faced pockets of tin, of just the right size to hold a playing card. I cut numbers from a wall calendar, 1 through 0, and cemented the numbers to the cards. By stacking them in proper order, 1 to 0, and by having a stack in each of the three pockets, the numbering problem simply disappeared. Lift the outermost card from the right-hand pocket and slip it into the back and the next number in sequence automatically appeared. Every tenth time around, a card in the next column is moved, and for every hundredth, one in the third.*

Original? Hardly. Counters had been used for years, working on the same principle. I wasn't inventing anything. I was simply trying to find some way of keeping out of trouble.

It was a crude-looking contraption at best, but after I had persuaded Cash Shockey to paint it all black, with GRIFFITH–BITZER lettered neatly across the top, together with the picture number, it was quite presentable.

Not that I presented it. I simply put it to use the next morning without saying anything to anybody. When I held the slate in front of the camera, with

---

* This device, greatly refined and improved, is still in use wherever pictures are made. Revealingly enough, it is still known as a "slate." (Author)

the numbers, white on black, clearly legible, Bitzer was so taken aback that he forgot to turn the camera.

Griffith looked at the slate from his seat beside the camera. His face was expressionless. He held out his hand and made a beckoning motion with his forefinger. I meekly surrendered the slate to him. He held it, studied it, fingered the numbers to see how they worked, then returned it to me.

Still without expression of approval or disapproval or anything else, he spoke in a reproachful undertone to Bitzer, "Billy! Why couldn't you have thought of this years ago and saved us all that trouble?"

Bitzer had nothing to say. His dusky face grew darker and his chin quivered slightly. He didn't look at me or at Griffith or anybody. I did a little quivering myself, inside. This might very well be the end of the line for me, because there is no surer way for a junior to be given the gate than by showing up the boss, and in public at that.

It was through this little episode that I came to know Sam Landers. Landers was a very strange man, physically and mentally. You've no doubt seen Toby jugs. Well, Landers had a face like those molded into Toby jugs and mugs, very wide and very squat and very much overstated, but of course without the tricorne hat. His body was built to the same general specifications, squat but not fat, a squashed-down giant. He never spoke unless spoken to, and his answers were all monosyllabic.

Sam Landers was a mechanical genius. He could do anything with anything mechanical. When the Trust threatened to drive all outsiders into extinction, Landers designed and built a camera that used no loop, no perforations, no shuttle, nothing that could infringe on anyone's patents because it operated on an entirely new principle. The film ran through as a continuously moving ribbon. The lens followed the aperture plate down during exposure, keeping in exact optical alignment. The shutter cut off the light at the downmost position and kept the film dark, while the lens and aperture plate returned to the top to catch the flowing ribbon of film in time to open again for the next picture. It was noisy—it sounded like a machine gun—but it worked. It was called the Griffith–Bitzer camera. Sam didn't mind. He knew who had designed and built it, and that was enough.

Landers had also designed and built a new type of laboratory for the processing of any quantity of film. Instead of racks he used small drums turned by power takeoffs from overhead shafts. These drums turned in shallow troughs, U-shaped in cross-section, holding just enough solution to wet the film. These drums could be lowered and lifted, turned and stopped, moved from tank to tank, all by mechanical power. The film was developed, fixed, washed, and dried all on one drum, with no handling of the film at all. It was the closest thing to continuous mechanical processing yet achieved.

As if this weren't enough, Landers also designed and built a camera in which the film ran horizontally across the lens instead of vertically. This enabled him to cut an aperture plate one inch high and as wide as desired, an inch and a half or more, producing a wide-screen picture. Bitzer derided the whole idea. "Only difference it makes is that instead of the picture jiggling up and down, it now jiggles sideways." Landers ignored the jibe. "You just wait," he said. "The day's coming when all you'll see is wide screen and nothing else."

I was on my way to the lab with some cans of film for Abe Scholtz when Landers surprised me by actually speaking to me. "Hear you're in bad with Bitzer," he said, his words emerging from a very small slit of his mouth.

"Suppose so," I agreed. I felt no great urge to enlarge upon the subject.

"Don't let it get you down," he advised. "D.W. loves it. Never happy unless everybody's jealous of everybody else."

I blinked a few times, trying to absorb this. Landers continued, "Bitzer hates my guts. Always has. Knows that if he lets down for a single second, D.W.'ll run me in to take his place. Same goes for everybody. Nobody here that can't be replaced. Nobody here that isn't itching to replace somebody. Plays one against the other, everybody against everybody else. Not satisfied with people who do the best they can. They've got to do *better* than their best or he'll run in somebody else who can, if he has to reshoot half a picture. So the more you show Bitzer up the better."

I couldn't see where this had any application to me. I was nobody in particular, just a raw youngster trying to hang on to a job. "I wasn't trying to show anybody up. I was just trying to make it easy for myself. I wouldn't have done it if I'd known. But I just didn't think."

"Damn good thing for you that you didn't. D.W.'s got his eye on you now. So give him something to see."

"And get myself fired?"

"Who'll fire you? Bitzer? Not a chance. Oh, Bitzer'd get rid of you in a second if he could, just as he'd get rid of me. But before Bitzer can fire anybody, he's got to clear it with D.W., and you can see how much chance there is of him getting away with anything like *that!* So keep up the good work, kid. Sharpen up your needle and ram it in as deep and as hard and as often as you can, and you'll live happily ever after."

The strange thing about all this was that I *liked* Bitzer. Not because he was likable, for he wasn't. He was a strict, demanding taskmaster in the Germanic tradition, because that was the one in which he had been reared. He never asked; he demanded. He never expressed approval; he expected the best and his mere acceptance of a duty well done was the highest praise he could bestow.

From various sources I had learned something of his background. As a mere youngster he had served his apprenticeship as a silversmith in the long-established firm of Gorham's in New York. He had spent so many years engraving formal announcements on copper that his handwriting had become an elegant example of the engraver's art. His hastiest scrawl had the light and shade, the grace and elegance of a wedding invitation. He had also worked as a creative jeweler, a worker in precious metals who could start with a blank piece of gold or silver, or even a gold or silver coin, and produce—well, anything that could be made of gold or silver.

His hands, stubby-fingered and thick, moved with the swift certainty of a born artist, as a sort of latter-day Cellini. His working habits were as precisely ordered as the mechanisms he worked with. He could take anything apart, find out what was wrong, correct it, and put it back together again without mishap of any kind, thanks to his methodical precision of working.

I watched him take a fine shutter apart one day. This was of particular interest to me, because I, too, had taken a shutter apart and I knew what to expect. In my case I had removed the screws from the front of the case and then I had lifted off the top. Whereupon something went *ping!* and the whole internal economy of the shutter blew up in my face and scattered small parts all over the floor.

Not so with Bitzer. Working with watchmaker's screwdrivers, he took the screws out one by one, placing each one in a neat row on a sheet of clean paper. He placed the first screw at the upper left-hand corner of the sheet and proceeded across the sheet, from left to right, each part in order of its removal. I held my breath when it came time to remove the front of the case, but it was wasted effort. Bitzer eased the top loose and lifted it with all the care of a demolition expert disarming a strange bomb. Nothing went *ping*. The spring that had done me in remained snugly in place. He removed it with the finest-pointed needle-nosed pliers I had ever seen, to place it in its own precise order on that sheet of paper, where everything else had been lined up like so many soldiers on parade. Next came the blades of the iris diaphragm, one after another, to take their places in line.

However, as Mr. Robert Burns has announced, the best laid plans of mice and men, et cetera, et cetera. This episode took place in Bitzer's home, where I had been sent to deliver an important telegram that had come to the studio. Mrs. Bitzer, a fine, brawny Irishwoman with a brogue and a temper to match, had a pet parrot that had the run of the house. And while Bitzer was studying the telegram, said parrot walked across the table, eyed all those tiny screws, decided that they would make excellent roughage, and proceeded to pick up the screws, one by one, to swallow them.

Bitzer turned just in time to see the parrot enjoying its meal. He made a mighty swipe at the bird, which squawked raucously and flew up to safety. The sweep of its wings scattered the rest of the small parts all over the floor. Bitzer used words about that parrot that were never heard in Sunday school. Mrs. Bitzer came hurtling in from the kitchen to see what had happened to her darling, and the shindy was on.

I made a swift strategic withdrawal of the kind known in military circles as getting the hell out of there. I had learned long ago never to be a third party to any family disagreement, for as sure as you do, both are bound to turn on you with their united wrath for meddling into something that is none of your damned business.

I walked back to the studio, thinking of a book that had been published recently. It bore the compelling title, *How to Be Happy Though Married.** It had a large sale, but the results, in human terms, were inconclusive. As far as I could recall, there was only one man who had ever solved the problem and that was Rip Van Winkle, who climbed up into the mountains and took a nice long twenty-year nap.

But that was all of no importance. What really counted was that regardless of his domestic life, happy or unhappy, Bitzer had spent at least the past fifteen years of his life competing with his one most unrelenting rival—himself. He had to be forever surpassing himself, and this demanded discoveries and inventions of the most revolutionary kind.

To my mind Bitzer's greatest discoveries were not of a photographic but of a human kind. He discovered Abe Scholtz and Joe Aller, and he may have discovered Sam Landers, the dour, monosyllabic mechanical wizard who had changed the old hand-development system into a smooth, continuous production-line process, in which the film never left the drums.

These were tended by bloused and bearded Russians who barely knew what they were doing. Everything was controlled by one man, Joe Aller, who moved from drum to drum carrying a red-glassed inspection light powered by a long cord that trailed behind him, to look at this drumload and that, to speak a single word in Russian or to merely make a motion of his hand to cause the drum to lift itself, move to the shortstop, thence to the hypo, and thence to the wash tank, always turning, never stopping, a continuous production line of thousands of feet of film always and forever under the eye of

---

* This book was published in 1910 by The Rev. E. J. Hardy, who stated that he got the title from a sermon by John Shelton (1460–1529). (Author)

just one man, and that man the top-ranking expert of film processing anywhere in the world.

Here was no faltering doubt of the future. Film was on its way to mass production for mass audiences. And the seer who had invested everything he
had, but most of all himself, was the great D. W.

To me, at my time of life and with my theatrical background, Griffith was
a puzzle to be solved, a challenge to the mind. This was not because of any
precocious gift for character analysis but a simple, normal desire, shared by
teenagers everywhere, to know what makes the wheels go around. I had
known stage directors, dance directors, musical directors all my conscious life.
These had fallen, to my mind, into three easy categories. There were the
Teachers, who sat and expounded patiently all that was to be said, done, or
conveyed by indirection. According to my father, probably the best of this
class was W. S. Gilbert, who, while rehearsing *Iolanthe,* admonished the
chorus girls with, "A little more virginity if you please, ladies." Then there
were the Showers, hams to the bone, who insisted upon getting up and acting out every part of every player. And finally, there were the Tyrants, the
loud, sarcastic, domineering slave drivers who could never get through a rehearsal without going into hysterics at least once. There were of course sub-
categories and line-crossing individual directors, but all of them, almost without exception as far as my observation went, were united in one fixed belief:
that their way was the only way and that no other way would do.

Griffith fell into none of these convenient pigeonholes. He did not teach or
preach, he did not act things out, and strangest of all, he never knew what
he wanted except in a broad general way. Obviously, if the scene called for a
confrontation and a fight, there had to be a confrontation and a fight. But just
how the confrontation was to be played and the precise blow-by-blow fight
was to be managed were always in question. His idea seemed to be that although he had a vivid mental picture of how that or any other scene should
appear on the screen, he realized that there were always physical checks and
balances to be overcome if he were merely to approximate the ideal of his
imagination. Hence the rehearsals.

These rehearsals were managed in accordance with the tradition of the
stage. A bare floor, plenty of kitchen chairs, the cast in street clothes ready
for a first run-through. But in Griffith's case, everyone connected with the
production was on hand with notebooks and sketch pads to determine the
settings, the props, the costumes, and everything else that went into the playing of the picture from first to last, long shots and close-ups, reverse shots and
cross-shots, the works.

Everything was played out fully with invisible props and invisible doors, windows, drapes, or whatever. This was easy for the cast. They could sim-ulate anything. But it called for the closest possible attention by the stage crew, from his incredibly capable master carpenter, Frank ("Huck") Wort-man, who could build anything Griffith could imagine, down through his equally capable prop man, Ralph DeLacey, to the lowliest of his second, third, fourth, or fifth assistants, who were really errand boys, forever on the run.* His first assistant was the big-bodied, brutal-faced, soft-spoken George Sieg-mann, whose ferocious appearance concealed a heart of purest mush.

Griffith's direction of these rehearsals was strictly ad lib, off-the-cuff impro-visations to see what would work and what would not. He started with a cen-tral idea from which the story grew and took shape and came to life through his manipulation of these living characters. It was his way of writing, and a very fine way it was indeed. Instead of working with pen or pencil, or through the mind and artistry of a professional writer, however skilled, he sculptured his thoughts in living flesh, to see and feel and sense what could be achieved and what could not, and to know in advance which scenes would "play" and which would not. This called for a sort of cut-and-try, or trial-and-error procedure. A simple scene, apparently meaningless in itself, possibly a mere "bridge" to carry the story from one phase to another, would be tried two, three, five, or a dozen different ways to settle at last into the one pattern that would work for everyone concerned: camera, setting, lighting, the placing of props, everything. This persistent haggling over trifles brought to mind the famous remark attributed to Da Vinci: "Trifles make perfection, and perfection is no trifle."

These rehearsals were no mere walk-throughs to determine positions. They were fully acted out to the minutest details. Mae Marsh, rehearsing for a picture called *Apple Pie Mary,*** played much of the action in an old-fashioned country kitchen. Here she pared apples from a pan held in her lap. She cut her finger slightly and carried it instinctively to her mouth. Inspected the tiny cut carefully and dismissed it as nothing. Continued paring, becoming tensely eager as she managed to peel one whole apple with a single unbroken skin. She threw it over her shoulder, then inspected the curled-up coil of apple paring to see if it would spell the initial of the one she would someday marry. She mixed dough, rolled crust, fitted pans, held the pans to eye level for trimming with a knife. A pause for discussion. Should she crimp the edges

---

* Among these may be listed Joseph Henabery, Erich von Stroheim, Monte Blue, Ed-ward Dillon, W. S. Van Dyke, Tod Browning, Elmer Clifton, and whoever else hap-pened to be handy and not otherwise engaged. They couldn't have chosen a better school in which to learn their trade. (Author)

** The final film was entitled *Home, Sweet Home.* KEVIN BROWNLOW

with her thumbs, to make ripples, or with a fork, to make a fluted edge? Decision: thumbs. More like the pies mother used to make.

And so the pie was made ready for the oven. Opens oven door, tests heat with hand. Too cool. Lifts stove lid with an iron handle, looks at fire. Needs wood. Gets wood from wood box at side of stove, forces it into stove. Stick a little too long. Has to wedge it in. Replaces lid, opens grate damper, opens stove-pipe damper. And with all of this conjured up out of empty air, so vividly that you could all but see the stove, the lid, the wood box, the dampers.

She washes smudged hands at an old-fashioned indoor pump beside the sink. Fluffs her hair at a mirror, quite a small one because she has to stoop and bend to see the reflection. Picks up damp cloth to wipe the table where she has been working.

Interruption from DeLacey. "What do you want on that table, Mr. Griffith? Checkered tablecloth or oilcloth?"

"Oilcloth, of course. Didn't you just now see her wipe it?"

Silent retreat by Mr. DeLacey while he resolves to be more observant in future.

These rehearsals, in which everything was not only worked out but *thought* out to the finest detail, told everybody everything about everything. Huck came away knowing exactly what sets to build and how to build them. De-Lacey had a clear picture in his mind of everything that would be needed. He could set about ordering the stuff to be sent out at any time. This would call for hunting and rummaging in secondhand shops, pawnshops, or even cellars and attics of old-timers who had such things cluttering their barns and outbuildings. Even Bitzer had ample foreknowledge of the sort of scenes he would have to light, and he could begin to plan how to go about it, what he might need in the way of extra equipment, and everything else.

Sometimes Bitzer would say, "Mr. Griffith, with Miss Marsh crowded into a corner like that we won't be able to see her face."

Griffith never resented intelligent questions. "Let's see, now," he'd answer musingly. "If we see her face, it will be Mae Marsh washing dishes. If we see only her back and arms, it will be every woman in the audience washing dishes. We'll play it with her back to the camera."

Griffith's dialect, if such it could be called, fascinated me. His was not the regional speech of Kentucky, which has a recognizable quality all its own. It was more of a personal idiom. Lillian Gish was spoken of as Miss Geeesh, very long-drawn-out. A bomb was always a boom, and a girl was always a gell. In normal conversation his voice was low, slow-paced, and assured, but at the times when he was directing and needed a certain amount of overstatement in a scene, he would become histrionic, almost hammy in his utterances.

Sometimes, when he was under the influence of whatever poet he had been reading, he would speak metrically, falling into an easy, natural, and most certainly unplanned blank verse.

He did not always shadowbox for his morning workout. If Miss Gish—pardon me, Miss Geeesh—were on the set, he would dance with her, not idly or prankishly but with the same earnestness of purpose that marked his boxing.

There was a dance tune that was sweeping the world, a French foxtrot called "Très Moutarde."* He not only danced to this tune but he furnished his own music, singing the melody with short, sharp, clipped tones in perfect time. "You must be a fox," he instructed his lovely partner. "Eyes sharp, darting!" And his eyes would become sharp and they would be darting from side to side. And no wonder, for as of that instant he *was* a fox, with all a fox's wit and cunning.

At other times he would sing. No idle humming for him but big, full-voiced tones that must have bounced from Mount Hollywood and set the neighbors to wondering what operatic star was rehearsing on the Griffith lot. And he could sing, too; really sing. Caruso was the big name in opera, but Griffith liked Titta Ruffo better. So he became Ruffo, and sang as Ruffo would sing, in long, very long-held tones, with all the power at his command. At other times he would challenge members of the working crew to a foot-race. His particular favorite in these races was a short, thickset, general handyman who had appeared from nowhere and who had stayed on for no special reason except that everybody liked him and he liked everybody. He was short, so he was called Shorty. His speech proclaimed him to be most unmistakably English, of the London dock variety (he had been a sailor who had jumped ship in Los Angeles), so he was known only as Shorty English.

It was an unforgettable picture to see Griffith, his long legs stretched to the utmost in mighty strides, his arms flailing for greater momentum, his coat billowing and trailing, his hair blowing because of a hat lost somewhere back along the way, his face aglow with joy as he tried his utmost to beat the bandy-legged little Shorty English, who ran with his head down, his arms close to his sides, and his terrier-like legs twinkling as he crossed the finish line in a dead heat with the master of the cinema world.

A moment to blow and regain breath, and then back to work, with a thrown-away remark to the world in general, "A man must perspire once every day to keep in reasonably good health." Not that he had to excuse his behavior to anyone. It was more a reminder to himself, to do something, any-

* This song had an enormous success in America as "Too Much Mustard." GEORGE PRATT

thing, to offset all those midnight hours of sitting, sitting, always sitting in that projection room, sitting and watching and wondering how he could possibly make his very best a little better.

There were also tragic moods that had to be exorcised by impromptu declamations. One of his favorites, repeated over and over again against the hammering and background chatter of stagehands (Hey, Pete, what the hell'd you do with my hammer, anyway?) was, "See this garment that I wear?/ It was knitted by the fingers of the dead./ The long and yellow fingers of the dead . . ." Nobody would pay the slightest attention to this. It was all part of working with Griffith.

A thing that kept preying on my mind was the black thought that I had arrived on the scene too late. I had been present through the making of a whole string of *little* pictures, not big ones. Things like the grim handling of *The Escape,* where Bobby Harron was changed from a bright young lad into a horribly grotesque, murdering monster by the effects of what was then smugly referred to as a social disease. He even showed a piece of film shot through a microscope showing the actual *Spirochaete pallida,* white corkscrews whirling and darting in some poor devil's bloodstream. I can still hear the horror in Griffith's voice as we watched this film in the projection room, saying, "Gahhhd! Can you imagine having anything like *that* in your body?"

Home, Sweet Home was virtually a remake of *Pippa Passes,* only instead of having the voice of a gay young girl bring cheer and faith to despairing mankind, the music of *Home, Sweet Home* changed the lives of a set of different characters, a sort of multiple story dominated by a single thematic idea.*

There were others, equally unimportant in my juvenile judgment. Oh, they were done to perfection, but they were *little* pictures, while what I wanted to see was how he handled crowds and mass action, as in *The Battle,* or *Judith,* or *Elderbush Gulch.*

Perhaps this day was over. I remembered from my schooldays a line to the effect that the sun at its zenith is already beginning to decline. Too bad, but there it was.

Then came the electrifying rumor that he was getting ready to do a really big one, a thing called *The Clansman,* from a novel by the Reverend Thomas Dixon, Jr.

I caught the next car downtown and hurried to the library, which was located on the two top floors of Hamburger's department store, at Eighth

* This, unquestionably, must have been a trial run for the massive effort of *Intolerance.* (Author)

and Broadway. I went straight to the fiction shelves and ran down the alphabet to the D's. And there it was! Dixon, *The Clansman*. I grabbed it before anyone else could beat me to it and took it home, reading the first few chapters on the streetcar.

It wasn't much of a story. Terribly biased, utterly unfair, the usual diatribe of a fire-eating Southerner, reverend or no reverend. For I knew that period and I knew it well. Grandfather Brown had served all through the Civil War with the 10th Massachusetts. He had been in every battle fought by the Army of the Potomac. Fredericksburg, Chancellorsville, Gettysburg. I'd heard all about these battles from his own eyewitness account. I'd also heard all about the aftermath, the horrors of Reconstruction and the rapacity of the political scoundrels who masked their robberies with a cloak of patriotism, the universally despised carpetbaggers.

I knew how earnestly people of my grandfather's class had tried to follow Lincoln's advice: "Let us . . . bind up the nation's wounds . . ." I also knew, from my own childhood travels in the South, how the Southerners kept tearing these wounds wide open again at every conversation, every meeting, every political rally. They were still fighting the Civil War, forty years after Appomattox. It was not so much the military defeat that hurt; it was the intense pain of their lacerated pride that rankled and burned and that could never be forgiven or forgotten.

I read all of the book entirely through that night in bed, and it was as bitter a hymn of hate as I had ever encountered. It was an old-fashioned hellfire sermon, filled with lies, distortions, and above all, the rankest kind of superstition.

The finish just about did me in. The actual book has to be read to realize that a minister of the gospel could seriously pretend that such a thing could possibly be.

A horrible Negro has killed a flower of young womanhood. For bestial reasons, of course. The girl's body is found, her eyes wide open, with the fixed, unseeing stare of death. Who could have done so foul a deed? Ah! They know how to find out, instantly. The eyes of the dead retain the image of the last thing seen at the moment of death. So they peer into the dead girl's eyes, using a powerful microscope, and sure enough, there staring back at them from out of the poor innocent victim's eyes leers the bestial face of that damned black bastard everyone hated!

After which, the deluge. It was burn, slay, kill without mercy. Which our heroes proceed to do, riding by night and disguised, even to their horses, in all-concealing white, so that nobody could ever know who they were, where they came from, or what they were by day.

I put the book down, sick at heart. The plot not only turned on a long-outworn superstition about dead people's eyes but it glorified cowardice. And to add sacrilege to cowardice, they rode under the symbol of a burning cross.

Oh dear . . . Now I *knew* I had come on the scene too late. For I knew Griffith's thoroughness, his dedication, his fanatic intensity of concentration on whatever subject he was handling. He would take every element of this book and make it a thousandfold more terrible than it could possibly be in print. And the result could not fail to be a complete and crushing disaster.

I looked at the clock. It was four in the morning. I turned off the light and sought sleep, which soon came despite my heavy and aching heart.

❧ 4 ❧

The Anatomy of Success

There is nothing either good or bad,
but thinking makes it so.
SHAKESPEARE, "HAMLET"

IT WAS once again time to count the house, set up a balance sheet, and take a good long hard look at just how things stood.

The result was most gratifying. We, as a family, were in better shape than we'd ever been before in all our lives. My father had been taken into Griffith's stock company from the very first day at his regular salary of forty dollars a week. My mother had been engaged at the same time as Frank Woods's assistant in charge of women. This was a peculiar, not to say unique, position that had been created for her. She was the official chaperone of the lot and she had a regular police badge to prove it. This badge, which designated her as City Mother No. 1, was strictly honorary and carried no power of arrest or anything else. Its scope was extremely limited and the law it was meant to enforce was nothing if not plainly clear: No Hanky Panky on the Lot. There were never any problems of enforcement. Not that everybody suddenly became good little angels overnight. Experienced sinners are nothing if not practical, and since all they had to do was to step across the street to be out of her jurisdiction, life went on much as it had before her elevation to power. Thus, justice was triumphant and all was well.

All was well with us as a family, too. We had been on salary, all three of us, for eight solid months without a break. Our salaries had remained the same: forty dollars for my father, thirty for my mother, and ten for me, but that total income of eighty dollars each and every week, rain or shine, month after month, gave us the greatest prosperity we had ever known. We were so very well off that we could afford to buy a piano for forty dollars, including cartage. This was not really a luxury but a necessity for a family of musicians.

The only reason—besides the lack of money—that we had never had a piano before was that you can't carry a piano as hand luggage on one-night stands. However, smaller instruments could be managed, so I had a violin, which I had bought, case and bow included, for ten dollars; and I had a flute, which had been given to me because it had a crack in it. (That crack didn't really hurt the flute at all, once I had learned how to cope with it: by soaking the flute overnight in water, the wood would swell and the crack close, so I could get quite a few hours of practice with it before the wood dried out and the tone became unreliable.) The violin was not really a good investment. I wanted one that would play the "Caprice Chinoise," while the best this one could manage was "Träumerei," a crippled rendition at that. But then, what can you expect for ten dollars, including rosin?

What really soothed and sustained my spirit was the experience, the good, hard, down-to-earth experience I had been forced to undergo as Bitzer's general factotum and everybody's errand boy. The whims and vagaries of the Pathé camera were by now old stuff to me. Nobody taught me, patiently and with long-suffering care, just what to do and how to do it. When Bitzer looked up at the sky and said, "There'll be clouds today. Get up on the roof and shoot some clouds," I went up on the roof and shot some clouds.

Not just any clouds. We were doing a picture called *The Avenging Conscience,* and Griffith wanted a lot of big, billowy, dramatic clouds to use as background for angels. Or grim, leaden, menacing clouds, preferably the kind with long black curtains of rain hanging down to touch the earth as they marched across the sky, suitable for devils and witches and imps of Satan. For this was a picture all about the murderous moods of a man long overdue for the loony bin. This called for symbolism, and I somehow became promoted to the symbolism department, mostly, I imagine, because shooting natural symbolism takes a lot of time and mine wasn't worth very much, so they could spend it freely.

I learned by doing. When the camera made a funny chugging noise, it meant that the upper loop was too short and the claws were tearing the perforations. Cure: use a larger upper loop. Too short a lower loop will do the same thing. Cure: larger lower loop. But not too large, because then the film will buckle against the feed sprocket and—*grunch!*—everything comes to a dead stop. After a very few such mistakes, a simple way of measuring both loops became self-evident. The film feeds into the camera and out again through a single large sprocket wheel. Before locking the film into the gate, measure the film inside the camera. If the length of film can be made to just touch the bottom of the camera, no more and no less, and if the upper loop is adjusted so there are just three frames' leeway, the lower loop will be exactly right and all will go well.

Except for a lot of exceptions, such as scratches, static, and in some cases, defective film itself, not to mention human errors, such as forgetting to put in the pressure pad, or to close the gate, or the door, or—or any number of things, such as an insecurely seated magazine, unlatched front boards, or forgetting to close and snap firmly the little lens in the back door through which focusing was done. The Pathé camera was commonly called a cracker box, because of its light wooden construction. It might with more justice have been called a Pandora's box, for all the troubles it could loose upon a poor defenseless cameraman. Something was forever going wrong with these Pathés, so something was forever having to be fixed, generally with the black sticky tape used by electricians. Almost anything could be done with tape and almost everything was. On-the-spot repair jobs were part of every cameraman's day, and I learned most of them in the privacy of my own rooftop, or garden, or lawn, or wherever.

For I was always being sent on more or less impossible missions. There was a time when I was standing outside the camera room, doing nothing in particular, when Griffith came by, paused, and without looking at me intoned, "Get me a peacock strutting on the green/and spreading all his glory to the sun." He accompanied this reading with graceful, molding gestures of both hands in the air, his eyes sightless and far away, lost in his own vision of what ought to be. He was like the Tenniel drawings of the White Knight in *Alice,* only of course without the mustache but with the same aquiline nose and that long, characteristic Hapsburg chin.

He moved on, without waiting for any questions or answers. I told Bitzer, who gave me one of our spare Pathé cameras and an old tripod that had seen better days, and away I went, headed for the Hostetter estate just down the street where they had peacocks as lawn ornaments.

I chased peacocks all over that lawn the whole day long. They strutted and they spread all over the place, but a certain coolness had sprung up between us and they did all their strutting and spreading as far away from me as they could get. One of them finally did spread his tail within camera range, but he was facing away from me, so it was all a total loss.

Well, it had been a long day and I became very tired, so I sat down behind the low-mounted camera and waited for the sun to go down. There was nothing to do for or with the camera. I was focused at ten feet, the finder parallax had been adjusted to that distance, so I was as ready as I'd ever be. In the meanwhile, it was good, very good, to simply sit there and rest, because peacock chasing is a tiring sport.

Unwittingly, I was doing what I should have done from the first, which was to remain motionless and therefore absolutely invisible to the animal world. Slowly, the peacocks moved toward me, occasionally making quick little rushes, stopping, and then spreading out their fans.

My heart nearly choked off my breath when one of them began his rush straight at the camera. Fortunately, the Pathé camera turns from the rear, so I was able to hold my arm and hand hidden as I turned the handle. Sitting and crouching as I was, I could see straight into the finder. The sun was almost down. A ray of strong light raked across the lawn from between two trees. And the peacock charged straight into that spot of light, stopped short, then raised his tail high to spread it in a full fan that just filled the finder from edge to edge.

I was so grateful to that peacock that I would have kissed him if I could have caught him. Griffith was delighted by the shot, which he praised in the highest terms possible to him, which was to murmur with soft content, "That is very fine."

The spider episode was another of my solo ventures. The direction, in the same mystical, faraway tone: "Get me a spider, weaving her web/to snare unwary blunderers/in the night." I didn't mind being instructed in verse. I was used to it. Griffith was up to his eyebrows in Edgar Allan Poe, who was the inspiration for *The Avenging Conscience,* and he couldn't help speaking in iambic pentameters of a sort, thanks to his love of Shakespeare and his hope of being a poet himself someday.

I knew what he meant, so I took to camera-hunting for spiders. One of the first and certainly the most disheartening things I learned about these pesky arachnids was that they spin their webs just at sundown, when the waning light is fading into no light at all. Furthermore, there was no telling where any given spider might decide to spin a web on any given twilight.

So I played the law of averages. Where a spider has built before, the same or another spider is likely to build again. There was a place in our garden where two strong rose canes were spaced about eighteen inches apart. This was where I'd have built a web if I had been a spider, because it was the best location in the garden. Besides, there were wisps of previous webs entangled in the thorns, so I knew it had been used before by at least one spider.

So I set up the camera and crowded in as close as I could. Knowing that the light would be dim, at best, I lined up from west to east, to get all the direct light I could on the star of my show.

My prima donna appeared much earlier than I had any right to expect. There was still a good hour's light left, and I felt sure of the job. Too sure. Because the light turned gray and in swept the night fog that blankets California as a matter of regular course at that time of year, and although the little lady spun her web exactly according to plan, the web was invisible. I could see her going through the motions, but I could not see the strands in that dull murky light. I ran into the house and grabbed up the first powder I could find—my mother's face powder—and blew it on the net. Also on the spider. Now I could see the strands but not the spider, because Miss Eight-legs resented being made up and she walked out on me in a temperamental huff.

Next night I set up again, but on the opposite side, reasoning that a full back light would show up the transparent strands while a front light would not. This time there was no fog. The low sun hung clear in the sky. My lady came out and threw her anchor lines across, then whipped over to the middle to begin working around and around, tacking the new-spun silk to the anchor lines with one hind leg. The web stood out clear and strong against the westering light. A shocking thought hit me. That very low sun might be hitting the lens. I jumped up and looked. It wasn't. Not quite, but very nearly. So I turned with one hand and used my hat as a lens shade while my star performer did her stuff.

Just then a fly came barreling in at full speed, as though late for an appointment, and ran bang into the net. The spider pounced. I'd always thought that spiders devoured their prey immediately, but no; this one whirled the insect around and around, wrapping it in silk until it was *all* silk, in a cocoon really.

I was still watching and turning, fascinated and revolted at the same time. The film ran out. I checked the camera for scratches. These show up as little specks of emulsion stuck tight to the polished steel of the aperture plate. No scratches. Nothing on the pressure pad, either. So I turned in the film and went home.

The shot was beautiful on the screen. The back light worked fine. The spider was spinning silver threads that stood out strong and clear. The jump of the spider brought a gasp from the people watching and Griffith's low, almost purringly satisfied murmur of "That is very fine." He added, in a businesslike tone, to Jimmy Smith, "We'll use just enough of the start to see what it is and then cut in just the jump, nothing more. Keep it short. As few frames as possible. A lot of people don't like spiders."

I felt an urge to apologize. "Mr. Griffith, I'm sorry about having to use so much film, but I had to waste four hundred feet just to get that little bit."

"Waste?" he asked. "What do you mean, waste? You got the shot, didn't you? Well, when you get what you're after, it's worth whatever it costs, no matter what. All right, Jimmy, let's run that reel we worked on last night. I think we can tighten up that garden stuff so it won't drag so much."

A few days later I was alone in the camera room making a new supply of ground glasses. Bitzer liked them to be thin, very thin, like microscope slides. There was an optical firm downtown that carried all sorts of glassware, and from them I was able to get wafer-thin slips of optically flat glass cut to fit the oblong brass frame that held the Pathé ground glasses. These had to be ground by hand, and since it was a long and time-consuming process that could not be hurried, I was the official ground-glass grinder. It wasn't much of a chore. Simply mix a very little triple-O emery with oil, put a drop between two of these little oblongs of glass, and work them with a rotary motion between thumb and forefinger with almost no pressure at all. Wash with alcohol and examine from time to time. When the glass becomes misty and just barely frosty enough to hold an image, it's time to use jeweler's rouge and oil to plane off the high spots of the microscopically fine grittiness of the abraded surface of the glass. Properly done, the finished glass was all but transparent, just misty enough to show Bitzer where the visual image was. The final test was to put the glass in the camera and study the image through Bitzer's focusing microscope. If you could see the image in clear, strong detail and yet *not* see the grain of the glass, it was right. To hit this balance exactly right was more a matter of luck than good judgment. But there was a lot of leeway. You could always regrind or repolish. It might take all day, but then, what else is time for?

I was working away on the ground glasses when Griffith suddenly appeared in the door of the camera room. He did not come in. He did not look at me or notice what I was doing. He was in one of his dreamy moods, far away from the world of here and now and seemingly in the grip of a fascinating inner vision. He looked with unseeing eyes at a spot above my head, a place where the gallery would be if he were speaking from a stage, and intoned with a deep, mystical voice, "Get me a lily . . . an *Easter* lily . . . holding its pure white virginal sweetness to the heaven it longs for . . . only to droop, to droop, to droop"—his hands were moving in expressive gestures as he spoke, so that I could *see* that lily—"to droop . . . and to die . . . stricken with shame . . ."

It was a performance, all right. Corse Payton himself couldn't have made it any hammier. He turned and left without waiting for any comment or acceptance or objection or anything else. The Oracle had spoken.

I hunted up Bitzer and told him what was up. He was disgusted to the point of open rebellion. "Symbolism!" he snorted. "More of his damned symbolism. It's not enough to have devils dancing up out of hell and angels flying out of clouds, but he's got to have spiders catching bugs and peacocks spreading tails. Why can't he come right out and show what he means in plain terms the way he's always done? Oh, I know what he's after, all right.

Somebody's done our Little Nell wrong and he wants to show it by having a lily droop and die. But how the hell can you make a lily droop on cue? You can't. Go tell him you can't do it."

I thought a moment and then said, "You tell him. I like it here."

He gave me a wave of dismissal. "All right. Do what you can. Only don't say I never warned you. There's just *no* way to make a lily droop and die, not unless you can get Sarah Bernhardt or, better yet, Anna Pavlova to play the lily. Better try Pavlova. She made it with a swan. Maybe she can do it with a lily."

There was a small initial problem of getting a nice fresh Easter lily. Ordinarily I would have simply told Ed Buskirk or Ralph DeLacey what was wanted and they'd get it. But the prop department was in far too much trouble as it was without taking on any more. It seems that they were trying to turn out twenty or thirty pairs of adult-size angel wings, made of papier-mâché and coated with feathers. The idea was to paint the wings with sticky, quick-drying shellac and then press chicken feathers onto them by hand. It was a good idea, but enough had gone wrong that the air was thick with floating feathers and profanity, while Ed and Ralph and a couple of helpers were trying unsuccessfully to work with shellac-wet hands in a bushel basket of loose feathers.

I somehow felt that it was not quite the opportune time to file any requests, however urgent, so I went out scouting and found my own Easter lily and brought it back to the camera room.

It was a nice lily, bright and fresh. Perfect casting for the part. But how do you get a lily to wilt? Well, any plant will wilt if it dries out. Heat wilts plants, too. So I'd have to use a combination of heat and dryness.

Result: a lily perched away next to the ceiling on top of a ladder. A camera on a low platform or parallel, lens even with the lily. Below, a gas stove turned on full blast. Around, a drapery of black cloth to hold in the heat. For light, a couple of strong Mazda bulbs, one for cross light, the other for fill. The idea: to use stop motion and take a picture a minute until the lily gave up the ghost.

But wait a second. If I took a picture a minute, that would be only sixty pictures an hour which, run at sixteen pictures to the second, would come to only four and one quarter seconds' running time. Griffith had said, most impressively, that the lily was to droop, droop, droop. Not drop dead. So I changed that to a picture every ten seconds. I had no idea of how long it would take the lily to droop, but that was as good a guess as I could make. If it didn't work, I could always get another lily and try again.

The stop-motion shaft of the Pathé camera was located below and a little to the right of the main drive shaft. Geared at a ratio of one to eight, and turning in the opposite direction to the regular handle, the synchronization was such as to have the shutter always closed when the handle was all the way down. So it was a simple matter to flip the handle over backward, wait ten counts, then flip again; then wait again, then flip again . . .

I don't know how long it took that lily to begin to wilt, but I'm sure of one thing: I wilted first, and by a wide margin. I am guilty of no impropriety when I say that it was hotter than the southwest corner of hell up under that ceiling, and that because of my ten-second interval between exposures, I couldn't climb down from that high platform for a drink of water or the reverse, or anything else.

Outside, I could hear people saying good night as they went home. After a while my mother came in to see what was holding me up. She asked how much longer I'd be, and I couldn't tell her because I'd never wilted a lily before. She left, and after a while she was back with some sandwiches and a bottle of milk. She left them on the platform where I could reach them and I ate, ten chews to the turn, while that lily actually seemed to look brighter and fresher than when I had begun.

By ten o'clock I was about ready to give up. Then I noticed that the lily was beginning to show definite signs of distress. A lot of gimp—as we used to say—had gone out of it, so this was no time to quit. I hung on. By eleven it was hanging on the ropes, dead on its feet, and by twelve it was down and out, and so was I. It had been a close match, though, and I climbed down from my cramped position on top of that parallel feeling that I had won no better than a draw.

I left the film in the laboratory with a note to Abe Scholtz telling him that this was a special stop-motion effect and to handle it tenderly because a lot of sweat had gone into the making of the scene.

Word that something extra special was in the works had gone out, and the projection room was packed when we all crammed in to see what it was all about. Even Ed Buskirk and Ralph DeLacey were there, still picking chicken feathers from between their fingers and out of their hair.

Griffith pressed the buzzer. The room went dark and the picture came on. And it was beautiful, simply *beautiful!* The blossom was facing three-quarters to the camera, and both Abe and Joe had done their prettiest to make this about as fine a still life as had ever graced the screen. There was a murmur of admiration that swept through the room, and that made me feel so good, so very good, that I tingled all the way down to my toes.

Then something happened. That central stamen, the long part that stands up from the middle, had been curving slightly upward. Now it began to sag, first at the middle and then at the tip, wilting and sinking and bending downward as the life went out of it. I could hear snorts and giggles and assorted snickers from all over the room. Then that stamen seemed to gather renewed life. It made a brave effort to get up again, almost succeeded, only to fall down, dead and defeated.

By this time the room was all but out of control. They seemed to think this was the funniest thing they had ever seen. But there was worse and more of it to come. The entire blossom began sagging and drooping and becoming more and more flaccid, until at last it hung as a limp, discolored, dangling mass . . .

Nobody even tried to hold in any more. They were not merely laughing, they were guffawing in an outrageous enjoyment of what was to me the bitterest kind of public disgrace. Billy Fildew turned up the lights and looked in through the port to join in the laughter. I sought Griffith's face, to see how he was taking it. He was laughing louder than any of the others, head back, mouth wide, tears of laughter in his eyes. "That," he announced to the listening world, "is without a doubt the *damnedest* thing I have *ever* seen!"

It had become so insufferably hot in the projection room that I had to get outside where there was some cool air. The last thing I heard on the way out was Bitzer's voice raising an even louder laugh by something he was saying about lost manhood. It was a black moment, a very black moment for me, indeed. And it stayed black, because the story spread and kept on spreading until all Hollywood was laughing at me.

Possibly the most ardent spreader of this misadventure was Frank Woods, who dearly loved a bawdy story, especially if it happened to be true. His favorite place for telling these stories was the Hoffman House, a restaurant downtown on Spring Street, where he dined at a large round table with certain of his cronies, such as Dr. Frank Crane and Harry Carr and I don't know how many others. I never went there myself, because the least you could get a dinner for was a dollar, but I heard about it from Elmer Clifton, who was ambitious enough to go without other things for the privilege of dining in distinguished company.

According to Elmer, Frank Woods had built the episode into a wonderfully effective act. Standing at the edge of the table, and illustrating the action of the lily with an extended forefinger, he had the entire café in stitches, or rolling in the aisles, or whatever theatrical term best fitted a hilarious response.

Enough was enough. I braced myself for the ordeal and confronted Frank Woods in his office to demand, with hurt indignation, why he wanted to keep running me down all the time.

He laughed. "Running you *down?* I'm not running you down, I'm building you up! Or haven't you sense enough to realize that?" He continued in a slow, temperate voice, "Who ever heard of you before this happened? Oh sure, people around the lot knew you were Bitzer's camera boy, but who else? *Nobody!* Remember, I mentioned your name ten or a dozen times every time I told about this, so if you ever have to go looking for another job anywhere around town, you won't have to explain who you are—they already know."

I was still sulkily sore. "I don't want to be known that way—not as a fool, anyway."

He was completely serious as he responded, "Who ever said you were a fool? I never did, nor D. W., either. He sort of liked you before, in a general way because you did your job and never complained. But you're in solid now because you *took direction,* which is all he's ever asked of anybody. He told you exactly what he wanted and you gave him exactly what he asked for. The result was ludicrous, but whose fault was that? Yours, for carrying out his orders, or his, for giving them? *He* knows. *I* know. And that's all that counts around here. Anything else on your mind?"

"Yes, sir. I was sort of thinking that now that I know how to handle a camera, I might feel around for another job somewhere else and start all over from the ground up."

He nodded gravely. "Well, there'll be no trouble about that. Anybody who's ever worked with Griffith for any length of time can pick his spot and go to work first thing tomorrow morning. But remember this: anybody you go to work for will be just another Griffith imitator. Now, who do you want to work for? A cheap carbon copy, or the one and only original, none genuine without the name blown in the bottle? How old are you now, anyway?"

"Sixteen. Going on seventeen."

He became very earnest, almost pleadingly so as he continued, "Well, you're young yet, with a lot of time before you, so why don't you be a little bighearted and understanding and give D.W. another chance? After all, you shouldn't shut a man out of your life for *one* mistake. He'll do better in future, I'm sure, if you'll be a little patient. Why not give him another chance and see how he works out? It *might* be to your advantage. How about it?"

I knew he was laughing at me, and that didn't brighten my mood in the least. I pumped up what little dignity I could to answer, "I don't know. I'll think about it."

"You do that. And, if you should decide to move elsewhere, let me know and I'll give you the biggest send-off I can. I'll tell 'em you're without a doubt the finest lily-wilter in town."

He couldn't hold the pose after that, so he simply leaned back and laughed in my face. There was no malice in the laugh, nothing but amusement. But I didn't enjoy being laughed at—no teenager ever does—so I got out of there and decided to lie low until the thing blew over.

My shame and my disgrace, which existed mostly in my own badly bruised ego, soon was swept away and forgotten by a much greater, indeed massive mistake made by Griffith himself.

Griffith had become—well, strange during the time I had known him. He had abandoned his old and by now famous philosophy of telling his stories in terms of suspense. During his Biograph days he had turned out picture after picture that followed one general formula. Put the good people in the worst possible trouble, build the troubles higher and higher until they become unbearable, and then come through with a crashing reverse that leaves everybody in the audience weak and exhausted with the blessed relief of a last-instant rescue.

But Griffith had become sick and tired of doing the same old thing over and over again. It had become, in his phrase, nothing more than grinding out one sausage after another. Sure, it worked. It worked fine and everybody made a lot of money, because audiences—*his* audiences—liked his brand of sausages very much indeed.

Now that he had his own studio and nobody to boss him, he was dead set on bringing poetry to the screen. And not just the everyday, cut-and-dried, school-recitation poetry of Longfellow or Bryant but the weirdly fascinating horrors of Edgar Allan Poe.

According to Bitzer, who had shot the old Biograph pictures, Griffith had always been obsessed by poetry in general and by Poe in particular. He had made a picture called *Edgar Allen* (sic) *Poe,* raven and all. Another, called *Faded Lillies,* was probably the root cause of my current disgrace. But these pictures had been turned out at such breakneck speed—at an average of two each week, year in and year out—and everything was so touch-and-go, that he had neither the time nor the footage to develop what he felt should be the full poetic values implied by such titles as *Pippa Passes* or *Enoch Arden* or anything else. Imagine the sheer concentration of values it must have taken to cram Jack London's *Call of the Wild* or Shakespeare's *Taming of the Shrew* or Dickens's *Cricket on the Hearth* into fifteen minutes of running time. Every inch, every frame of film had to be compressed into the tightest possible essence of story values to get such ideas on the screen at all. Small wonder that after five years of this sort of work, Griffith had become the master editor that he was, and that his staccato cutting of nothing but "net" values had put him far and away above and beyond any and all competitors.

If there is truth in the saying that limitations reveal the master, those Griffith worked under had forced him to become what he was. Not that he liked these limitations. He wanted more and more time and scope in which to expand and develop his ideas. Biograph would hear nothing of such foolishness. Movie programs were thought of as the poor man's vaudeville or music hall or variety show, in which variety was of the essence. The ideal program would be four or five one-reelers, all on different subjects, a knockabout comedy, illustrated songs, and from 1911, a Pathé weekly newsreel.

Out of the five one-reelers there might be one or two that were not half bad. It was a sort of grab-bag deal, designed to spread the risk. But to make one five-reeler was to gamble everything on one shot. So why take a chance?

Griffith was an all-or-nothing gambler. Biograph was not. Hence the split.

Now that he was his own master and could do as he pleased, Griffith went all-out for freedom unlimited. Or almost. Old habits die hard. The vaudeville idea of serving up a mixed grill of short turns that would be sure to please some of the people some of the time still clung to him. He made *Apple Pie Mary* as just another Biograph of the familiar home-folks pattern that had served him so well in the past. The same was true of *The Battle of the Sexes,* started in New York but finished in Hollywood.

But the urge to expand was irresistible. He used *Apple Pie Mary* as the second of four stories to be bound together by a single link, the oldest and most familiar heart song he could think of, *Home, Sweet Home.* So now he had four stories in one, all fully played out to build up into a massive production in six reels. He had always wanted to use symbolism, so now he tried it by having grotesque figures representing Lust and Greed battling with his hero, who aspired to his heart's desire, a literal, visible angel. Griffith was flying now, but flying with one foot on the ground, so to speak, and with that foot deeply rooted in experience and tradition.

There was nothing very new or daring about playing allegory in the literal terms of living actors. The idea of portraying Greed and Lust and Avarice and all the rest goes back to the first stirrings of stagecraft, from the Greek tragedies to the pre-Elizabethan Moralities. A perennial theatrical hit was *Everyman,* a morality play always up to date. Horror stories were probably as old as mankind and used in the caveman days to keep little toddlers from straying out into the open, where they might be gobbled up by some low-flying pterodactyl.

I remembered a certain winter night when I was living in school-exile with my grandparents in Delta, Ohio. A blizzard was howling in from Canada. Even with the fires going, the rooms were cold as I lay huddled in bed reading Poe's "The Tell-Tale Heart" by the light of a flickering oil lamp. Between the screaming of the gale, the clattering of loose shutters, the beating of hail and sleet upon the windows, and the wavering black shadows cast by the unsteady flame of the lamp, I scared myself half to death reading that story.

So I knew what was in Griffith's vision as he stalked slowly through the bedlam of a set being constructed, competing with the noise of hammers and saws to declaim, with expressive gestures and with a voice pitched to a low and ominous monotone, "They are neither beast nor human,/they are neither man nor woman . . . /they are *ghouls* . . ."

So we had ghouls. We had devils. We had peacocks, personifying Vanity, and we had spiders. We also had an owl that refused to act but that simply sat on its branch, staring fixedly at Griffith as he made funny noises and waggled his fingers from his ears and did everything else he could think of to provoke a response. It was no go. The owl refused to act, so it ended where all other non-performing actors land, on the cutting-room floor.

This time the big thing was angels. Not just one or two angels but a whole flight of angels, or as many as the prop department could make wings for.

For this we needed a much bigger stage than anyone had ever built before. So one was built, a monstrous platform of some fifty by three hundred feet. The angels, played by as many pretty young girls as could be found in the neighborhood, had to be swung from heavy piano wires from overhead rigging. This called for what amounted to a full theatrical gridiron assembly to be built all along both sides of the set. Wires and pulleys and cleats for securing the lines in place had to be rigged, mounted, and tested with sandbags weighing some two hundred pounds each. No; the girls didn't weigh that much, but there had to be that much margin of safety.

The girls were assembled, fitted with harnesses to which the wings could be attached, dressed in angel robes, and crowned with identical long-flowing blond wigs. They were then hoisted, one by one, until their feet were about fifteen feet above the floor. This took time, and by the time the ninth or tenth girl had been hauled up into position, angels numbers one and two began to be very sick indeed. They were lowered and made to lie down and sniff smelling salts. During this, the other girls who had been hauled up decided to join the act, so they too got rid of whatever breakfast they had aboard. Pretty soon all we had was a lot of sick angels lying around the edges of the stage, with Ed Buskirk sending Charlie Muth, one of our best drivers, on a hurry-up trip for a couple of dozen more vials of smelling salts.

In the meanwhile, we had Eddie Hungerford's Pierce-Arrow, top down, standing by at the edge of the platform, with the camera mounted on a high tripod in the back of the car, everything lashed down tight and turnbuckled for greater security. The camera was loaded with undeveloped negative of the cloud shots I had taken every time the clouds had been there. Tests had been taken from the end of each take, and these tests had been blown up into four-by-five paper prints, from which Griffith could make his selection. These tests also enabled Bitzer to determine the position of the frame line, which was marked on the undeveloped negative for proper placement in the aperture gate. So we were all ready. Everything was set. All we had to do now was pull up the girls and run the camera through the angels, and that should do it. As this was a double exposure, the angels would "ghost" through the clouds, but that was all right. Angels were supposed to be ethereal beings, anyway.

So the camera was ready, Griffith was ready, Eddie started his motor, and we were all set to go when we discovered that our angels were turning slowly around and around, heading every which way.

So now it was a matter of letting them all down again, so some sort of stabilizing device could be affixed to each angel. This turned out to be a simple yoke of strong black carpet thread attached to each harness and held by hand by someone off-camera. It was now a matter of mustering all hands and the cook to each hold a thread to keep our angels from flying backward out of heaven.

By now, after all this delay, the day was waning toward the danger point. It might have been well to call it off for the day. But this could not be done, because Griffith had scheduled a showing of the picture at Pomona for that night at seven. This was not a preview. It was, in the theatrical sense, an out-of-town tryout to test audience reaction and thereby spot the weak points and the strong points as well, to reduce the one and to augment the other. For this he not only needed but he had to have this angel shot developed, dried, printed, dried, and cut into the reel by showtime.

So it had to be done and it *was* done, in the last rays of the low-hanging sun. Eddie Hungerford ran his Pierce back and forth among the angels, and Bitzer shot the scene three or four times for insurance.

Griffith left immediately for Pomona, taking all seven or eight reels of *The Avenging Conscience* with him. Not that the theatrical release would be that long but because he needed the audience to tell him where to cut and how much to bring down the footage.

There was intense activity in the laboratory. Abe Scholtz did his stuff with his usual thoroughness. No time to wait for the film to be air-dried. It went through an alcohol bath, and as soon as it was dry enough to handle, Joe Aller took over, also using alcohol to rush out the prints.

Charlie Muth was standing by with his Packard ready for the run to the rescue, a law-defying race to Pomona with the angel scene. The picture was under way by the time he could get there, but he was not too late. Griffith himself spliced the scene into the reel that was next to be run, so it was there and on time and ready to go, but only just barely.

And when it came on, the audience laughed. With reason. The angels were not really flying but just hanging there, like so many sides of beef in a meat market. They were not serenely happy and joyous as angels are supposed to be. They were the sickest, most woebegone angels anyone could imagine. Griffith, in the projection room, stopped the machine before the laugh could build to unquenchable proportions. He swiftly ran down the film to where the normal action began, and the show continued. Nobody in the audience paid any attention to this. Film was forever breaking and they accepted this as such.

In the postmortem that followed the showing, many different opinions were advanced as to what was wrong with the scene. For one thing, the angels weren't flying in the right position. They should have been flying like birds, with heads forward and bodies back, with flowing draperies and gracefully moving wings, and not like so many white socks hung out on a washline to dry. There were many other ideas and suggestions as to how to stage the scene, but Griffith came through with the best idea of all, which was to throw the whole damn thing out and forget it.

Somehow this made me feel a lot better about my little mistake. Mine hadn't cost much. Thirty-five cents for the lily, eight dollars' worth of film, and seventy-five cents for my time and labor, while Griffith's cost many thousands; he wasn't saying how many and nobody felt it diplomatic to ask.

Somehow, despite all the wild chances Griffith had taken with the film, the first-night audience in the big Clune's Auditorium thought it was wonderful. They followed it every inch of the way with breathless intensity. The allegories didn't bother them a bit, possibly because as youngsters they had been thrilled by the same bedtime stories of ghosts and goblins and evil spirits and guardian angels as everyone else. To say nothing of the grisly horrors of *Grimm's Fairy Tales*, full of blood and terror and the blackest kind of witchcraft and treachery. The idea of a man being tortured all but out of his mind by an imaginary murder was as simple as ABC to them, because they too had committed murders, every one of them, in the world of their imagination. So this was not a real film about real people, but a sort of fairy tale, to be classed with *Sleeping Beauty* or *Cinderella,* meant to be enjoyed but not necessarily to be believed. Griffith had outguessed everybody once again by knowing his audience not only thoroughly but exhaustively, inside and out.

∽ 5 ∽

Sorcerer's Apprentice

If at first you don't succeed,
Try, try again.
COPYBOOK MAXIM

THE deeper we got into the rehearsals and preparations for *The Clansman,*
the less forbidding the prospects. True, the story had everything wrong with
it. But if so, what about the universally acclaimed *Hamlet,* that blood-soaked
compost of murder and madness, treachery and double-dealing that ends
with a whole stageful of assorted corpses—and without so much as one
single laugh in the entire show?

Maybe *The Clansman* would score a similar hit *because* of its defects,
not in spite of them. I didn't know. It was all far beyond me. All I could lay
a firm grasp on was that in this, my first really big one, there would be
compensations. There would be compensations, indeed.

Consider the camera. During the Kinemacolor days it had been strictly
hands off and no peeking because of the Trust situation. But by now I was
not only allowed to see and handle the Pathé camera, but I had been forced
to use one as part of my job.

This was not the result of any plan. I was simply turned loose with a
camera and a magazine of film and it was sink or swim, survive or perish.
The only reason I was given these jobs in the first place was that my time
wasn't worth much, so they could afford to squander it.

By the time we got around to actually doing *The Clansman,* I was wise
enough to the multiplex vagaries of the Pathé camera to meet any challenge it could offer and meet it head-on and be sure of coming out with no
worse than a draw. I now loaded and prepared Bitzer's camera for him so
that he had nothing to do but line up, focus, and compose his picture.

Composition. That was the thing. That and an infallible instinct for
exposure were the secrets of Bitzer's truly wonderful photography. It was

also the secret of how he managed to make slender short-statured Henry Walthall into the giant he appeared to be in *Judith of Bethulia.*

"Perch him up on something," explained Bitzer. "Box, couch, throne, anything. Squat the camera down as low as you can without overshooting the set. Then play Blanche Sweet as far away as you can in the background, at full length; then he'll look big and she'll look little and that's all there is to it."

But there was more, much more to it than that. He had an instinct for such things that I couldn't grasp then and can't explain now. Things seemed to fall into place for him. Even in the little close-up he took of me playing a violin, he arranged the drapes and adjusted the lighting of the background as carefully as though he were creating a masterpiece. Which, if the result counted for anything, he was, considering the material he had to work with.

Composition. That was everything. Exposure was important, too, but that was a matter of scientific judgment. Art isn't. And Bitzer was an artist first of all, and a lot of other things to round him out as a human being. He was also a humorist in a bitter sort of way, easily at home with the Germanic sort of black comedy known as gallows wit. Knowing of his home life made me realize why this had to be.

But the real Bitzer was Bitzer the artist, first, last, and all the time, and his art was the art of pictorial composition, in which lighting is not a separate element but the key factor, the essence of any fine picture in any medium. Good lighting, good picture; bad lighting, bad picture; wonderful lighting, wonderful picture. But before you can light anything you have to have something to light, and that's where pictorial composition becomes the all-important thing.

Rembrandt to the contrary notwithstanding, there is nothing very useful from a cameraman's point of view in having a half-lighted face suspended against a background of densely impenetrable gloom. But as for Vermeer, ah! there's the lad who knew how to use daylight the way we had to use it, with natural reflections from natural sources and with light backgrounds that could be shaded and lightened this way and that, so as to play light against dark and dark against light. And when I heard, from Cash Shockey, that Vermeer used a camera obscura built almost exactly like a Graflex, only without shutter or plates, and drew what he saw on the ground glass, Mynheer V. was our boy no matter what any art critic had to say.

Not that we had access to museums full of masterpieces to study. Located as we were at the far edge of the Far West, we depended mostly on pictures collected from old bookstores, which were surprisingly well stocked, with their wares low in price. I found a copy of Dante's *Inferno,* with pictures by Doré, in Holmes's bookstore on Main Street. This was a big book with a big price, but since it was so valuable an educational textbook in the art of pictorial composition, I recklessly spent the sixty-five cents it cost and took my treasure home for detailed study in the technique of compelling the eye to focus on the heart of the composition.

So although I was not yet a cameraman or anything like one, I was on my way and progressing steadily toward my goal, with the examples of masters at work all around me. Certain values had become crystallized. I knew the weird and wonderful ways of at least one camera, the Pathé, and I knew exposure through knowing what the right exposure looks like in the camera. So now with Doré for composition and Vermeer for lighting, there was nothing very much left for me to do except grow up. This would take time. Too bad, but there it was. Bitter as the truth was to face, I would have to become a little less gangly and awkward, and I would most certainly have to overcome my distressing habit of falling over my own feet before I could hope to impress anyone with the idea that I was an extremely gifted artist with a world of experience and a man of such portentous dignity as to over-awe even the most skeptical of producers.

Well, if I couldn't be great myself, I could help others to extend their already established greatness, so I braced myself for the making of *The Clansman,* much as Pickett's men must have done before the charge at Gettysburg or Raglan's Six Hundred before riding into the valley of death at Balaclava.

And after all that bracing and braving myself up to meet the challenge of a really big picture, nothing much happened. As a matter of record, the first thing we did was to ride up over Cahuenga Pass, turn to the right at the top, and coast down the steep crooked road of Dark Canyon to where a narrow dirt lane led the way over bumps and roots and deep holes to a natural parklike clearing on the northern slope of Cahuenga Mountain. And here we stopped, got out, and shot off fireworks.

More accurately, a strange little man with a Mephisto beard and all but a short stump of his left arm missing managed the fireworks.* His name was Fireworks Wilson and he had been managing pyrotechnic displays for years. Having only one arm didn't bother him a bit. He could clamp a whole assortment of fireworks under his stump, fuses dangling forward, a lighted fuse in his teeth and a mortar in his one free hand, and go about his business as briskly as anyone. The lighted fuse that he wore between his teeth was not the familiar punkstick of our childhood days but a fiercely flaring paper

---

* *Photoplay* (June 1928, p. 36) mentions Walter "Slim" Hoffman as an explosives man on *Birth*. KEVIN BROWNLOW

tube of hissing fire. Whenever he turned his head to talk to us over his shoulder, and the gush of fire from between his teeth brushed threateningly close to the cluster of fuses held under his stump, we all drew back with instant unanimity. Not that we were afraid. Merely cautious.

Fireworks Wilson spoke scornfully, "What you scared of? I never had an accident in my life. Never."

His words may have been meant as reassurance, but they were voted down by the silent witness of that stump. I couldn't help but wonder what had happened to that left arm. I couldn't convince myself that it had been lost because of a hangnail, and it didn't seem reasonable to suppose it had been nibbled off by mice.

Anyway, Fireworks Wilson had some effects to show us, so we watched, poised for instant flight, as he set up his equipment. Traditionally, a battle calls for bombs bursting in air, so Fireworks set up a mortar—a metal tube some eighteen inches long and about three inches in diameter, mounted on a flat base with the business end pointing upward—and dropped a tightly wrapped paper package into the tube with a fuse dangling on the outside.

"Now watch," he said, as he applied the hissing firestick to the fuse. His advice was wasted. We were already watching with the greatest possible intensity. I moved a few feet to my right, ostensibly to get a better view, but actually because there had been a rather large live oak tree back of me that might be an obstacle in case of a precipitous withdrawal to a safer distance.

The fire hissed down through the fuse and disappeared into the mortar. There was a moment of intense silence, broken only by the distant call of a mountain quail. Then all hell broke loose. There was a stunning blast that shook the ground and all our nerves at the same time. The projectile shot up and up, growing tinier and tinier as it rose. All hands braced for the truly tremendous concussion that seemed sure to ensue. Instead, there was the faintest possible little *pip* from above, and that was that. We regrouped to find out what had happened.

"Got it upside down," explained Fireworks Wilson. "That was the bomb down here, firing charge up there. Nothing to worry about. Happens all the time."

He scuttled over to his car to get another mortar to replace the one that had been rather badly shattered by the misplaced blast. I say "scuttled" because that was exactly his way of moving. He could dart in any direction with astonishing agility, crouched over and making himself as small as possible. Probably a sort of conditioned reflex acquired through long handling of unreliable explosives.

He came back with a new mortar and a new bomb and a new firestick hissing and gushing flames from between his teeth. He had some difficulty placing the mortar in an upright position. The ground sloped down toward the river and it was of hard-baked decomposed granite that could not be scraped or shaped like soft soil. However, he managed to poise it somehow with some loose gravel under the lower side, after which he dropped in the new package, lit the fuse, and scuttled back out of the way.

This time the thing worked according to plan. There was a *whuff!* as the firing charge propelled the bomb into the air, followed by a *wham* as the bomb burst in air the way it was supposed to. It was a perfectly splendid effect, but there was one thing wrong with it. Too high. You can't shoot men charging into hand-to-hand conflict on the ground and still include bombs bursting fifty or a hundred feet over their heads. There had to be some way to see the bombs and the soldiers at the same time in the same shot or nobody would know what was happening.

This was explained to Fireworks, who dismissed the whole problem with a careless wave of his one remaining hand. "Nothing to it," he said, looking more like Mephisto than ever with another firestick spluttering from between his teeth. "Got just the ticket right here." He took one of the several fuse-dangling packets he was still carrying under the stump of his left arm and held it up for display. "Hand grenade. Perfectly safe. Nothing in it but half a pound of blasting powder. What you want to do is light it like this . . ." He held the dangling fuse up to the firestick. It caught immediately, and the fire ran down the fuse with such unexpected speed that we had no time to back away. ". . . And you want to watch that fuse . . . watch it carefully—and just as the fire reaches the charge—not too soon and not too late—especially not too late—you throw it—like *this!*"

Fireworks hurled the bomb into the air just as the fire reached the charge. It arched up and over, and just as it was coming down, *poof!* a big hot flame blew in all directions, giving off a cloud of white smoke that drifted away slowly in the slight breeze. "See that?" he exclaimed proudly. "Perfect. Ab-so-lutely perfect!" He added warningly, "Only you got to time it just right. Too soon and you get a lot of wiggly white trails from the fuse. Too late and you might get scorched a little. Now, you get yourself twenty or thirty men to stand around to throw these things over your battle and you'll get the damnedest finest bombardment you *ever* saw!"

"Suppose the boom is thrown too soon and it lands down among the soldiers?" asked Griffith. Fireworks stared at him. He didn't know that Griffith always said boom for bomb or gell for girl. But he gathered the meaning and replied somewhat scornfully, "Nothing to worry about. All they have to do is kick it out of the way."

"But suppose they kick it into someone else's way and it goes off?"

Fireworks sighed with an expression of exasperation. "Look, Mr. Griffith. You're staging a battle, right? You want realism, don't you? Suppose someone *does* get hurt a little. Not much. A foot blown off or something. What you want to do is hustle right on down to where he is and get a good big picture of it, and I tell you, sir, it'll *make* your picture. Yes-sir-*ee*-sir, it'll *make* your *picture!*"

Griffith disagreed. What Fireworks didn't know was that Griffith had shot battle pictures before and that he knew more about the ways and means of getting effects without casualties than Fireworks ever dreamed of in all his philosophies. So did Bitzer, and it was Bitzer who took over and gave Fireworks Wilson the Word.

Use very little powder, just enough to blow the packet apart. Load the packet with sawdust and lampblack, which will scatter and *look* like a terrific explosion. Fireworks snorted in disgust, muttered something about sissies, but he complied. After all, this meant the sale of a thousand or more of these powder puffs, as he called them, and business being business, and lampblack and sawdust being cheaper than powder, he agreed to make up as many as Griffith ordered. But at a price, of course, because these special bombs would call for special handling, and special handling came high. Griffith dismissed the entire subject with a careless wave of assent. Results were everything, cost nothing. Fireworks scuttled away toward his car, radiating happiness. He did not rub his hands together in gleeful anticipation of all those fat juicy profits because there was just no way he could rub one hand together. But he came as close to it as any one-handed man possibly could.

Cars kept arriving, bringing more people to assist in planning the battle. Frank Wortman and George Siegmann had been with us in the first car. Others brought Elmer Clifton and Erich von Stroheim and Tom Wilson and Herbert Sutch, and I don't know how many others, because I was far too intent upon what Griffith and Bitzer were discussing to bother with anything else.

The battleground-to-be was ideal for the purpose photographically. A sort of ridge of high ground curved around the rim of a gently descending slope of clear ground that ran down to where the dry-as-dust riverbed of the Los Angeles River lay baking in the sun. There were little clumps of trees clustered on both sides of this open area, with small hills rounding up here and there in the background to provide splendid locations for artillerymen to rake the field with grape and canister, the two favorite close-range charges of the Civil War cannoneers.

Not only the geography but the orientation of the field happened to be perfect. When shooting big stuff you must shoot either north or south, never east or west. On this location all the camera angles from the ridge would be shooting north, which meant cross light from the right during the morning, and from the left throughout the afternoon. A flat, dead-on light is no good because the shadows fall away back of the subject and there is no modeling, while a back light is murderous when there's any smoke in the air, because the smoke blinds everything and you can't see what's going on in the background.

Then came the matter of laying out the trenches and gun emplacements. Here Siegmann and Huck Wortman had to be at their most alert to capture every slightest word or gesture from Griffith, who surveyed the scene and voiced his vision of what was in his mind in more or less obscure poetic terms.

With the Battle of Petersburg in mind (as the titles later revealed), he spoke of men on both sides huddling under a hellish rain of fire during a massive artillery duel, after which the gallant heroes of the Confederacy charged in a body across the intervening ground, to be slaughtered in their tracks by the murderous fire of the entrenched Yankees, and to be driven back by the sheer weight of overwhelming numbers. But not before their leader, the Little Colonel, had plunged their sacred banner, the Stars and Bars, straight down the cannon's throat.

Gestures indicated that the Confederate trenches were to be on the right. In order to be visible at all, the cannons would have to be mounted in plain sight on the little hillocks within camera range. By putting one thing together with another, Siegmann and Huck managed to piece out just about how much of what equipment would be needed and where it was to be placed. Nobody asked any questions. All they wanted to find out was *what* he wanted, or more accurately, what he wanted it to look like on the screen. It was up to them to find or contrive the material and methods to bring this into being. This derived from the long centuries of stage tradition. It was the director's job to let the working crew know what he had in mind. It was up to them to bring it into being. And woe betide the stage director who lost his patience and said, "Why don't you just fly another scrim and stop fooling around with those silly lights?" Because he'd get the prompt answer, "Why don't you mind your own business? Listen, mister, you want to come up here and do it yourself? Okay. Just show us your paid-up union card and we'll sit back and let you." Or, if they really wanted to put him in his place, they'd say, "Aw, shut up! One more peep out of you and we'll hit the bricks, and then where'll you be?"

I had learned by this time, from various sources around the studio, that Griffith had been an actor on the road with the cheapest kind of rip-and-tear melodramas, not for just a little while but for ten long starving years of doing everything and getting nowhere, so he knew all about stagehands. He never made the mistake of telling anybody how to do anything. Instead, he put them on their pride and let human nature take its course. So when he said, "Let's have eight or ten cannons up on that knoll," it tossed the whole thing right into their laps and it was up to them to make good, or else.

The same held true for Griffith's many assistants, who had come out to discover what was in his mind. George Siegmann, that evil-faced, gentle-hearted, soft-spoken human elephant, sensitive to Griffith's every whim, yet powerful enough to bend everyone else to his will, was there to apportion out duties to Elmer Clifton, Herbert Sutch, Erich von Stroheim, and a strange sort of self-styled aristocrat who called himself Baron von Winther. Stroheim was disliked because of his enormously offensive arrogance, but the baron was despised because he was so obviously a phony. One of our actors expressed it all by remarking, "I don't think he's a baron, but I wish his mother had been." I had to chew this comment over mentally for quite a while before I caught the pun, but it was worth it.

There were many others: Howard Gaye, Monte Blue, George (afterward André) Beranger, Donald Crisp, and of course Fred Hamer. Hamer had served in one of His Majesty's many little wars and he knew all about warfare from the private's point of view, including any number of barracks-room ballads that Kipling never heard of and couldn't have had printed anyway. And of course Christy Cabanne was there, because he had been in on an earlier Biograph called *The Battle* and he knew all about directing battles. In fact, he claimed that he had directed *The Battle*, which amused Bitzer, who knew better, while it bothered Griffith not at all.

For Griffith knew from his father, who had fought for the Confederacy, that nobody has ever directed any battle, real or staged, all by himself. The commanding general can indeed direct the disposition and state the objectives of his forces, but after that it is up to his subordinates to carry out their assignments if victory is to be gained. As a respected military authority has said, wars are won or lost by sergeants. And with this in mind, Griffith had supplied himself with as many sergeants as he could muster, each to perform an assigned function.

So we explored the entire field, now empty, that was to become a battle-ground. Herbert Sutch, a well-nourished man of early middle age whose speech and pink cheeks said he had come from Devon, was in charge of procuring and maintaining the many muskets that would be needed. Civil

War muskets existed in great quantity, procurable from a military-surplus house in New York called Bannerman's, but they had all been converted for use with metallic cartridges. Instead of being loaded from the muzzle with ramrods, they had been fitted with a simple flip-up receiver into which modern brass cartridges could be slipped. Snapping down the flap, firing, and raising it up again would extract the spent shell. Easy. Easy but not authentic. However, this authenticity had to be bypassed. Our soldiers would have to be recruited from the army of the unemployed, skid-row bums who would be eagerly glad to shoot and be shot at for three dollars a day and lunch. There would be no time to drill them in the manual of arms, circa 1860. The cartridges themselves were a little problem for Sutch to solve. How do you get thousands of rounds of Civil War blank cartridges? Answer: you don't, you improvise. So Sutch improvised. Home-loading tools were available, instruments to punch out the spent percussion caps and to install new. Fireworks Wilson could supply all the black powder needed —black powder to produce white smoke, not the faint haze of the smokeless powder in universal use for the past thirty-odd years—and instead of paper wads, which could cause injuries at close range, it was a simple matter to hold the small measured charge of specially mixed, extra smoky black powder in place simply by pouring a small amount of soft melted wax into the upturned cartridge case. This was not the hard paraffin wax of commerce but a special wax, very soft and greasy and made mostly of lard, that would come out as a harmless spray when the musket was fired.

Yes, and there were such tiresome details as getting sandbags for parapets and placing the trenches in such a way as to enable the camera to see the soldiers all the way back to the end of the battlefield. And uniforms, for which a strange little dumpy gentleman of Middle European origin and presently engaged in the suit-and-cloak business was to be responsible. This voluble little dialectician, whose name was Goldstein, had much more than soldiers' uniforms to supply. There was also the matter of period clothing for the men, hoop-skirts for the women, even specially made ragged clothing for the blacks, and not only peaked hoods and white garments for the Ku Klux Klan but also fully concealing white coverings for their horses. Imagine having to provide a tailor to make hand-fitted, custom-tailored costumes for horses. And then there was the matter of cannons.

There were real Civil War cannons a-plenty scattered all over the Eastern part of the country. No village square was complete without at least one. In Delta we had our courthouse cannon; ours was not one of your commonplace artillery pieces on wheels but a massive naval gun brought from nobody knew what particular gunboat. But there were no period ordnance out here in the Far West, so it was up to Huck to make them up for us—guns, carriages, caissons, and all. Fireworks Wilson would provide the charges.

Horses. Horsemen. This was easy, because we were in the land of the cowboy and his bronc, so getting clansmen in quantity was simply a matter of having Siegmann put out the word and we'd be over our heads in horsemen.

I didn't realize it at the moment, but what I was witnessing was a Griffith rehearsal of a battle. True, there was no action to be run through, but by the time we had finished, everyone in any capacity knew his purpose in the general scheme and Griffith had nothing to do with the preparations from then on. He knew, because he knew his men, that when he appeared on the field ready to shoot, every trench, every gun emplacement, every costume, every detail would be set and ready, and all he would have to say was "Fade in" and the battle would be under way.

Which reminds me: Griffith never called "Camera" or "Cut" as was customary with other directors, but always "Fade in" and "Fade out." Every shot began and ended with a fade. I didn't know why until it finally dawned on me that Griffith himself never knew in advance whether he would need or not need a fade to open or close any scene he ever shot, even in the close-ups. So everything faded in and everything faded out and he was ready for anything. He might want to open a sequence by fading in on a close-up. He never knew. He would never know until an audience told him.

For Griffith depended absolutely, even slavishly, upon audience reactions. Whatever audiences responded to was right, no matter how wrong it might seem from any other consideration, and anything audiences did not respond to was wrong, regardless of how finely enacted or how beautifully photographed. That was why he had previewed *Home, Sweet Home* and *The Avenging Conscience,* not once or twice but dozens of times, in out-of-the-way places. These were mostly secret forays into the hidden villages of the surrounding countryside.

Griffith took his own car, driven by his own driver, a tall, thin, tight-lipped man known only as Mac. He took Rose and Jimmy Smith and a stack of film cans containing the latest of many cut and recut versions of the film in progress with him. He might go anywhere. He once went as far afield as San Luis Obispo, far up the coast halfway to San Francisco. These trips were closely guarded secrets, not for the sake of hiding anything but for the sake of being sure that there could be no such thing as a studio claque in the audience to distort reactions.

This was exactly opposite to the traditional out-of-town tryouts of the legitimate theater. Producers of plays in New York never opened "cold." They'd take their shows to Philadelphia or New Haven or Boston, which were known as "dog" towns, from the old medical saying about trying any new medicine on a dog before using it on human patients. Here they exhibited their wares before sophisticated audiences in order to discover and remedy defects before launching their shows on ultra-sophisticated Broadway.

Griffith sought out the most *un*sophisticated, least theater-wise audiences he could find. I kept asking myself why he should go so contrary to established custom. The answer came from several sources, all old-timers, who came through with what seemed to me to be the final, the definitive answer.

Griffith had been an exceedingly bad actor. It followed that he could be employed only by exceedingly bad producers at an exceedingly bad salary. He traveled the length and breadth of the country, appearing in turkeys of the rankest raw melodrama. This meant appearing before the cheapest of audiences, the great army of the unwashed, who paid ten, twenty, and thirty cents—the familiar ten-twent'-thirt' price scale of the barnstormers of jerkwater towns and city ghettos.

Then, by a quirk of ever-unpredictable fate, these same town-and-country yokels became the audiences upon which the nickelodeons depended for their life, liberty, and pursuit of happiness.

Griffith knew this. He also knew the psychology of the cheapest of cheap audiences as no New York producer ever could. He was not alone in this knowledge. Al Woods had been there before him, and Al Woods had become his guide in the art of giving the yokels the thrills of their lives. I doubt if he ever worked with Al Woods directly. But that didn't matter. My father and mother never worked with Gilbert and Sullivan, either, yet they held both in worshipful esteem.

Ten years of seeing audiences of the lowest caste go wild over the crassest of raw melodrama. The hell with the subtleties of Galsworthy, Shaw, or Wilde. What these horny-handed sons and daughters of toil wanted was a full-course theatrical feast of tragedy and comedy, not delicate tragedy but raw blood, and not witty comedy but blatant slapstick. Everything had to be spelled out in black and white: deep-dyed villains and the purest possible heroes and heroines.

There were rules never to be violated. The hero must never stain his hands with blood. The heroine must be pure to the point of pathological absurdity. Devices had to be invented to bring this impossible state of affairs about.

One of the standard gimmicks was the Mysterious Stranger, who appeared briefly in the first act to declaim (with gestures) to the audience, " 'Twas on just such a night as this ten years ago that that foul caitiff who calls himself Reginald van Millionbucks visited upon my beloved sister a fate far worse than death. The search may be long and the quest forever in doubt, but I have sworn to bathe my hands in his heart's blood e'en though it be at the cost of my own. But hist! He comes! I go!"

So the Mysterious Stranger disappears, not to be seen again until the last moments of the last act, when the heroine is strapped to the railroad tracks, a train bearing down upon her at full speed; the hero is strapped to a log moving inch by inch toward a whirling saw blade; the orphan asylum is a mass of flames; and the Old Homestead is in the very process of being foreclosed to turn dear old Denman Thompson out into the cold; or, as an alternative, the outcast, disowned heroine is dying in the snow outside Grace Church, while the choir inside is singing "Nearer, My God, to Thee"; and all hell is breaking loose, when the Mysterious Stranger reappears to fire a blast from a double-barreled shotgun straight into the heart of the cowardly villain, who proceeds to die in writhing agony all over the stage as the lovers are united, the girl rescued, the Old Homestead saved, and nobody goes over the falls to their death after all.

This was the picture audience of the day. Raised on blood-raw melodrama, they had no palate for delicate nuances of cinematic artistry. They wanted to have exciting things happen and keep on happening, with every character clearly labeled, so there could be no mistakes in the hurly-burly of action they so dearly loved. And Griffith believed in his innermost heart that it was his duty to—well, in the oldest and most misunderstood of theatrical phrases—to give them what they want, to feed their hunger.

But with a difference. In the big cities giving them what they want meant giving the first-night critics what they thought was good theater. Out in the sticks giving them what they want meant making them laugh, making them cry, and making them wait, which was the gospel according to Al Woods, and which Griffith followed with religious fervor.

One thing and one thing only prevented Griffith from applying this formula according to his own best judgment. He labored under the handicap of being a born artist and a poet to boot. He could never entirely trust his own instincts. Hence the secret tryouts, the mysterious disappearances about which he said nothing. Otherwise, he would have gone soaring high into the empyrean, where they could never follow him. Like Antaeus, he drew his strength from the earth.

There was nothing high-flown or arty about *The Clansman* as Griffith shot it. Everything was of the earth, earthy. Carpetbaggers were crooked, crookeder, crookedest. Ralph Lewis played Stoneman as a thinly veiled caricature of Thaddeus Stevens, the fanatically vengeful senator who regarded all Confederates as traitors deserving nothing less than the most condign of punishments, making him a hateful image of blind cruelty. He and his characterizations were lifted straight out of the old rip-and-tear period of Griffith's acting experience without breaking bulk. A villain was labeled, "This is a villain: hate him," as clearly as though he had worn a sign to that effect around his neck. Walter Long became a terrifying monster as Gus, the black rapist-murderer. Walter made no effort to look like a real Negro. He put on the regular minstrel-man blackface makeup, so there could be no mistake about who and what he was. Lillian Gish was the perfection of Wordsworth's poetic dream of the dawn, like a nun, breathless with adoration. Mae Marsh was her own adorable self, a prankish little hoyden cute as a bug's ear, the sort of kid sister everyone would love to have. Elmer Clifton was a gay young blade in his brave blue-and-gold, the beau ideal of the gallant youth of song and story. Walthall was nobility personified, representing all the best in human nature, untainted by the slightest stigma of the worst. The Little Colonel would fight, yes, but only in defense of his sacred homeland. He never killed anyone, even in the heat of battle. He was content to charge the enemy, ram the flag into their cannon's mouth, and then retire to his ruined mansion, covered with honor and with very little else, such being the fruits of defeat. But he bore his disaster bravely as a gentleman should, never complaining, never repining. And so on throughout the length of the picture. Type-casting absolutely, not because Griffith wanted it so but because his audience, that million-headed but singlehearted monster, had to have its villains and its heroes clearly labeled so it could know whom to cheer for and whom to hiss.

I now felt secure about Griffith and his *Clansman,* however revolting the original story might be. Griffith controlled his studio and everyone in it. There was no doubt of that. But the peanuts-and-popcorn audience controlled Griffith, and as long as he lived, thought, and had his being with the strictest of compliance with their unspoken wishes, he could do no wrong.

❦ 6 ❦

The Tremendous Trifles
of Perfection

Little drops of water, little grains of sand,
Make the mighty ocean and the pleasant land.
JULIA A. FLETCHER CARNEY

THE actual shooting of *The Clansman* began tamely enough. We needed an exterior setting for a small town, and for this we needed nearby space. There was a large stretch of vacant, weed-covered land just across the street where Sunset Boulevard curved to the west and let Hollywood Boulevard start from scratch at that division point. So the land was leased, and Huck Wortman and his gang of long-seasoned stage carpenters put up our Southern town, complete with slave quarters and whatever else was needed to recreate an antebellum town of the Deep South, circa 1850.

There was no question as to what the town should look like or how it should be dressed. I doubt if there was a man on that work crew who hadn't been out with a "Tom" show, as the *Uncle Tom's Cabin* shows were called. There were Tom shows scattered all over the country by tens and dozens. It was not so much a show as an institution, a part of the American scene for the past sixty-odd years. Little Evas had grown old in the part, playing nothing else, to the effect that it was firmly believed throughout the profession that no actress could really *play* Little Eva until she was at least forty years old. Stage crews had been constructing Tom sets for so long that there wasn't a detail of the Civil War period, inside or out, that they hadn't built, up to and including wobbly ice for Eliza to flee across, one jump ahead of the bloodhounds, which were usually Great Danes.

So the Southern street came into being on what became known as the Griffith Lot, as distinct from the Griffith Studio or the Griffith Ranch, where the battlefield was being organized. The Cameron house was built on the studio grounds, just inside the gate at the western end, along with Piedmont Street, which ran back to where the dressing rooms were hidden by a return piece that blocked the camera vision. That studio-entrance roadway had become one of the most useful of properties. Street scene after street scene had been built there. A Western street, a fishing village, a warehouse district, a city slum—all wonderfully handy to the carpenter shop, where the fronts could be constructed and set up right on the spot.

Force of habit instilled by years of backstage training kept our staff of old-time stage carpenters building all this scenery in sections that could be folded up and shipped to any op'ry house in the country. The picket fences came in sections that could be "struck" at any time and set up again anywhere else. We had flowers galore, all made of cloth and mounted on steel spikes that could be thrust into the stage or the earth to turn the bare ground into a garden of lush profusion. Grass mats, made of raffia woven into burlap, could provide a velvet lawn wherever it was wanted. Old, weathered stone walls could be lifted and placed anywhere by any stagehand, because they were made of light shells of cast plaster painted to look more like the real thing than the real thing itself. Brick walls were easy. They came in conveniently sized castings that could be nailed up anywhere, while if the script called for a broken-down slum interior, the scenic artist could paint broken plaster with lath showing beneath so realistically that you could almost get splinters by rubbing your hand across the painted place.

Thoren's garden, back of the carpenter shop, had been turned into an artillery park, filled with wooden cannon lined with iron pipe that would gush flame and smoke at the touch of a fuse. The gun carriages and caissons were accurate to the finest detail because two years before, in 1912, a New York newspaper had published a very cheap reprint of the great *Battles and Leaders of the Civil War,* originally published by the Century Company back in the eighties. I was very familiar with this publication, because that expensive, four-volume edition, printed on heavy coated stock, was the prize of my grandfather's library, and I had spent long winter evenings as a boy, sitting on the floor with these books open in my lap, searching the rosters of the many battles for my grandfather's name, and finding it, too, in every action of the Army of the Potomac from First Bull Run to the Wilderness, that bloodiest of campaigns, which ended the war.

This cheap modern reprint, made to sell for a few dollars and correspondingly shoddy, nevertheless contained close-up pictures of all the military equipment and therefore became the bible of our construction crew. True, the gun carriages, and especially the trails of the cannon, were made of thin plywood, and the rivets were merely rounded wooden buttons glued in place, but they had been painted with a black paint containing graphite, so they gleamed with the authentic sheen of polished iron.

This same book, of which we had a dozen or so copies, was the fashion plate for Goldstein's costume house, which was on an around-the-clock schedule to turn out the uniforms and period clothing for every character from high-born ladies to the lowliest of Negro field hands. Goldstein, himself of theatrical background, knew better than to make smartly well-fitted outfits for the common soldiery. One glance at a Brady picture proved that the real uniforms had been turned out in quantity far from the field of action and that nothing fit anybody. So the soldiers were outfitted with uniforms that were too loose or too tight, too long or too short, and therefore technically accurate as army issue of that or any other war.

The first scenes to be shot were of the village across the car tracks on the Griffith lot, showing the despised carpetbaggers filling Negro field hands with as much whiskey as they could drink, then providing them with already-marked ballots to stuff, a dozen to a man, into the boxes through which these newly freed blacks exercised for the first time their right to vote. The whole episode ended with a general celebration, a victory dance in which these blacks kicked up a great deal of dust with their bare-footed, wildly enthusiastic African exultation.

I personally thought all this was terribly overdone and much too obvious. But Griffith didn't, and he was the boss, and an extremely happy boss at that. I had never seen so much delight in any man's face as he showed through this and all the remaining sequences to come. Win, lose, or draw, he was having the time of his life, and I can't believe that the thought of success or failure ever entered his mind. This was good, this was right, this rang true to him, and he enjoyed it to the utmost.

We had another dance, this one on the studio lot on the lower stage; it was interrupted by a call to arms, and all the bravely uniformed officers kissed their lovely partners in what might very likely be a farewell forever as they hurried away to battle. My notebook covered the entire sequence with a single quote: "On with the dance, let joy be unconfined." (Although I believe I used the word "unrefined" in place of the original.) So Griffith had lifted the entire sequence from a familiar, school-taught poem. But why not? He wasn't making the picture for highbrows who knew everything. He was making it for his own particular, well-studied audience, and he had to make everything in terms that they could understand instantly and without thinking. If it wakened some dormant recollections of Friday-afternoon school recitations, all the better. For he knew what he had learned in the hardest of schools, the school of failure, that these, his people of the streets who would make or break him with their approval or disapproval, would never believe anything that they did not already know.

That, I think, is why we had to make the long and dangerous trip to Big Bear Valley, high in the mountains, to shoot the sequence of the black rapist chasing the darling little pet sister of our noble hero to her death. There was plenty of shrubbery and trees and craggy rocks right there on his own battleground, but the people, *his* people, knew all about *The Trail of the Lonesome Pine,* so we had to go to where there were pine trees and plenty of them, or his audience, the Griffith audience, would never believe that all this was actually happening in the Deep South.

We knew in advance that it would be a long, hard, man- and machine-testing ordeal. The roads were built for wagons, not automobiles. But the city roads were paved, for the most part, so we made fairly good time as far as Pasadena, after which it was sand and ruts, ruts and sand, all the way.

We were in Charlie Muth's car, a strong, heavy Packard. Griffith, Bitzer, and Miriam Cooper were in the back seat. I was given the front seat next to the driver, not because I rated any particular consideration but because I had to cradle the all-precious but ridiculously fragile Pathé camera in my lap.

The trip across the mountain slope of the San Gabriel valley was a matter of fighting sand and ruts and potholes all the way. Sometimes we would get stuck, or Charlie would kill the engine, which meant getting out and cranking it back into life. On our left a strong wind whistled down from the mountains, while at our right the immense vineyards of the Guasti people stretched away as far as one could see. Luscious grapes growing in blowing sand. It didn't seem possible but there it was.

After a long hard fight through the sand and gravel, we finally arrived in San Bernardino, where we felt the blessed relief of a pavement under our wheels. But not for long. We were worn out, sun- and wind-burned, and sore to the bone from all that swerving and jolting. Charlie Muth pulled up at the hotel, and we climbed stiffly out to enter the lobby where Siegmann, Long, Clifton, and Eddie Hungerford were waiting for us. They were rested and refreshed from what had been to them a delightful trip, except for the blasting of the sand-laden wind. It developed that while we had been fighting sand, they had been rolling merrily along a well-paved road not far from the Santa Fe tracks. How had they found it? Somebody told them. Mental note: it pays to ask questions, especially in a country where the last official survey had been made in 1854 and where the current roads were not mapped, except in cheap, giveaway folders that were of little use except possibly as fly swatters.

A bath, a meal, and a night's rest and we were all braced and ready for the real test, that of climbing what was euphemistically called a service road, which squirmed its way up to the eight-thousand-foot level of Big Bear Valley. A third company car had joined our little entourage, a Pope–Hartford driven by "Dutch" Schultz and carrying George Beranger, Mae Marsh, a stage carpenter, and a big wicker basket of costumes.

We pulled away from the hotel in an orderly procession, with Griffith's car in the lead. But it was no follow-the-leader game. Each driver had been asking questions, and each had been told of the best and easiest road up the mountain by local yokels who enjoyed playing practical jokes on ignorant Easterners.

So we in the leading car soon found ourselves all alone on an old road that ran out past the Patton insane asylum to a place where the road turned sharply to the left and headed up a wide, dry, rocky wash. It was bumpy and it was bad, but it could have been worse, because there is no way you can fall out of a dry riverbed. True, your car might turn over, but that would be nothing compared to plunging over a thousand-foot cliff. And we could see such cliffs, too, with the road woven back and forth over them like a tangled string. It was a disheartening sight to one brought up in the flatlands of the East.

The road, if such it could be called, soon became disgusted with the deep sand and high boulders of the wash and took flight up the steep shoulder of the pinched-in canyon walls. I use the term "flight" advisedly, because the hacked-out shelf that pretended to be a road pitched so sharply upward that Charlie Muth had all he could do to keep the Packard inching upward and onward in its lowest gear.

If the pitch of the road had been at all even, there would have been no problem. We could have agreed that the car couldn't make it, the trip would have been abandoned, and everyone would have been happy. But the road had been built on the roller-coaster principle, with sudden pitches and dips, with the result that Charlie would coax his Packard, laboring and groaning and pinging, somehow over the top of the ladderlike ascent, only to tramp down hard on the throttle and hurtle down the intervening dip at all-out speed in order to rush the next rise with as much gathered momentum as possible. This made for thrills and it could have been fun of a dubious sort on a hard, level, well-tended roadway. But this roadway was anything but hard, level and well-tended. It was full of rocks and bumps, it had not been tended at all, and wherever the winter rains had cut gulleys across the road, they sloped alarmingly downward toward the bottom of the canyon, now hundreds of feet below. Even worse, these gulleys came naturally enough at the lowermost part of each dip where our speed was greatest and our chance of survival least.

This sort of entertainment did not last long, because the clutch began to slip more and more, until finally it lost its grip entirely and the engine spun while the wheels did not. It seems unnecessary to say that we stopped. The problem became one of finding some way to stay stopped, because on that roof-steep slope no hand brake was to be trusted. So we piled the largest rocks we could find back of the wheels, while Charlie got out and under to see what could be done about that non-cooperative clutch.

Fortunately, automobiles were designed for home repair, with every man his own mechanic. Charlie knew exactly how to fix the clutch. He opened the large steel tool box that rode on every car's wide running board and found a sprinkle-top can of talcum powder, the kind mothers use on babies. He crawled under the car, and while I held down the clutch pedal to keep it open, he carefully dusted the leather facing, after which it was as good as new.

Griffith made some remark about this being a "Percy" car, because of its use of baby powder, after which we removed the rocks, climbed in, and away we went, groaning and snorting and careening alarmingly every time we crawled past the many washed-out places in the road.

Our seating arrangement had undergone a certain change. The car was open, of course; all cars were open with what were called one-man-tops, so named because they could be raised or lowered by one man, provided he had two other men to help him. The top was down and folded across the rear, and Griffith sat on the top, his long legs dangling over the back, perched up high and facing backward. Not that he was afraid. Never. But he could see better from that position, and in case the car *should* happen to go over the side, he had merely to slip to the ground and observe its progress for use in future pictures. Bitzer wasn't at all scared. He sat stolidly in his place, eyes slightly closed and face a dusky green, for protection against sunburn. Although it may seem vainglorious on my part, I was the least alarmed of the lot. This was because I knew my own strength and my own agility. I had the whole front seat area to myself, with no encumbrances of any kind, except that Pathé camera in my lap, and at the first hint of the car going over the cliff I'd have been up in the air like a kangaroo and halfway up the mountainside before the first dislodged pebble had had time to trickle over the edge of the drop.

Although it hardly seemed possible, there was worse to come. Thus far we had been climbing up one face of a single shoulder. Now we came to the switchbacks, where the real fun began. The turns were so narrow that the

Packard, designed for city streets, could not possibly cramp its wheels hard enough over to make a turn at one pass. So at every turn it was a matter of back and fill, back and fill, like an inexpert driver trying to get out of a bumper-to-bumper parking space, in order to get around at all.

Going upward was not so bad. The front wheels would be stopped by the steep cutbank of the road. But backing up, with the wheels cramped hard around, was another matter, because the rear wheel had to be carried right to the edge of the brink and there stopped, while gears were shifted, wheels turned to the opposite limit, and the clutch engaged against the spinning flywheel. Full power, of course. You do not risk a stall when one wheel is dangling over an abyss.

Here Bitzer suddenly became very useful. The moment these maneuvers began he would hop briskly from the car and stand well clear at the back, where he could signal Charlie by hand motions just how far to come and when to stop. After the car had safely negotiated the turn, Bitzer would hop to the running board and ride there, fireman fashion, to the next switchback, after which he would jump clear and resume his duty as traffic director. The exercise did him a world of good. His face lost that greenish tinge and he seemed to be actually enjoying the trip. I began to curse my own slow-wittedness. Why couldn't *I* have thought of that? I offered to trade places with him, to save him all that jumping in and out, but he said no, I had to guard the camera, and besides, he had a better eye for distance than I.

After an eternity of backing and filling and crawling over the high side of the washed-out places, we came to the top of the ridge and rolled out on a fine, broad, level road that followed the rim of the mountains through forests of giant pines. We rolled along in great style, enjoying the fresh clean ozone and the scent of the pine forest and looking out over the vast expanse of the valley we had left and wondering how it could happen that so beautiful a road had to be reached by so miserable an approach. The only reasonable explanation seemed to be that the authorities had given the job of building that access road to some of the more disturbed patients at Patton, as a sort of occupational therapy.

It was thirty miles to our destination, but the day was fine, the road good, the Packard powerful and easily capable of doing thirty miles an hour, so it seemed to be almost no time at all before we swept over the dam that had created Big Bear Lake and pulled up at the Pine Knot Lodge, only to find the other two cars waiting for us, with our people badly worried and discussing the matter of sending out a search party to look for us.

The landlord, learning of how we had come, said, "Why the hell—beg pardon, ladies—why in the world did you come *that* way? Hell's bells, that road ain't been used in years, not since the new one was put in, anyway. What ever made you *try* such a fool thing? Look, if you was bound and determined to commit suicide, I'd have lent you a gun. I got lots."

"Fellow in San Bernardino told me," said Charlie, in an injured, wait-till-I-get-hold-of-that-guy tone of voice.

The landlord nodded understandingly. "That explains it. Them San Berdoo jokers can't rest until they get hold of some greenie and then fill him up with all the lies they can lay their tongue to, and then they lay back and laugh the rest of their lives on account of all the trouble they put him to. Come on, folks, your cabins are all ready."

I asked Eddie Hungerford later how he'd made it with his big Pierce-Arrow. "No trouble at all. New road, thirty miles longer but a cinch. We just *coasted* up, didn't scarcely shift gears hardly ever, except on the switchbacks."

"How'd you find out about it?"

"Well, I asked the guy at the garage and he told me to take the road you folks took, said it was thirty miles shorter, but there was something fishy about the way he said it, so I phoned up here and got the straight dope."

"You *phoned?*"

"Sure. They got phones these days. Or didn't you know?"

That night I made a note in my book: "Ask and ye shall receive. But be sure to ask the right questions of the right people or there's no telling *what* you'll receive."

(This habit of using the reverse blank side of my notebook pages for personal observations was to cause me a lot of embarrassment in the days to come. It happened this way: one day during the shooting of *The Clansman* I came back from an errand and saw Griffith seated beside the camera on the upper stage, going through my notebook with absorbed interest, reading all my silly little immature observations on the reverse side of the pages. He snorted at some, smiled at others, and stopped to give one particular page his closest attention. He closed the book, put it on the slate where I had left it, then took it up to study that page again. Then he put the book down and sat staring into space, lost in reverie.

(I moved to my place back of the camera and pretended not to have seen, for many of my notes had been slightly on the irreverent side. I waited uncomfortably until his attention was distracted, then took up the book with exaggerated nonchalance to pretend I was looking for a scene number but actually to discover what I had written that had captured his attention.

(It was nothing but a semi-punning effort at juvenile smartness, an affliction that is part of the process of growing up. It was an observation of Griffith's method of direction and it read, very simply: "Take care of the emotions and the motions will take care of themselves." Not much; but it became the ruling influence of my life when I myself became a director, many long years later. Not because I had written it. No. Because Griffith had given it the *cachet* of his absorbed attention, which was validation enough for me. Or for anyone.)

But to resume: if we had plowed through all that sand and climbed that abandoned road to find pine trees, we had succeeded beyond all possible expectation, because these pines were not merely large but monumentally huge. This was success with a vengeance, because these towering giants with cones the size of footballs bore not the slightest resemblance to the thin and scrawny piney woods of the Deep South, the scrub growth from which turpentine and rosin are distilled. But they were pines, so the letter if not the principle of realism had been achieved. This satisfied Griffith, who liked to have everything as much larger than life as possible.

So we shot scenes of Walter Long, playing Gus, chasing Mae Marsh, the Little Sister, up hill and down dale, and through thickets, and finally to the pinnacle of a high, pointed rock from which she would theoretically plunge to the rocks far below in obedience to the better-death-than-dishonor rule that governed all pure young maidens of that time and place.

These were the most peculiar chases I had ever seen. I had done some running in my time. When danger pressed, the idea was always to get the hell out of there as fast as possible. Not so with Griffith's characters. "Run low, low!" he'd call, repeating, *"Run low!"*

So Walter Long, in his burnt-cork makeup and his carefully hand-ripped ragged clothing, ran with a low, staggering gait, almost like a hound with nose to earth, meanwhile maintaining a precarious balance with his outstretched arms working like a high-wire acrobat's balance pole. His eyes were leering wildly and his mouth was wide open, while white foam ran from his lips down over his chin.

This idea of foaming at the mouth to indicate bestial passion was so firmly fixed in Griffith's mind that the prop box always contained dozens of small bottles of hydrogen peroxide. Small bottles were best. The larger sizes lost strength after a while, but a good full swig of fresh peroxide well sloshed around in the mouth could convert any man into a slavering monster in a matter of seconds.

So we'd shoot a scene of Walter staggering and wavering after his prey, leaving a trail of white foam as he went, after which he'd come back for a fresh charge of peroxide and we'd do it over again, and again, and again, until he ran low enough and wildly enough to convince Griffith that that was about the best—or worst—he could do. And so to another setup and more of the same, until we had had Walter Long chase Mae Marsh over most of Big Bear Valley.

Mae Marsh was required to run in an entirely different way. A dozen or so quick fluttering steps, a pause to look back in fear, then more quick fluttering steps, then another look back, and so on, until she was finally stopped by reaching the pinnacle of the rock from which there could be no more fluttering but only a long, swift, unhesitating, no-chance-to-look-back plunge to the bottom.

I am forced to admit that I was thoroughly disgusted with this sort of running and fluttering. Griffith was a great director, there can be no doubt of that. But there was one thing of which I was very sure indeed: he had never, never in his long and varied career chased a fifteen-year-old girl, or he'd have known, as I knew, and as every other teenager knows, that these little devils can go like a bat out of hell, and that the chance of any adult's catching one of them is practically nil.

And so, after shooting these chases frontward and backward and crosswise, we finally got to the scene where Little Sister is trapped on the top of the pinnacle, agonizes as she makes the hard choice between death and dishonor, and—we cut away to Gus, reacting in horror as he sees what he has brought about. This cutaway was made of necessity, not choice. We were shooting out of sequence and there were many more scenes yet to be taken in which Mae Marsh was to appear, and so, much as Griffith loved realism, he did not make her take the jump. Not that he couldn't have done so. Our stagehands could have rigged a net under that point into which she could have landed as safe as a baby in its cradle. But he didn't think of it, nobody thought of it, and that was that.

Then there was the business of discovering the poor crumpled body at the foot of the pinnacle and the swearing of vengeance in the manner hallowed by two thousand years of stage tradition, stretching from Aeschylus to Clyde Fitch, after which we settled down in a beautiful meadow to play a tender love scene between Elmer Clifton (North) and Miriam Cooper (South).

This, too, was in the sacred tradition of the theater: the son of the villain in love with the sister of the hero. It had been an unbeatable, ready-made, tried-and-true situation guaranteed not to rip, ravel, or bag at the knees ever since Shakespeare dramatized that squabble between the Montagues and the Capulets in a thing called *Romeo and Juliet,* the stoutest war-horse of them all. Griffith *had* to use it. It was something his audiences had come to love and cherish over the years and he could not, would not, disappoint them.

That was all. We loaded up and went back down the mountain much faster than we had come up. Too fast. Our cars had but two mechanical brakes in the rear and they could not be used continuously or they'd burn out. The cars could be held back by keeping them in low gear and letting compression do most of the braking, but this was all pretty dubious because cars *will* build momentum, and it was all Charlie could do to keep the Packard from taking the bit in its teeth and running away with us. The switchbacks were particularly tricky because the car had to be brought to a standstill in order to back and fill its way around those sharp hairpin turns.

We reached the bottom with a multiple sigh of relief and headed for home along the narrow but paved roadway flanking the Santa Fe railway tracks. The rest of the trip was without incident, except for two punctures and a blowout, but these were not really incidents because everybody had punctures and blowouts as a normal and expected matter of routine. No trouble, of course. Everyone carried repair kits and blowout boots as a part of the normal equipment, so nobody paid much attention to these roadside repair stops.

The film turned out fine. Beautiful shots, well worth the time and trouble to go up there to get them. But when it came to the actual matter of cutting the film, one shot was missing. Griffith felt that he simply had to have a shot of Mae Marsh actually making the jump from the pinnacle to the rocks below. So he sent Bitzer and me and a dummy representing Little Sister back up the mountain for that one short scene.

We traveled in Eddie Hungerford's Pierce, and the trip was easy, now that we knew the right roads to take. But there were certain difficulties connected with the scene itself. Bitzer set up his camera so as to include the jagged rocks at the bottom and all but the very top of the pinnacle itself. My job was to manhandle the dummy up to the top and throw it over the edge and down to the rocks when Bitzer gave the signal.

This was not the usual straw-stuffed scarecrow type of dummy but a carefully weighted, correctly proportioned, and costumed replica of the girl herself, a sort of taxidermed Mae Marsh. The figure was limp and heavy, something over a hundred pounds, and my job of hauling her up that cliff from handhold to handhold was no picnic. Even worse was balancing that kneeless mass of fake femininity in an upright position on the needle top of that peak.

Bitzer began to turn the camera and signaled to me to let her go. I did, but the dummy did not let *me* go. Something—a ribbon or a belt—caught on my arm, and for one unbalanced instant I was very close to going over the drop attached to the dummy. However, I managed to break free, with much waving of arms to regain my balance, and the scene was saved. Otherwise Griffith would have had a shot of not one but two dummies making the drop, which would have ruined the scene.

The rest of the picture was one long disjointed jigsaw puzzle to me. I saw every scene while it was being shot. I had to, for it was an essential part of my job to keep a record of the action and the scene numbers in my notebook. And yet nothing seemed to go together, nothing seemed to fit. Oh, there were a few sequences that made sense, like the assassination of Abraham Lincoln in Ford's theater, but this all took so long to shoot, with so many individual shots from so many different angles, that I couldn't see how they could possibly be put together in anything much better than a series of set pieces, like the old-style panoramas during which one man turned the crank to reveal the pictures, one after another, while a second man delivered the lecture.

The setting was correct enough because Huck and his men had authentic still pictures of the real theater to guide them. The playing of *Our American Cousin* on the stage of this theater was as accurate as anyone could wish, because we had the old playscript to go by, together with old engravings to pinpoint every detail. So Lord Dundreary was there, famous whiskers and all, and so was Laura Keane; but did Griffith *have* to drag this scene out and out as though he were making a separate production of it?

Then there were close-ups of Joseph Henabery as Lincoln, endless close-ups of him doing this and that and the other thing, adjusting his shawl, pulling it up around his neck, getting shot and slumping forward. Then there were separate shots of Raoul Walsh, playing Booth, coming into the theater, creeping along the wall, getting to the box, firing the shot, rushing through to leap to the stage to cry, *"Sic semper tyrannis!"* and limping off the stage, with everybody standing around doing nothing to stop him, which seemed utterly silly to me. For I knew stagehands from way back, and it did seem to me that one of them would have clouted him with a stage brace while another dropped a sandbag on him, while if *they* missed, there would be no getting past the man on the door. No; it was all wrong, but I said nothing because—well, if I knew more about direction than Griffith did, I'd be directing and he'd be working for me. So, things being as they were, I let him go his way while he let me go mine, which seemed to be the only fair way of compromising the situation.

Bitzer did something that I thought was utterly outrageous. Here we had this big set on the lower stage, and it was L-shaped, with one side open to let the light from a long row of big white flats shine into the set. That was standard procedure. Shooting with sunlight only, that was the only way to light that or any other set. But with Booth dressed in black and creeping along the far side of the wall, it was impossible to pick him out from all the others. So what did Bitzer do? Believe it or not, he had the men bring in a mirror, a big, pier-glass type of mirror made so ladies could admire themselves at full length, and he had this mirror mounted on a high parallel and he had the grips move the mirror to shoot the hot sunlight directly upon Booth and to follow him wherever he went, just like a spotlight in a theater. This surely was exceeding all bounds of reason, for who ever heard of the sun shining in a dark theater at night? But it was their funeral, so I let them have their way.

Some of the other sequences seemed to make fairly good sense. The grouping of the scene of Lee's surrender was an exact replica of an engraving Griffith was holding in his hand, a unique example of a picture being directed by a picture.

The battle scenes were really good. Lots of smoke, lots of bombs, lots of charging around, some of it more realistic than comfortable. Howard Gaye, playing a Southern officer, came running to our parallel, to call excitedly up to Griffith after a particularly violent scene, "Those men are utterly crazy! Why! I—I actually had to *defend* myself!"

Tom Wilson, who had been doubling in brass all through the picture, was a big, strong, heavyweight boxer who had served as Jim Jeffries's sparring partner. Tom had a good throwing arm, so he stood on the camera sidelines throwing hand grenades up and over the battle scenes to get the effect of bombs bursting in air. He held one of them a fraction of a second too long and nearly had his hand blown off. The doctor—we had two or three on the set—who saw this rushed to his side with bandages and Vaseline in hand. Tom eluded the doctor and ran to the foot of our high platform to call up, "I ain't dogging out on you, Mr. Griffith! See my hand?"

He held up his right hand. It was black and wet with dripping blood. Griffith called down sharply, "Look after that hand at once! Doctor! Take care of him!"

Tom ran toward one of our company cars, chased by the doctor with his Vaseline and bandages. The hand was saved, but Tom Wilson had a mottled white hand for the rest of his days. I could see how Fireworks Wilson had lost his left forearm.

Griffith's staff of assistants—Clifton, von Stroheim, Siegmann, Raoul Walsh, Fred Hamer, and whoever else happened to be standing around doing nothing in particular—managed the actual staging of the battle. Each controlled his own small group, sending them in, pulling them back, making them stop to fight, all in accordance with the master plan Griffith had set up. This called for close visual coordination.

In staging the charge, the Confederates in the extreme background had to be started first, those in the middle ground next, while those in the foreground last of all. Why? Because of the smoke. Start them all together and the smoke in the foreground would blot out everything that was happening.

What bothered me throughout the shooting of the battle was that it was all so chopped up. After all, a charge is a movement in which a body of men sweep forward all together. But with this charge, everything was chopped up into bits and pieces, with a separate shot of assistant-director Henabery's group leaping out of their trenches to go racing forward, every man yelling at the top of his lungs, to be followed by an exactly similar shot of Christy Cabanne's group doing precisely the same thing. And so on and so on, all through the first long hot day of the battle, including a similar series of shots of the entrenched Union lines braced and ready and firing at the onrushing enemy, one repeated action after another.

Probably the most puzzling of all the shots, to me at least, was the climactic moment when Henry Walthall, playing the Little Colonel, did the bit about seeking the bubble reputation at the cannon's mouth. I knew perfectly well that I was nothing but a punk kid with only the slightest of knowledge of camera angles, but even with my limited experience I knew better than to take that close-up shot with the camera squatted way down and shooting up to include nothing but the gun and the sky, with nothing at all of the background. From that angle it was impossible to see anything of Walthall's run toward the cannon, nothing of the storm of death raging all around him, nothing but a plain, ordinary, everyday close-up of the man himself, a shot that could have been made on a corner of the back lot with no other actors at all. And yet Griffith and Bitzer spent as much painstaking care with this shot as if the entire battle depended upon it. So Henry ran in, stabbed the shaft of his Stars and Bars down the cannon's throat, gave the famous Rebel Yell, and dropped back out of sight. Oh well, it was their baby, not mine. So I scribbled in my notebook, "Hank delivers the mail," and let it go at that.

Then there was the time we rode out away east of town to where a shallow river, called the Rio Hondo, wandered down from the mountains toward the sea. This was all open country: no buildings, no utility poles, nothing but fields and trees and dirt lanes, ideal for our white-robed clansmen to go galloping on the white-clad horses, bearing a burning cross as they raced through the countryside, hell-bent on rescuing whoever needed rescuing.

These scenes delighted Griffith. He kept laughing aloud and exclaiming, "Good old Al Woods! You can't beat a run to the rescue, it just isn't possible!"

There was seemingly no satisfying his appetite for these chases. We shot our thundering herd of white horses and white horsemen over skylines, along the river banks, back and forth over the tree-bowered lanes, and across wide verdant fields. We also shot them from every angle, from Bitzer's angle high on a platform to my angle with the tripod squatted as low as it would go on the side of the narrow country lanes to get the effect of shooting up at the horses.

These horses ran awfully close to my camera, only a few feet away, and I would have felt nervous about it, except for the assurance of one of our cowboys who said that a horse would never run down a man, never, not if he could help it.

There was one run-by when the horses *couldn't* help it. There were seventy-five or a hundred of them pounding down at a dead run when they somehow became bunched up and crowded. The horses on my side of the lane came plunging straight at the camera, but true to that wise cowboy's words, they leaped *over* the camera. It would have been a perfect shot except that the last horse over happened to hit the front magazine of my camera with a hind hoof, to rip the silly little holding screws right out of the camera and to send both magazines spinning with raw film streaming out of one of them like ribbons out of a stage magician's hat. Fortunately, it was the front magazine that lost the film, not the back one. So we had the shot and all was well. Repairing the camera was nothing. I had learned from my first old relic of a still camera how to stuff match sticks into stripped wood threads, so it was only a matter of minutes before my camera was all ready to go again.

Not that there had been anything to worry about. Bitzer, on his high safe parallel, had the shot, so if I'd missed it there'd have been no great loss. Nor any disappointment, for that matter. Nobody expected anything of me, so if I'd spoiled my shot, they'd have shrugged it off with "What can you expect from a kid like that?" This was a warmly comfortable position to be in. If I failed I failed, surprising nobody. But if by any miraculous chance I happened to succeed, as in the cases of the peacock and the spider (but not the lily), whatever I had done was thought to be wonderful. You can't beat odds like that. Nothing to lose and everything to gain. No wonder the world belongs to the young. They have all the advantages, none of the risks. Except those of their own making.

One thing that gave me more and more comfort as the picture progressed was the faithfulness with which Griffith clung to his tried-and-true Biograph principles. He was most emphatically *not* striving for natural realism but for a sort of cartoonist's projection of the outstanding features of his various character types.

For many years before my time, public thinking had been molded and hardened into fixed conceptions by the cartoonists who had created John Bull and Uncle Sam as national images; bloated monsters wearing clothes covered with dollar signs for the soulless corporations; and local politicians as instantly recognizable caricatures that were more revealingly characteristic than the men themselves ever could have been.

In literature, Charles Dickens had been a sort of literary cartoonist, projecting word-images of characters whose essential characteristics were stressed at the expense of everything else. Griffith admired Dickens very much indeed, and what we admire we emulate. So Griffith's characters in *The Clansman* were really caricatures, and for that very reason became somehow inoffensive.

Best of all, he steered clear of all that superstitious nonsense about the dead retaining their last sight imprinted inside their eyes. The plot turned on an incident so simple and so human and so easily recognizable by the people of his audience that it could not possibly insult anyone. Walthall, in despair because of the plight of the South after the collapse of law and order through the scheming of the carpetbaggers and scalawags, happened to see some Negro children scaring one another by playing "ghosts" with the aid of some white sheets. So Negroes are afraid of ghosts. Why not capitalize on this fear? Memories of old tales about Headless Horsemen and ghost riders must have helped. At any rate, the worst he could have had in mind was a scare campaign, without the slightest premonition of what this might become in the hands of ignorant terrorists in the years to come. And that's all the clansmen became in the picture, white-clad ghosts riding through the night to terrify the ignorant and the superstitious. For remember, under the rigid rules of the rip-and-tear melodrama, the Hero must never Stain His Hands with Blood.

Under the same inflexible rules, the villain not only can but absolutely *must* resort to every vile trick his diseased imagination can dream up. So we had flights and fights, our dearly beloved but horribly downtrodden innocent people being trapped by the hate-inflamed mobs, all in the best old Biograph tradition.

I don't know how or when Griffith became so obsessed by the idea of having his good, innocent, lovable people crammed into a death trap, with yelling savages swarming at them from all sides. It may have been a line from that old poem we had to learn in school: "And how can man die better/Than facing fearful odds . . .?" In any case, he had used it time and time again in his Biograph pictures, and now he used it again, doubled and redoubled, with the troubles of our dearly beloved good people coming not as single spies but in battalions.

The picture was eventually finished, after what had seemed to be a terribly long time of shooting, not mere thousands of feet of film but miles of it. So much of it was so old hat that the things I really remembered were side-lights that seemed to have nothing at all to do with the picture itself.

There was a day, early in the shooting, when the word came that the Patents case had been settled and that the Trust had lost on all counts. This was tremendous news, for it grabbed that sword of Damocles from over our heads and flung it into oblivion. This, if anything, should have been an occasion for a great celebration, complete with dancing in the streets. It wasn't. Nobody paid much attention to it one way or the other. There were a few grins, a few wry jokes about narrow escapes in the past, after which it was business as usual.

Griffith's personal habits of shadowboxing, dancing whenever Miss Geeesh was available, or singing at the top of his lungs went on as usual.

Up to this picture he had been content to sing the most effective parts of the more flamboyant operatic arias. Canio's famous *"Veste la giubba,"* from *I Pagliacci,* got a thorough working over, but only in open tones, not Italian. He would sometimes also observe, in full voice, that the stars were brightly shining, this from *Tosca.*

But during the time we were shooting the chases, or run-bys, of the clansmen pounding hell-for-leather down the narrow lanes or open fields of the wide open spaces just east of the little crossroads called El Monte, Griffith would stride back and forth between shots while the horsemen were re-grouping for another run, singing two notes, high, almost falsetto in pitch, that were related to nothing I had ever heard before. They were taken from no opera, no song or tune that I had ever heard before. "Ha-haaaaah-*yah!"* he'd sing, at full voice, repeating these two notes at different spacings, sometimes doubling them up or extending them in a bewildering variety of improvisation. "Ha-ha—Yah! Ha-haaa—Yah! Hi-yah! H-yah! Hi-yah! Hi-haaaaa . . . *Yah!"*

I drew a staff on the back of a page of my notebook and took the notes down. They were simple enough. Naturally nobody can place a key signature or determine scale position from only two notes. It takes three to make a triad, the fundamental building block of all musical notation. But it did seem to me that the long-held upper note was the dominant sounding the long-drawn-out "Ha-haaaah!" with his voice dropping two tones to the mediant, with the interval sometimes cutting abruptly from high to low, sometimes with a sort of moaning glissando, sometimes with a long, silent break after the first note, to be followed by an explosive staccato *"Yah!"*

None of the working crew paid the slightest attention to Griffith's vocalizing. They were used to it and so was I, but the persistence with which he worked out every possible variation of two notes fascinated me, and I couldn't help wondering what he had in mind or what he was reaching for.

Another time Griffith's obsession with music showed itself was when we took a very long shot of the battlefield strewn with dead and with Lillian Gish running from corpse to corpse, looking for her beloved.* Correction: she fluttered from corpse to corpse. A lot of little quick steps, a pause, a look, then some more quick little fluttering steps, another look, and so on. It was during the making of this scene that Griffith exclaimed, with a sense of sudden inspiration, that the Lohengrin Wedding March, the familiar "Here Comes the Bride," was in exactly the same time and rhythm of the equally familiar Funeral March from the Chopin sonata. It seemed to astonish him that two such opposite sentiments, the extreme of happiness and the extreme of grief, should be couched in exactly the same musical terms, except that one was in the major mode, the other in the minor.

These are the sort of peripheral observations that somehow cling to the mind. Another was the time when I went to the camera room for something and found Bitzer there with Frank Woods, Barry, and that man of mystery, Harry Aitken. I don't know what had gone before, but Bitzer was saying, "Oh sure. Why not? The money's doing *me* no good. Get it for you soon as the bank opens in the morning."

I think it must have been Aitken who asked, "Why not give us a check now? Save you all that trouble."

"I don't have a checking account. It's all in savings. Don't worry. I'll get you the ten thousand tomorrow morning and that's a promise."

"We need it now, for the payroll."

Bitzer shook his head. "Sorry. It's past four. Bank's closed."

"We'll open it. Come on. Let's go."

They hustled him out toward the car waiting outside. It struck me then, for the first time, that there was more to making a picture than shooting long shots and close-ups. There was also the matter of finding the money to pay for everything that went into the making of a picture, and this could be a severe problem with a producer like Griffith throwing money right and left with both hands.

---

* This is a famous scene from *Hearts of the World*, but Karl Brown clearly remembers it being shot and included in the original prints of *The Clansman*. KEVIN BROWNLOW

Somehow the whole situation reminded me of an all-too-familiar scene in many a melodrama, or even legitimate drama. You know it, of course. The young lord is about to lose everything to his creditors, but he doesn't because Old Jeems, or Waters, or whoever the faithful old butler may be, comes forward to state, apologetically, that he has saved a bit here and there from his wages and the master is welcome to it, such as it is. It always turns out that this bit amounts to several thousand pounds, which saves the day, not only suggesting that the white-haired old servitor of his master and his master's father, the old Earl, for fifty years come Michaelmas, is not only faithful but—to my cauterized mind—has been snapping up unconsidered trifles, together with a private understanding with the tradesmen, in order to have piled up all that dough.

Anyway, Griffith got the money and Bitzer got a piece of the action, so everybody was happy and the show could go on. Studio rumor had it that *The Clansman* had turned out to be an extremely expensive venture, some said seventy-five thousand, others one hundred thousand. If so, Bitzer had bought himself ten or twelve percent of the picture. Not that it was so much a reckless gamble as a protective shoring up of his personal income. For if Griffith went broke, Bitzer's three hundred a week would stop. He was bound to get *something* back, which, together with his salary, would repay his investment in half a year. So he hadn't been so recklessly stupid after all, and who could tell, he might even make a little something extra from the investment if things went at all well.

One of the real standouts of my memory was a private, secret scare that drove me almost frantic for the few moments it lasted. We were shooting the scene where Walthall returns to his ruined mansion after the war. I knew what the action was to be. He'd come in, look the place over, then walk to the front door, where he would be greeted with open arms—just the arms, nothing more, reaching out through the door. This was like Mae Marsh washing dishes with her back to the camera. Show only enough to establish the point and force audience imagination to fill in the details. Instead of it being one woman, it was every woman welcoming her returning hero. An old Griffith trick, standard operating procedure by now. Make the audience *imagine* what *must* be happening . . .

Well, if there was one thing Griffith simply would not stand for it was having the camera run out of film at any time or for any scene. I checked the front magazine myself by turning the wheel and sensing the weight of the remaining footage. There was a good generous fifty or sixty feet left, plenty for that simple walk. So we were all set and ready.

Griffith was ready, Walthall was ready. Griffith called, "Fade," and the camera began to turn. I made my note of the scene: "W. ret. home, goes in."

But he didn't go in. I've never seen a man dawdle and fool around the way Walthall did in that scene.* He seemed to be killing time, stopping everywhere to look at everything, while the wheel of that front magazine kept turning faster and faster as the roll became smaller and smaller. If I'd known Walthall was going to spend the rest of his life walking that forty feet from gate to door, I'd have put on a fresh full four-hundred-foot roll, but I hadn't, so I had to suffer, suffer, suffer, while he seemed to be deliberately killing time so as to get me fired as he stretched that simple little walk into a whole production all in itself.

That front magazine wheel seemed to be racing faster than I'd ever seen it go before. Would he *never* reach that door? Somehow he did. Somehow the arms appeared and drew him inside. And the wheel was still turning, but at a perilously fast rate of turn, when Griffith intoned, "Faaaade . . ." Bitzer faded, stopped the camera, then called, "Test, please." Walthall came out of the house and stood facing the camera. Bitzer turned off the test, and just as he had finished, the wheel stopped turning as the end of the film ran through.

Bitzer looked at me strangely. "What are *you* so green about?" he asked.

"Nothing. Nothing at all. Change film."

Griffith wanted to take the scene again. I didn't mind. With a fresh full four hundred feet of film on the camera, Walthall could dawdle all he wanted to for all I cared. And strangely enough, that's just what he did. For some reason Griffith wanted the pace to be slow, slower, slowest. And it was all in a single unbroken long shot, too. This time I had time to really watch the scene instead of worrying myself sick about running out of film.

And honestly, I thought it was pretty bad. No action, no suspense, nothing. Not even a change of expression. Walthall simply walked in, stared, moved toward the door, slowly surveying the ruin of his previously immaculate mansion, which was now battered and stained and ruined by war. Griffith didn't even bother to take a close-up, which was unlike him. I couldn't understand it. Surely here, if anywhere, was the place for a big full-head close-up of Walthall, his eyes brimming with tears and his lips trembling ever so slightly. But no. Griffith passed up this wide-open chance to milk the scene of its dramatic impact, so that was it. I could sort of halfway understand. Griffith was probably tired and worried about the money situation and he was not really functioning at his best. Too bad, but there it was.

---

* In the prints we now see, the reason it takes Ben so long to reach the arms of his mother is that his return is intercepted by Flora as the whole family's temporary surrogate. Their passage of wordless inter-greeting runs fifty-seven feet. GEORGE PRATT

But as I have said, the shooting finally came to an end, and none too soon, either. Studio gossip had it that practically everybody except his contract players and staff members had been working more or less on credit or deferred payments to make the picture possible at all. Goldstein had been persuaded to take a share of the picture in lieu of cash, and it was said but without verification that Griffith had contributed all his salary and all his earnings from previous pictures to the project, keeping nothing for himself and living on credit at the Alexandria.

What Aitken, who was by now spoken of as Mr. Moneybags, had put in nobody knew. However, it was the general impression that by splitting up the cost of the picture among a number of investors, the risk would be so widely spread that nobody could be too badly hurt. So no one was in any very real danger of being wiped out.

Except Griffith. A massive failure at this point of his career would unquestionably destroy his every chance of shooting for the skies and would reduce him to the treadmill task of grinding out Biograph-type sausages for the rest of his life, because nobody, nobody at all, would ever back him again for a really big one.

❧ 7 ❧

The Proof of the Pudding

They pay off on results.
POPULAR SAYING

I SAW very little of Griffith and nothing of the film during the weeks to follow, because I had been given the additional job of shooting the titles. This didn't seem to amount to much, just at first blush. Stick up the title card, square it in the frameline of the camera, and grind away, a foot of film for each word. Someone had figured out that a word a second was the average audience reading speed, so that was it. Ten words, ten feet; fifty words, fifty feet. Nothing to it.

But these title cards, printed with white lettering on black cardboard stock, turned out to be more of a problem than you'd think. For one thing, the black stock is no longer black when you hit it with the full force of C-filament Mazda lamps from each side. It becomes a medium or even a light gray, because the greasy printing ink on that rough stock picks up the light and reflects it back. Furthermore, the white ink is not really perfectly white but semi-transparent, with the black showing through from underneath. The result was a smeary sort of dim gray on gray, no good at all.

Idea: why not shoot the title cards on positive film for greater contrast? True, positive stock is slow, so it meant shooting in stop-motion, and it took forever to get a shot of a long editorial title, but at my rate of pay, time didn't matter.

It should have worked but it didn't. Why not shoot the titles with a still camera using lantern plates? This gave a negative of very black letters on perfectly transparent glass. Now print these negatives on more lantern plates and the result was razor-sharp clear letters on an absolutely black background. Never mind the little pinholes and dust specks. They could be blocked out with regular retoucher's opaque. Now illuminate these plates from the back in a regular light box and that's it, a foolproof system.

[84]

Not that these titles were something to shoot and forget. They were being cut into the picture as Griffith did his editing on a day and night schedule. We now had a third projectionist added to our original two. George Richter, a thin, sallow, hopeless-looking youth, took his turn at hand-grinding the projector, on the alert to stick a slip of paper into the uptake reel every time the buzzer sounded, a signal that a change of cutting was to be made; the slip, caught in the reel, would tell Rose and Jimmy Smith where the cuts were to be made.

More often than not, the changes were to be made in the titles, of which there were two kinds: the editorial and the spoken. Every time Griffith would see one of these titles on the screen, he'd find some way to change it: the word order or the punctuation or something else. This meant that Frank Woods would have to rewrite the newest revisions of the latest titles and have the downtown print shop make up new ones, which I, in turn, had to shoot on lantern plates, print the plates on more lantern plates, then shoot the result on positive film stock, which became the negative for the picture, and—but you get the idea. It was a long and complicated process because we were ignorant and didn't know any better. There were better ways of getting the same result, but we—or more correctly, I—didn't know about them, so I spent all of my days and most of my nights shooting and re-shooting revised, re-revised, and re-re-revised titles, a whole new batch every day.

If there were any out-of-town previews of *The Clansman,* I never heard of them.* Nothing strange about this. Studio people were not supposed to know; otherwise they'd be there cheering things along, which was one thing Griffith most assuredly did *not* want.

It was during these day-and-night title sessions that I came to know and really appreciate Frank Woods's place in Griffith's life. He was a sort of elder statesman, because he knew everybody worth knowing, and being inflexibly, fanatically honest, and incapable of misrepresenting anything to anyone, not even to me, he was trusted and respected absolutely by Griffith. He was always "Mr. Woooods" to Griffith, who never even asked, much less ordered him to come on the set to help straighten out some dubious point or other, but who left the set himself to go to Frank Woods' office to ask for his advice. Once in a long while, Woods would come on the set to present an idea or to ask for guidance, and it was a strange sight to see old Frank Woods, wearing his ridiculous tam-o'shanter-type cap of rough

---

* There were previews in Riverside, California, January 1 and 2, 1915, according to Eileen Bowser. KEVIN BROWNLOW

tweed, with a button on top the size and shape of a flattened tea biscuit, leaning over, with the sun glistening on the snowy-white stubble of his unshaven face, while he consulted with Griffith in murmured tones about matters of immediate importance.

That stubble was not a sign of carelessness or indifference to his public appearance. It was merely that his working day, his real working day, did not begin until night. Then he would visit his favorite barber (nobody but actors ever shaved themselves) and have his face lathered and steamed and shaved and reshaved and creamed and lotioned to perfection before going to work as host to the visiting greats at his favorite seat at the head of his favorite table in the middle of the Hoffman House café. Frank Woods knew absolutely everybody worth knowing and a good many that were not. A printer and newspaperman himself, and keenly aware of the power of the press, he entertained mostly newspapermen and columnists, writers and editors, some of whom were his oldest cronies, like Bob Davis and Ben De Casseres, with whom he cut up old touches about the care and feeding of authors like O. Henry, the most popular and the most difficult writer of the day. And of course little words, little stories, little human-interest anecdotes, delivered in Frank Woods's inimitable manner, somehow found their way into the conversation, with the result that Griffith was ceasing to be a man and was rapidly becoming a legend.

Not that he lied or misrepresented even by inference. Frank Woods was incapable of deceit or misrepresentation. He told the absolute truth at all times, but he told it with such art and such gusto that the truth became entertainment at its best, which is an art that almost surpasses art. For, as everyone knows, nothing is so unreasonable as the truth, and it's a rare personage who can make the truth believable.

It was probably Frank Woods's doing that had the picture world waiting and counting the days for the first glimpse of Griffith's most ambitious effort to date, the showing of *The Clansman* at Clune's Auditorium.

It was a packed house, with swarms of people standing around outside, hoping for cancellations so they could get in anywhere at all, even in the top gallery. I never saw or felt such eager anticipation in any crowd as there was at that opening night. We three, my father, my mother, and I, had been given choice seats saved for us by Frank Woods. My parents, old-stagers at the business of opening nights, were all keyed up to a state of high tension, while I—well, I was feeling a little sick because *I* knew what the picture really was, just another Biograph, only four times as long. I simply couldn't help feeling that it had been a tragic mistake to build up such a fever pitch of eager anticipation, only to let them down by showing them what was bound to be just another movie. Only longer, much longer, three hours longer. What audience, however friendly, could possibly sit through that much of nothing but one long, one very long movie of the kind they had seen a hundred times before?

My first inkling that this was not to be just another movie came when I heard, over the babble of the crowd, the familiar sound of a great orchestra tuning up. First the oboe sounding A, then the others joining to produce an ever-changing medley of unrelated sounds, with each instrument testing its own strength and capability through this warming-up preliminary. Then the orchestra came creeping in through that little doorway under the proscenium apron and I tried to count them. Impossible. Too many. But there were at least seventy, for that's where I lost count, so most if not all of the Los Angeles Symphony orchestra had been hired to "play" the picture.

Not that I hadn't known about a special score having been prepared for the production. Joseph Carl Breil had been around the studio a lot, talking with Griffith, so I knew what was up. But Carl Breil was no Beethoven. Thus far he had produced only one song, "The Song of the Soul," which had become a great favorite among those who liked that kind of music, but he was no great shakes as a composer in the grand manner. Oh, he was capable enough in his own limited way. He *was* a musician, there was no denying that. He could arrange, he was good at instrumentation, and he could conduct. He could do just about anything known to music except think up tunes. Well, maybe Griffith had supplied that lack. We'd soon find out, because the orchestra pit was crammed to overflowing with the finest performers in Los Angeles and more, many more instruments of different kinds than I had seen anywhere before except at full-dress, all-out symphony concerts. He had the big doghouses, as we called the double basses, and a lot of little doghouses, as the cellos were called, with as many fiddles as there was room for and enough brass to make up a full brass band all by itself. And as for the kitchen, or hardware shop, as the drum section was called, there was everything known to percussion, while at the console of the massive pipe organ sat a little man lost in a maze of stops and manuals, ready to turn on the full roar of that monster at the tip of a baton. Yes, it was a complete orchestra, all right. I even glimpsed two or three banjos in that crowded orchestra pit, but what they could be doing there was more than I could imagine.

The house lights dimmed. The audience became tensely silent. I felt once again, as always before, that strange all-over chill that comes with the magic moment of hushed anticipation when the curtain is about to rise.

The title came on, apparently by mistake, because the curtain had not yet risen and all I could see was the faint flicker of the lettering against the dark fabric of the main curtain. But it was not a mistake at all, because the big curtain rose slowly to disclose the title, full and clear upon the picture screen, while at the same moment Breil's baton rose, held for an instant, and then swept down, releasing the full impact of the orchestra in a mighty fanfare that was all but out-roared by the massive blast of the organ in an overwhelming burst of earth-shaking sound that shocked the audience first into a stunned silence and then roused them to a pitch of enthusiasm such as I had never seen or heard before.

Then, of course, came those damned explanatory titles that I had shot time and time again as Griffith and Woods kept changing and rechanging them, all with the object of having them make as much sense as possible in the fewest possible words. Somehow, the audience didn't seem to mind. Perhaps they were hardened to it. They should have been, by now, because whenever anybody made any kind of historical picture, it always had to be preceded by a lot of titles telling all about it, not to mention a long and flowery dedication thanking everyone from the Holy Trinity to the night watchman for their invaluable cooperation, without which this picture would not have been possible.

The orchestra sort of murmured to itself during the titles, as though to reassure the audience that they couldn't last forever. And then . . . the picture, gliding along through its opening sequences on a flow of music that seemed to speak for the screen and to interpret every mood. The audience was held entranced, but I was not. I was worried in the same way that young fathers, waiting to learn whether it's a boy or a girl, are worried. I was worried, badly worried, about the battle scenes, and I wished they'd get through fiddle-faddling with that dance and all that mushy love stuff and get down to cases. For it was a simple, open-and-shut matter of make or break as far as I could see; and I could *not* see how that mixed-up jumble of unrelated bits and pieces of action could ever be made into anything but a mixed-up jumble of bits and pieces.

Well, I was wrong. What unfolded on that screen was magic itself. I knew there were cuts from this and to that, but try as I would, I could not *see* them. A shot of the extreme far end of the Confederate line flowed into another but nearer shot of the same line, to be followed by another and another, until I could have sworn that the camera had been carried back by some sort of impossible carrier that made it seem to be all one unbroken scene. Perhaps the smoke helped blind out the jumps. I don't know. All I knew was that between the ebb and flow of a broad canvas of a great battle, now far and now near, and the roaring of that gorgeous orchestra banging and blaring battle songs to stir the coldest blood, I was hot and cold and feeling waves of tingling electric shocks racing all over me.

The Confederate charge was simply magnificent. Once again, there was nothing choppy about it, no sense of scenes being cut one into another. That whole line of men simply flowed across the field, stumbling and dropping as they ran somehow into solid sheets of rifle fire from the Union entrenchments, while bombs, real bombs and not Fireworks Wilson's silly little powder puffs, burst with deafening roars among these charging heroes. Oh yes; I knew. I knew perfectly well that the backstage crew was working furiously to create these explosion effects just behind the screen, but I was too caught up in the magnificence of the spectacle to care *how* it was achieved.

And that scene with Walthall snatching up the flag and racing forward with it: holding it high and waving it defiantly as he ran with it in one hand and his drawn sword in the other straight at the cannon, to mount the parapet, and then—in a single, magnificent, overwhelming glimpse of one man, alone against a sky full of bursting bombs, thrusting that standard down the cannon's throat and shouting his defiant yell, while the trumpets in the orchestra split the air. Nor were those trumpets alone. I think every man in that packed audience was on his feet cheering, not the picture, not the orchestra, not Griffith but voicing his exultation at this man's courage—defiant in defeat, and all alone with only the heavens for his witness.

Suddenly I remembered; and with the memory came shame, deep and bitter, for this was the very scene I had convinced myself was so very bad, so utterly silly. And yet it was the greatest of them all, inconceivable except in the mind of an inspired genius. Of *course* he was right. For every man stands alone, in the ultimate moment of truth. How could I have been so stupid as to have missed anything so starkly obvious, so universally true?

The same humiliation came repeatedly to drown me in shame through the length of the showing. I was forced to admit to myself over again how pitifully little I knew about anything at all. There was that scene of Lillian Gish fluttering and running, fluttering and running over the death-strewn battlefield looking for her beloved, not as any human being would make such a search but as a ballet dancer might pictorialize it. I thought it was awful when it was being shot. But it was heartbreakingly effective on that night upon that screen before that particular audience, especially with the orchestra, that beautiful orchestra, interweaving the twin themes of love and death, just as Griffith had thought of them at that one magic moment on the battlefield. For she wasn't a woman at all but a spirit, a will-o'-the-wisp, floating over the field of death. She was even more than that: she was the spirit of *all* the women of the Civil War, who still lived in the memories of their daughters and granddaughters, whose hearts had been searching among the dead for the living after every one of the many major battles.

The long sequence in Ford's theater made me feel sick at heart because I had been on the scene as an active participant, and yet I had seen nothing, felt nothing, sensed nothing of what was happening before my eyes. Those many shots and cross-shots, those confusing scenes of the silly little farce taking place on the stage while Booth was creeping up on his prey, of Lincoln fussing with his shawl, and of the people in the audience laughing at the play, all these flowed together in a sort of vision that began with the full set and then crept in and in by imperceptible degrees. Once again, I could *not* tell when and where the cuts were made, because I was so fascinated by the way the camera crept in and in, ever closer to the inevitable tragedy.

And that mirror business that I had thought so silly—it was nothing of the sort. It *picked out* a symbol of death itself, a figure all in black with a ghost-white face and a short, villainous little mustache; you never knew or cared where that light came from, so compelling was this poetic vision of Nemesis. And Lincoln was *not* fussing in any old-womanish manner with his shawl, for Booth was approaching the box with death in his hand, and Lincoln drew the shawl around his shoulders with a little shiver that made you feel sure he had felt the cold chill of the wing of a black angel sweeping from that unguarded, open, black-yawning doorway behind him. And during all this, the people on the stage and the people in the audience were laughing as though there could be no such thing as death in the world, nor that it would strike within a very few seconds to fell the nation's most dearly beloved man—not President or leader, but *man,* because he had fulfilled every man's dream of rising from the most ignoble of obscurity to the highest level of greatness possible to any mortal creature.

The shot—the scream—the leap—the shouted slogan—and the massed rising of the audience—the hysteria—the volcanic eruption of shock and agony, grief and terror—during all this, when it was happening in my very presence, had prompted me to do nothing more than make a few silly and ridiculously juvenile comments about stagehands!

But how could I know? How could I guess that this sequence was not to be cut, not to be edited, but was to be orchestrated with an exquisitely sure rhythm of point and counterpoint, with the instrumentation of grimmest tragedy against the bubbling froth of carefree laughter?

It was hopeless. From then on I simply sat and watched and listened and wondered about how blind people could be, myself most of all.

Somewhere during my self-castigation a title came on reading INTERMISSION. So soon? I asked my father the time. He pulled out his watch, snapped open the case, and said it was nine thirty. Preposterous. Somehow during the past fifteen minutes, or not more than twenty, an hour and a half had sneaked away.

We went out with the rest of the crowd to stretch our legs and, in true backstage fashion, to eavesdrop on the comments of the others. There was enthusiasm, yes; lots of it. It had been exactly as grandpa had described it was the consensus, only more real. There were also a few professionals who were wisely sure that Griffith was riding for a fall. "You can't shoot all your marbles in the first half and have anything left for your finish" was the loudly expressed opinion of a very portly, richly dressed gentleman. "That battle was a lulu, best I've ever seen, and that assassination bit was a knock-out, I ain't kidding you. But what's he going to do for a topper, that's what I want to know. I'll *tell* you what's going to happen. This thing is going to fizzle out like a wet firecracker, that's what it's going to do. Don't tell me, I know! I've seen it happen too many times. They shoot the works right off the bat and they got nothing left for their finish. You wait and see. You just wait and see."

Chimes sounded from inside, to signal the end of the intermission. Loud-mouth threw his cigar away and shouldered his way back inside. I crept to my place with a sense of cold foreboding. I knew what was coming: no more action, no more battles, nothing until way down at the very end, which was a virtual repeat of *Elderbush Gulch,* only with renegades instead of Indians, and with clansmen instead of the good old tried-and-true United States Cavalry, complete with flags and pennons, bugles and flashing sabers, and if need be, a full-screen shot of the flag itself with the National Anthem blared out by a regimental band for a surefire finish that would bring 'em up cheering.

Yes, this would work. Of that there could be no possible doubt, no possible doubt whatever. But it was so old, so very old as to be threadbare.

And yet it wasn't the finish that worried me so much as the long, dull, do-nothing stuff that I knew was slated for the bulk of the second half. Stuff like the hospital scenes,* where Lillian Gish comes to visit Henry Walthall, she in demurest of dove gray, he in bed with a bandage neatly and evenly wrapped around his head. Now what in the world can anyone possibly do to make a hospital visit seem other than routine? He'll be grateful, naturally, and she'll be sweetly sympathetic, but what else? How can you or Griffith or the Man in the Moon possibly get anything out of such a scene?

---

* In the prints we now see, the hospital scenes Brown refers to occur before the inter-mission. GEORGE PRATT

Answer: you can't. But *he* did, by reaching outside the cut-and-dried formula and coming up with something so unexpected, and yet so utterly natural, that it lifted the entire thing right out of the rut and made it ring absolutely true.

Since this was an army hospital, there had to be a sentry on guard. So Griffith looked around, saw a sloppy, futile sort of a character loitering about, and ran him in to play the sentry, a fellow named Freeman, not an actor, just another extra. Well, Lillian passed before him and he looked after her and sighed. In the theater and on the screen, that sigh became a monumental, standout scene, because it was so deep, so heartfelt, and so loaded with longing for the unattainable that it simply delighted the audience. But not without help. Breil may not have been the greatest composer the world has ever known but he did know how to make an orchestra talk, and that sigh, uttered by the cellos and the muted trombones softly sliding down in a discordant glissando, drove the audience into gales of laughter.

Another scene that struck me as being way off key when it was being shot was the one where Mae Marsh, as Little Sister, is preparing a homecoming feast for her beloved brother, the heroic Little Colonel. Now *you* know, and *I* know, and everybody else knows that she could have scrounged around somewhere to rustle up something decent to eat. Eggs, maybe, or a chicken or two. But she had corn in the house, so she shiftlessly parched some corn and let it go at that.

But on the screen, and before that eager audience, what a difference, what a world of difference there was! Just *look* at that girl. Poor, yes; so very poor that all she has to offer for a homecoming celebration are a few grains of parched corn in a dry pan, nothing else at all. But the spirit, the magnificent spirit of that girl shone through with such poignancy that it brought tears of pride from all around. I could hear snuffling and coughing, and my mother was delving into her purse for her handkerchief. But was Little Sister sorry or apologetic for the poor welcome-home meal that was the best she could provide? Not a bit of it, for her head was high and her eyes were bright and she even added a touch of royalty to the occasion by draping a sort of shawl of raw field cotton around her shoulders and making it into ermine by dabbing it with tails of black soot from the bottom of the frying pan. And Carl Breil, bless his larcenous soul, added the crowning touch by letting his orchestra sing something very like "Land of Hope and Glory" in a softly muted undertone, the tune that won Elgar his knighthood.

There was a question in my mind as to which represented the higher heroism, the brother charging through shot and shell in the heat of battle to glorify himself before the world, or this fifteen-year-old girl, alone and unseen in the quiet of her impoverished kitchen, making a royal feast of a handful of dry corn and a royal occasion of it all with the help of a few wisps of cotton and some dabs of black soot from a kettle? One reached the peak of momentary bravery, the other the long-sustained pride of a girl whose spirit could *not* be humbled but who held her head and her heart proudly high despite the most grinding of poverty.

Thinking of this, and remembering that Napoleon had said that the greatest courage was the two-in-the-morning kind, made me vote overwhelmingly in favor of Little Sister. And so, I believe, did the audience.

If so, then what of Griffith's long-established principle of making the audience love a character and of then putting that same character in the direst possible danger, only to stage a rescue at the last instant? Because he had made the audience love Little Sister, he was going to put her in the gravest possible danger, but he was *not* going to rescue her. She was going on over that peak to her death. I knew, because I had thrown her over myself. How could he dare to do such a thing? Audiences would never stand for it. They'd hate him. And they'd hate his picture for letting such a thing happen to this heroic little girl.

But before that came the interminable walk of Walthall to the doorway of his ruined mansion, the walk that had nearly cost me my job. I waited with squirming anxiety for that scene to come on, and when it did appear, I was caught up, along with the rest of the audience, with what seemed to me to be the most restrained yet most powerful scene I had ever seen. Of course, Carl Breil helped enormously. As Henry's eyes drifted over the smoke-blackened pillars and the broken gates and windows of his formerly immaculate home, little hints of happy memory came fleeting past from the orchestra. And when he reached the door and the arms came out to greet him, the muted strings brought a lump to every male throat and a flow of tears from the eyes of the gentler sex. I looked at my mother. She was frankly weeping; and I didn't feel so absolutely indifferent myself.

I endured the "drama"—all that stuff with Ralph Lewis being shown up as a fake when he wouldn't let his daughter marry George Siegmann because he was a mulatto—all because I was itching to get to the part where Walter Long chased Mae Marsh all over Big Bear Valley, running low and dripping with peroxide.*

What came on the screen wasn't Walter Long at all. It was some sort of inhuman monster, an ungainly, misshapen creature out of a nightmare, not

---

* In fact, the Big Bear Valley episode comes much earlier in the film, four hundred shots before Siegmann says to Lewis, "The lady I want to marry is your daughter."
GEORGE PRATT

running as a human being would run but shambling like a gorilla. And Mae Marsh was not fluttering, either. She was a poor little lost girl frightened out of her wits, not knowing which way to turn, but searching, searching for safety, and too bewildered to know what she was doing. So she ran to the peak of that rock, and when the monster came lumbering straight at her, she . . . well, all I can say is that it was *right,* absolutely, perfectly, incontestably right.

And did the audience hate Griffith for letting them down? Not a bit of it. When the clansmen began to ride, the cheers began to rise from all over that packed house. This was not a ride to save Little Sister but to avenge her death, and every soul in that audience was in the saddle with the clansmen and pounding hell-for-leather on an errand of stern justice, lighted on their way by the holy flames of a burning cross.

Ah, but those rides. Sure, there were people in trouble, bad trouble, fighting in trapped positions for their lives, but the concern of the audience didn't seem to be at all with the plight of the besieged. On the contrary, their hearts and souls seemed to be riding with the clansmen, who kept pounding through, over hills and through streams and along lanes, all of them in a long-continued, never-slackening charge.

A thing that hit me like a paralyzing electric shock was to hear Griffith's voice—not his real voice, of course—but the brasses imitating his voice as he sang that "Ha-Haaaah—Yah!" over and over again. Griffith had undoubtedly sung it for Breil, who wrote it down and then orchestrated it for trumpets, trombones, and horns, backed by the thunder of hoofs created by the sound-effects men behind the screen.

The effect was tremendous. There was one shot in particular that made the audience duck and scream. The horses swerved from their path in a huddled bunch and ran straight for the audience, to *jump over* the screen as though to land right square in row M of the orchestra seats.

I watched this shot with the greatest of interest because I had never seen it. True, I had shot it. That was the one where the horse kicked the magazine off the camera as he passed over me. But I had never seen it, because although I was turning the camera as a sort of reflex action, I personally was huddled down in as tight a knot as I could manage, with both my eyes screwed tightly shut. Not that I was frightened. No, never that. But I was a cameraman and cameramen have to protect their eyes. So I was only doing my duty by looking—no, not looking, but *guarding* the company's best interests.

So everyone was rescued and everyone was happy and everyone was noble in victory and the audience didn't just sit there and applaud, but they stood up and cheered and yelled and stamped feet until Griffith finally made an appearance.

If you could call it an appearance. Now I, personally, in such a situation would have bounded out to the center of the stage with both hands aloft in a gesture of triumph, and I would probably have shaken my hands over my head, as Tom Wilson had told me was the proper thing for any world's champion to do at the end of a hard-fought but victorious fight.

Griffith did nothing of the sort. He stepped out a few feet from stage left, a small, almost frail figure lost in the enormousness of that great proscenium arch. He did not bow or raise his hands or do anything but just stand there and let wave after wave of cheers and applause wash over him like great waves breaking over a rock.

Then he left. The show was over. There was an exit march from the orchestra, but nobody could hear it. People were far too busy telling one another how wonderful, how great, how tremendous it had all been.

The street cars were all crowded. My father and mother managed to get a rear seat together on the fourth or fifth car, and I took the little wooden bench that ran sideways just back of them. The conversation was all about the picture and what a miraculous experience seeing it had been. I lost all this babble in a seething sea of my own thoughts.

It was not, I decided, so much what you shot as what you did with it after you had it on film. Not that what you shoot doesn't have to be good. Not at all. Silk purses are not to be made out of sows' ears. But once you have the silk, what you do with it makes all the difference. Directing a picture, it seemed to me, was something like a cameraman making a negative. The subject, the composition, the lighting all have to be right. But all you get is a negative.

I had done enough experimental work myself, in my own spare bedroom, to realize that even the finest negative is only the first step toward the final result, the print that is to be shown. And there were so many, so very many different ways and methods of making prints—carbon, gum bichromate, projection prints, toned prints that could be made in any color, managed prints that could be controlled every step of the way with shading here, brightening there, until a final result was obtained that could be very fine or that could also be perfectly awful.

Somewhere in this welter of confused images came a new concept of Griffith. I was not wrong in thinking that some of his scenes had been pretty bad, definitely overdone and in some cases actually hammy. But how was I to know that these *had* to be so because he was intending to use only the shortest of flashes, measured in frames and not feet, and that he had to punch everything possible into these shots or the effect could never be felt? So I began to feel less bad about myself, even though ignorance is no excuse, and better about Griffith, not so much as a great man but as a great craftsman. And the heart of his craft was in what we fumblingly called cutting, or editing, or some other such inadequate term.

What he really was—it seemed odd to think so—was a great composer of visual images instead of notes. What I had seen was not so much a motion picture but the equivalent of Beethoven's *Eroica* or his Fifth. That picture had been perfectly orchestrated and the instrumentation flawless.

This turn toward music as a parallel set me to thinking about Carl Breil and the wizardry of his effects. I thought particularly of Freeman's sigh. There was something I had heard before in that sigh, some identifiable strangeness, if I could only place it. It seemed to me that this had been inspired if not copied from the "Windmill" passage in Richard Strauss's *Don Quixote*. I made a mental note to go to the library and pull down the score and check it out for myself.

The car stopped. My father shook my arm. "Wake up, son. We're home."

We got off the car and walked home. Lily greeted us with loud joy, but we were all too drained to pay much attention to anything but sleep.

I crawled into bed and stretched out in the dark, fully resolved to relive that picture through and count the many places where I had been wrong and Griffith right.

But something went wrong with my good intentions, because suddenly it was daylight and the house was full of the aroma of fresh coffee.

It was another day, and time to go to work.

❦ 8 ❧

The Winner's Circle

Great oaks from little acorns grow.
COPYBOOK MAXIM

THE enormous, worldwide success of *The Clansman* was not entirely un-
assisted. Griffith, who was a modest and retiring gentleman of the old school
of Kentucky, had three publicity men who were not. Bennie Ziedman, Wil-
lard Keefe, and Jack Lloyd, directed by the master mind of Frank Woods,
transmuted Griffith from the figure of a highly successful director of nickelodeon movies into a living legend, the miracle man who had done everything, originated everything, and who was now the Great Master of Masters.

This, supposedly, is about as far as any publicity campaign can carry anyone. But they surpassed even this. Perhaps by design but more probably
through sheer momentum, they made Griffith fashionable. And from the
tyranny of fashion there is no appeal.

Fashion, that irrational compulsion to be first with the latest, decreed
that Griffith was great, *The Clansman* was great, and that all who had not
climbed aboard this latest and most opulently glittering bandwagon were
ignorant oafs groping blindly in the outer darkness. For even the President
himself had declared that seeing *The Clansman* was like seeing history by
flashes of lightning, a phrase lifted bodily from a century-old comment on a
performance of *Lear,* written by Coleridge or Hazlitt, I forget which.*

So Griffith was "in," and in conformity with the old proverb, "Them as
has, gits," everything that had ever been done in the development of pictures
was accredited to him, whether he deserved it or not. And so it suddenly
became common knowledge that he had invented the close-up, the iris, the
fades, the use of parallel action, the flashback, and everything else that
seemed worthy enough to be laid in reverence at the feet of this newest idol.

* Coleridge (as I did *not* know at seventeen) said that seeing Kean as Lear was like
"reading Shakespeare by flashes of lightning." (Author)

As usual, Griffith was given great credit for many things he had not done, while he was given no credit at all for the really enormous advances he had brought to the whole wide world of picture making.

The greatest of these was the lifting of the lowly nickelodeon storefront theater, with its tinny honky-tonk piano and its windowless, foul-air smelliness, to the grandeur of a great auditorium with a great orchestra and a great picture that ran three hours and filled an entire evening with thrills and excitement in a setting of opulent luxury such as the great masses of working people had never dreamed possible for them. This sort of thing was for the idle rich who went to the opera to see and be seen. But after that first opening night at Clune's Auditorium in Los Angeles, anybody could be a millionaire for three hours and a Griffith snob for the rest of his life.

Probably the surest test of the power of any innovation is the opposition it engenders. This is no independent discovery of mine. Sir Isaac Newton beat me to it way back in the seventeenth century by announcing that action and reaction were equal and opposite, a law that seems to have no exceptions, physically, emotionally, or politically. The power of *The Clansman* was great enough to brew riotous opposition that put blood on the streets in some quarters and that filled columns and pages of newspapers and magazines with attacks, counterattacks, demands for censorship, and other demands for even greater freedom of expression on the screen. Equal and opposite. Never fails.

What was of much more immediate interest to those of us actually working in the Griffith studio was the sudden cascading of money, money, and yet more money into the studio itself. Not that everybody got immediate and substantial raises. Our salaries remained the same, but with the important difference that they were dependably sure to *be* there every payday. There were exceptions, of course. Bitzer's ten thousand kept doubling and redoubling and increasing and multiplying until he couldn't be bothered with picking up that measly little three hundred a week but simply let it pile up in the cashier's office until it grew into two or three thousand, or enough to make a trip to the bank worthwhile. Not that the money did him any good. He was still nailed hand and foot to that same old contract, from which there was no escape. Goldstein, the costumer, made so much money from his share that he went into the picture business on his own, planning an even bigger and much more controversial film than *The Clansman*.

The real benefit came through the fantastic expansion of activity within the studio itself. Directors, stars, cameramen, and crews for half-a-dozen companies were hired. The carpenter shop was working day and night, turning out sets for the stages, while other crews of carpenters, plumbers, electricians, and maintenance men were swarming all over the place building more and more new structures to house this influx of talent.

Every inch of Thoren's formerly weed-covered property had been covered with ramshackle buildings thrown together for temporary use. With no more linear space available, the builders took to the air, and nearly everything new was built as a second story on something old. Stairs sprouted everywhere, and we had to climb up to the new rehearsal hall, the new dressing rooms, the new drafting rooms, the new projection rooms. The stages were being covered and electrified, so that shooting could proceed in good weather or bad, day or night. Cooper Hewitt lights came in various sizes and shapes, from overhead banks to sidelights to the so-called foot warmers, low horizontal lights that held only four or five tubes and could be fitted under the front of the camera as a low fill light. And of course we had an ample supply of the good old stage-designed automatic arc lights designed and built by the Kliegl Brothers, lights that were always mispronounced as klieg lights, giving rise to countless puns about who knocked the L out of Kliegl. But these were ills that could not be cured and so had to be endured, like the forever misused reference to the limelight. In the old days the only source of light for a spotlight was a cylinder of lime made white-hot by a jet of gas. These primitive spotlights had been replaced by hand-fed arcs for many years, but celebrities and politicians were still referred to as being in the limelight, a term that simply refused to die, even though the actuality no longer existed.

We were all as eager to try our splendid new lights as youngsters with new toys. They were really wonderful. There was nothing that couldn't be done with them. Back lighting was a cinch. You could hit a profile with a 100-amp. spot and get a line light that would knock your eye out, as the saying went. You could also burn one into the back of a frizzy-headed blonde and make her look like a haystack afire.

We all crowded eagerly into the projection room to see the first tests of these new lights. They were beautiful, very beautiful, except for one thing: the picture flickered abominably. Hasty consultation. Conclusion: we were using alternating current, the alternations were out of step with the shutter, and there was nothing to be done about it except to install a motor-generator unit that would deliver direct current to the lights, which would then be steady, and all would be well. This would run into money, but with the kind of money that was pouring into the studio nobody cared. So heavy concrete foundations were formed, a huge AC motor was married to a DC generator, the juice was turned on, and the song of the motor-generator set was heard in the land, never to be silent as long as a company was shooting inside. We soon became so accustomed to this high-pitched, ear-piercing whine that the studio seemed to be deserted and corpselike whenever that set was silent. Electricity had become the life of the studio, to remain so forevermore, as far as we could see.

While all this was going on, we were getting people, people, more and more people. Douglas Fairbanks came leaping and cavorting in from the New York stage to do his stunts under the direction of John Emerson, with the extremely able help of Anita Loos, Johnnie Leezer* running the camera. (These first releases of the new Triangle schedule did not appear until September 1915.)

Anita Loos fascinated me. Here was a mere slip of a girl, who should be wearing a middy blouse and going to high school, and yet who was filled to the brim with more wit and wisdom than anyone I had ever encountered. A child prodigy, maybe. We'd had them on the stage, so I knew it was possible. But she was so quick on the trigger, so fast on the comeback that I finally pumped up nerve enough to ask her, with due humility, how in the world she could possibly manage it.

She thought this over for a moment and then answered, in a low conspiratorial undertone out of the side of her mouth, "As long as I can hang on to my copy of Voltaire, there's nobody going to catch me without a snappy comeback."

However, this was not the entire truth, as I discovered later. She really did think up her own gags, some of which I thought were very funny. For instance, in a Fairbanks picture in which he leaped and hurdled through a fashionable health resort, Anita named one of the very fat lady characters Mrs. Helfer-Eaton, while the thin sick one who was always gulping pills she named Mrs. Fuller-Germes. Then, in a parody on Sherlock Holmes, with Fairbanks bouncing around with a huge magnifying glass in his hand and a deerstalker cap on his head, he opened a cabinet labeled DEADLY POISONS to disclose a bottle marked Cyanide and another tagged Rat Poison, while snuggled between them was a familiar, square-faced bottle with a well-known label, Gordon's Gin. I thought these were all extremely funny. But then it must be remembered that I was not yet seventeen.

The real secret of her invariable success was that she made no secret of her use of Voltaire, and whenever one of her own gags misfired, she'd blame it on Voltaire. Nobody can afford to think of Voltaire as being anything but brilliant, so the gag was accepted instantly as being pure, 24-carat

---

* Leezer photographed *Mystery of the Leaping Fish* (1916), with Karl Brown as assistant. KEVIN BROWNLOW

wit. Frank Woods and Griffith both agreed that Anita Loos was one of the brainiest young women alive. For once I had to differ—silently, of course—with them. For with smartness like that, who needs brains?

DeWolf Hopper arrived. He was a fine actor who had been superb as Friar Tuck in DeKoven's *Robin Hood,* but he had recited "Casey at the Bat" so many times that all his past glories were forgotten and he was known merely as the world's best reciter of "Casey at the Bat." Naturally he was cast as Casey in a picture called *Casey at the Bat,* what else? The action takes place in a town called Mudville. Fortunately, Mudville was just over the pass, perfect in every bucolic detail, in a tiny rural village called Lankershim. The setting was perfect, Hopper was perfect, everything was perfect, except that the only action is that Casey strikes out. And since everybody knew the poem and knew he was going to strike out, the finished picture seemed to lack something. Suspense, maybe.

Sir Herbert Beerbohm Tree arrived, to do his famous interpretation of *Macbeth.* George "Tripod" Hill shot the picture, while Victor Fleming, a racing-car driver turned cameraman, was another of our new crop of photographers. We had so many new directors, cameramen, actors and actresses that I gave up all idea of keeping track of them. They were everywhere, doing everything from slapstick comedy to Shakespeare.

All of this overnight, mushroom-growth expansion came through a sort of three-way agreement between Griffith, Mack Sennett, and Tom Ince to release a picture a week from each of the three studios, to be shown as a triple bill, a full evening's entertainment in big theaters throughout the country, complete with orchestra and organ and backstage sound effects, as a sort of follow-up attempt to ride the great success of *The Clansman.* For the idea of a big show, lavishly presented in a big showhouse, was the latest popular rage, and the idea was to strike this particular iron while it was good and hot.

During all this, Griffith was in and out of town, following the various gala openings of *The Clansman* from coast to coast. Somewhere along the line, the title of *The Clansman* was changed to *The Birth of a Nation,* which seemed to all of us inside the studio to be an extremely ill-advised attempt to add historic dignity to what was already a runaway popular success. For a title is really a trademark of sorts, and once a trademark has been burned into the public mind as a symbol of some one particular thing, why confuse everybody by giving it another name? You might with equal folly abandon such names as Kodak, Pears Soap, Beecham's Pills or Sozodont for something grand and exalted and in our crude way of putting it, hifalutin'. But *The Clansman* was too big and its momentum too great to be swerved from its headlong career by anything so trifling as a change of title. People knew by now what it really was: a chance for everyone to leap into the saddle, protected by an impenetrable disguise, and ride hell-bent on a mission of retribution for the foul death of everyone's beloved Little Sister. Vicariously, of course. But then, what great literature is anything other than the vicarious sharing of the great experiences of great heroes?

The studio itself went through a bewildering number of name changes. Let's see, now. First it was Mutual, then Fine Arts, then Triangle, then— but who cared? To everybody in town it was the Griffith studio and that was enough.

Then there was that sudden influx of girls. Girls to the right of us, girls to the left of us, girls to the front of us giggled and tittered. Winifred Westover, Pauline Starke, Bessie Love, all in their early teens, became part of the stock company, along with the older, wiser young marrieds, such as Adele Clifton, Gracie Wilson, and Daisy Robinson, seasoned performers all.

There was also a whole stable of girls, drawn from the neighborhood, who worked in the newly built, long and narrow building where they did nothing but assemble release prints all day long.

Their work was theoretically easy. The prints came from the laboratory as separate scenes, some of them very short. To join or splice these into a continuous thousand-foot reel meant that the emulsion had to be wetted, scraped from the end of the film to clear a strip of clean celluloid just one perforation-width wide, cemented with amyl acetate, and then pressed to the celluloid side of the adjoining film. I said "theoretically," because in practice these girls never managed to get the emulsion absolutely clear of the film, with the result that the joined place, now two films thick, was never solidly welded together, especially at the edges. These edges had a tendency to curl up and eventually to break in the projector.

Film breakage was a commonplace, everyday happening, even with new release prints. The projectionist simply stopped the machine, pulled down the film, made a hasty repair with a paper clip, and then continued. The clipped place would be recemented during the rewinding of the reel, hurriedly and not very expertly. After all, he was hired to run a projector, not to join films, and if it broke again at the same spot, that was the next fellow's headache, not his. If he happened to be handling a film of any prestige, such as the imported *Quo Vadis,* this was a good time to nip out a foot or so of the print to take home to the kids. I got a fine strip of the hand-colored *Birth of a Pearl* from a projectionist in Danbury that way. It was a good long strip, too. It showed the big shell opening all the way from a narrow slit to its fully opened position, revealing a beautiful girl who rises to her feet. This was fine for me but not so good for the flow of motion in the picture itself. First they'd see the shell, then *flick!* it was wide open and there was the girl.

In the meantime, our platoon of girls was kept busy cutting and scraping, cementing, and winding on to the next place to be joined. They were pretty girls, too, some of them. And lonely. They cast many a languishing glance at the rich young celebrities who were constantly passing and repassing their long tunnel of a workroom, which was walled with windows left partially open to allow the fumes of the film cement to dissipate.

But in that close-guarded room, only the fumes were allowed to dissipate. Nobody ever went near those girls or even gave them a second glance. I wondered why, and with me to wonder was to ask. So I asked Kern, the beefy, blocky, blond-headed German who was in charge of the assembly room and who was constantly patrolling the aisle, advising here and correcting there, how come?

"You vant know?" he asked, with a certain gleam coming into his eyes. "I show."

Before I could guess what he had in mind, his arms were around me, with his hands locked behind the small of my back. He squeezed. I had never felt such pain in all my life. He saw the agony in my face (I would not have yelled before all those girls if he'd killed me), and he relaxed the bear hug slightly. But he still held me so close that I could smell the day-before-yesterday's beer on his breath as he said, "I am German rassler from docks of Hamburg. Vun more little sqveeze und I make your *kidneys* bleed!"

There was one particular girl in that lineup who was prettier than a picture and who turned the full dazzling power of her thousand-watt smile on me every time I passed. But I paid not the slightest attention to her. She was attractive, yes; very attractive indeed. But I felt that I was far too young to risk any entangling alliances. Especially with Kern.

The expansion of the studio accelerated at an explosive rate. More directors, more cameramen came and went with dizzying frequency. Billy Fildew was taken out of the projection room and given a camera. I was with him on his first picture, serving as second, or back-up, cameraman. The picture was *Daphne and the Pirate,* starring, of all people, Lillian Gish! It seemed unimaginable that so sensationally successful a beautiful young star could be cast in a swashbuckling sea story directed by Christy Cabanne, but there it was. I think the decision to make this particular picture was influenced by the fact that there were two old square riggers available from the Ince company. One, the *Alden Bessie,* was a round-bottomed whaler; the other a sharp-prowed clipper, the *John C. Fremont.* So we put to sea, not in a pea-green boat but with pea-green complexions that everyone developed as soon as the ground swell caught these empty old hulks and started them well on their way toward a new world's record for plain-and-fancy rolling. Few if any experiences can be less enjoyable than rolling under a broiling sun in an ancient whaler, reeking of the fishiest of stenches, that of whale oil that had gone rancid fifty years ago and that was becoming more and more rancid by the minute.

One incident that impressed me as being typical of our sudden change from the lowly movie to the lofty cinema was the time when Cabanne asked our leading man, Elliott Dexter, to walk the plank as called for in the script. Whereupon our hero spoke with crushing dignity, "I was engaged as a *personator,* sir; *not* as an acrobat!" Whereupon Tom Wilson, playing a bandannaed, ear-ringed pirate, spoke contemptuously, "Aw, hell, *I'll* do it. Gimme his clothes." The change was made, the scene was shot, and nobody knew the difference when the scene reached the screen.

This business of doubling in brass extended to everyone on the lot. Now that Griffith was not shooting but was merely lending the prestige of his name to the Triangle* pictures, Abe Scholtz's talents as a negative developer were no longer needed in the laboratory. This was now being run on a production-line basis, with everybody's films being treated the same and no babying for anybody. So he was pulled out of his darkroom and put on the camera. Cameramen, like Frank Urson, were moved up to direct the safe-and-sane, director-proof action pictures, full of hairbreadth escapes by daredevils driving flying wheels.

Strange, weird, and impossible story ideas kept coming out of Frank Woods' office. There was one, *The Flying Torpedo,* that was so fantastically impossible that I doubt if Jules Verne himself could have made it acceptable. Here it is: sometime in the far-distant future our shores are being threatened by an unnamed but terrible enemy. His fleet is already in battle array and firing salvo after salvo of heavy shells to destroy our cities. What to do? Ah! Our brave inventor comes up with a brilliant answer. Blast him out of the water with guided missiles controlled by radio impulses.

Guided missiles indeed! Who ever heard of such a thing? And radio impulses to boot. Ridiculous. H. G. Wells had supplied us with plenty of science fiction like *The Invisible Man* and *The War of the Worlds,* but they had been nothing like as hare-brained as this.** However, the man who brought the idea in, a fellow named McCarthy, was a sort of radio nut himself, and

---

* Fine Arts was the trademark for the Griffith studio, the other two angles of Triangle being Keystone (Mack Sennett) and Kay-Bee (Thomas Ince). KEVIN BROWNLOW

** The Urban film, *The Battle in the Clouds,* shown in the U.S. in December 1909, features a guided missile. GEORGE PRATT

he made it all sound so very convincing that the company fell for it. So the idea was approved and put into production. There was no trouble about the flying torpedo itself. Fireworks Wilson had been firing display rockets for years; it was no trick at all for him to bury a rocket in a fancied-up conception of what a rocket might look like far in the future, and the thing worked like a charm.

There was no trouble about the bombardment destroying cities, either. Fireworks Wilson himself stood on a high parallel and threw contact-triggered torpedos into the toy cities and scattered them high, wide, and handsome. But when it came to getting shots of the enemy battle fleet firing salvos from offshore, that was an entirely different matter. There was no trouble about making up a fleet of toy battleships. Our carpenter shop could make anything. Fireworks Wilson could fix the toy guns so they'd fire beautifully. The trouble was with the water.

These toy battleships were set afloat in a shallow tank filled to the brim with water. Since it was a night shot, black cotton velvet supplied all the background that was needed. The lighting was held down, so there was just barely enough to get an image. This was all very good thinking, because the fakier the shot, the less you see of it the better. However, one thing could *not* be hidden A tub of water is a tub of water, and little ripples are little ripples, and there's no getting around it. They shot it this way and they shot it that, but no matter how they shot it, the scene still looked like toy ships in a baby's bath.

I knew perfectly well that any old-line stage crew could lick a problem like that without half trying. For the art of stagecraft is the art of illusion, and our old-timers were quite literally magicians in this highly specialized line of work. One of my most vivid childhood memories was of a scene in a melodrama where the heroine is strapped to the railroad tracks that run from the far horizon straight down to the proscenium apron. Way back, miles away, a train ran across the back, headlight shining, whistle sounding faintly as it curved toward the front before disappearing on the O.P., or opposite-prompt, side of the stage. The whistle came nearer and nearer, and the rumbling of the rails and the chuffing of the train, now invisible, came nearer and nearer. The villain, silk hat, black mustache, and bediamonded ultra-rich costume, stood concealed in a ground row of bushes waiting blood-thirstily to see the gory result of his evil scheme.

Now the train appeared in the distance, coming straight downstage, headed for our helpless heroine, who struggled in vain and cried out in futile attempts to bring help. The headlight of that train became brighter and brighter and more and more dazzling as the train roared out of the background heading for our heroine and the audience as well. The locomotive was now in plain sight, headlight blindingly bright, smoke pouring from the stack in great noisy puffs, drivers turning, rods clanking, the very theater itself rumbling and shaking under the great weight of the onrushing monster. Could *nothing* save that poor heroine? Yes! For on rushed our hero, dressed in Bedford cord, his pure silk ballet shirt open at the neck, his wavy blond hair set in a permanent wave as he leaped to bar the way of that train by waving a lantern back and forth, high and low. There was a loud screeching of brakes as the monster slid to a stop bare inches away from our heroine—a great, towering locomotive that puffed and shot plumes of steam far out from either side, while the train crew in pin-striped coveralls leaped to the ground to help our hero free our heroine, while the villain, at one side, clenched his teeth, shook his fist defiantly at heaven, and cried out, "Foiled! Foiled! Foiled again!" as the curtain fell amid thunderous applause from the audience.*

But even though I felt certain that the bombardment scene could be licked by going back to the first principles of stagecraft, I still hesitated about offering my ideas to McCarthy. He would probably tell me to go do something undignified to myself. So I went to Frank Woods and told him I thought there was a quick and easy way of getting the scene. He looked at me wearily and said, "Quick and easy, eh? That's what they've been telling us all along, how quick and easy everything was going to be. Know how much we've wasted on that one scene alone?" He paused to shake his head as he regretted the folly of ever undertaking such a picture in the first place. He pulled out of his slump to speak with resigned hopelessness as he said, "Well, I might as well know the worst now as later. How much is this going to cost us *this* time?"

"Well, I don't know much about the overhead, but—"

He cut me short with, "*Overhead!* Don't ever mention that word to me, it spoils my whole day. How much will it cost over the line?"

"Over the line?"

"Yes. How much over and above the fixed charges like salaries, transportation, film, and so on. How much for extra equipment?"

"Well, I'll have to fly a ground row as a teaser or tormenter—"

"Never mind the backstage lingo. We know you've been in the theater, you've mentioned it often enough. Now give it to me straight. How much actual dough?"

---

* The effect of a locomotive approaching head-on toward the footlights seems first to have been used on the American stage in 1896, in Lincoln J. Carter's melodrama, *The Heart of Chicago.* GEORGE PRATT

I had to think for a moment and do a bit of counting on my fingers. Better to overstate and come in safe than to underguess and have to beg for more. "Well, I'd say about fifty cents, maybe sixty-five." He stared at me uncomprehendingly. I was quick to reassure him. "It won't go over that. If it does, I'll pay for it out of my own pocket, and that's a promise."

"As much as all that?" he asked, trying to be severely shocked and not succeeding. He thought it all over very carefully as though struggling with a momentous decision, and then said, "Tell you what I'll do. I'll accept that estimate and go you one better. Here's a whole dollar. Take it. Spend it. Don't stint yourself. Give it the works. Oh, and another thing. The details of this agreement must remain strictly between us. You're the only producer on the lot who has ever had the entire budget of his picture given to him cash in advance, and if it ever got out, they'd all be after me for the same thing. Understand?"

I said yes, sir, and got out of there before he could change his mind and want his dollar back.

Preparing the equipment was ridiculously easy. Cash Shockey painted a row of battleships in line on a piece of compo-board six feet long. They were done in a nice, even, misty gray, the gray of things seen at a distance of five or more miles. The men in the carpenter shop profiled it for me, stiffened it with a strong batten, glued and nailed to the back so it wouldn't waver or wobble in the wind. They made me a pair of upright supports that would hold the profile of the ships at any desired height, and supplied C-clamps to hold it firmly in place. Fireworks Wilson gave me all the squibs I wanted and refused payment. These squibs, which were popular with children, were little paper tubes filled at intervals with small charges of flash powder. They could be held in the hand and fired, *piff, piff, piff,* one charge after the other, quite harmlessly. Small holes were bored in the profiled ships where the guns ought to be and the squibs were forced into place, dozens of them for the entire fleet. Tommy Thompson, our head electrician, wired these squibs so they could be fired on cue from a small dry battery.

And so off we went in Dutch Schultz's big Pope Toledo, heading for the beach at Santa Monica, where there were never any crowds and we could work without disturbance. Ed Buskirk came along and so did Tommy Thompson, ostensibly to be of service but actually because a ride to the beach was a rare treat and they weren't passing up any rare treats. Cash Shockey cut himself in on the deal for the same reason. And at the last moment Props, our studio dog, came running out to leap into the car and settle himself down for a nice long ride.

Props was a dog who had joined the Griffith studio as a permanent fixture as soon as he discovered that the workmen carried lunches and that lunches could be wheedled out of workmen by a wag of the tail. Other dogs tried to join the club without success, because Props was a greyhound of sorts who could outrun and outdodge anything on four legs. It didn't take many nipped tails and sore bottoms to convince the canine population of the area that Props had an exclusive franchise on the lunch-cadging concession in the Griffith studio. Props soon became known and loved by all, and the cup of his happiness ran over, especially when someone was going on location and it took only a leap and a wag to become one of the party.

Props was also considered a potent mascot, and when he jumped into our car, we all felt sure we were going to have the best of good luck.

We parked at the beach near the Santa Monica pier and set up the profile, adjusted the squibs and the wiring, and then we had nothing to do but wait for the sun to go down and the light to become just gray enough to match the gray of the profile. The profile was adjusted until the bottom edge was in exact line with the horizon. The gray looked awfully dark against that brilliant sky and sea. But the sky would pass through gradations of gray as the day waned, until it would become absolutely black. The trick was to catch it at the exact moment when the gray of the distance matched the gray of the profile.

I kept watching, watching, watching through the camera as the two colors came closer and closer together. One thing was absolutely certain: there would be no doubt about this being sea because it *was* sea, with an incoming tide and three-foot-high breakers, with rows of pelicans gliding and diving in the water just a little way offshore.

The magic moment came. I closed the camera, slipped the pressure pad into place, double-checked everything, and began to turn. After twenty feet had gone through, I gave the go-ahead to Tommy Thompson, who touched wires together. There was one horrible moment when nothing happened. If anything had gone wrong with the wiring, there'd be no time to find it, because that moment of color matching could not last for long and it would be twenty-four hours before the light conditions would occur again.

But then the guns began to fire, and fire, and kept on firing. I didn't know how long it took a crew to fire and reload a sixteen-inch gun, but these crews of the future were managing it in something between two and two-and-one-half seconds. But maybe in fifty years or so big guns could be fired that fast, who could tell? Almost anything could be happening by 1965.

By the time those squibs had burned out, the light was gone, so swiftly does the light change at sunset. But we had plenty of film in the box before the light change destroyed the illusion, so we packed up and headed for home.

Thus far I had not spent any of Frank Woods' dollar, so I splurged by offering to stand treat for beers all around. The offer was gratefully accepted, and Dutch pulled up at the first saloon we came to. I couldn't go in with them because it would be four years and three months before I would be allowed to enter a saloon. But Tommy Thompson took the dollar, and I waited outside with Props until they came out again. Tommy was an honest man. He gave me the sixty-cents change and away we went, not to stop until we drew up at the studio gate.

The shot was wonderful on the screen. Everything worked exactly right. That was a real fleet on a real sea, and if you don't believe it, just look at those pelicans, swooping and diving and sailing in formation over those tumbling breakers. Griffith smiled and murmured, "That is very fine." Which was reward enough for anyone. Praise from Caesar . . .

I went back to the camera room well pleased with the world in general. It occurred to me that I ought to settle up with Frank Woods in a businesslike manner. So I found a sheet of paper and began by writing at the top, "Rec'd from Mr. Frank Woods, the sum of one dollar." (I was quite proud of that contraction. I had never been able to tell which came first, the "i" or the "e" in such words, but the contraction takes care of all that.) Accounting for those four beers took a little thought. However, "Entertainment, 40 cents" covered that nicely. For in a swindle sheet, entertainment, like charity, covers a multitude of sins. All that remained was to write, "Amount returnable, 60 cents," and to sign it, and the job was done.

I went over to Frank Woods' office. Woods and Griffith were standing together outside their office door (they shared offices), and since they were talking earnestly, I kept decently apart so as not to eavesdrop. Certain words came to me anyway, such as Griffith saying, "No, I'm leaving for New York in the morning . . . ten o'clock . . . I'll sign it and send Banzhaf out . . . say about eleven . . . See you when I get back . . . Keep in touch . . . Goodbye."

There was a handshake and Griffith was gone. Frank Woods turned and stared at me peculiarly, perhaps wondering what I had overheard. I hadn't overheard anything, so I approached him and held out the paper and the sixty cents and said, "Mr. Woods, I have completed the shot—"

"Yes, I know. I saw it. Very good. Very good indeed. Was there anything else?"

"No sir. I just wanted to submit my expense account and—and—er—complete the transaction."

He took the paper and glanced at it. "Entertainment, eh? Now *where* have I seen that word before?" His tone became sharp and his eyes piercingly alert as he continued, "Out with it! Who did you entertain and what with? Come now, come! I'll only find out anyway."

I felt hot and flustered, like a criminal hauled before the bar of justice, with all my imperfections on my head. "Well," I managed to say weakly, "everybody was so good about everything—wouldn't take anything—went down to the beach with me to make sure nothing could go wrong—that I —well, I stood them to a glass of beer each." He continued to bore his eyes into me, and I explained hastily, "I didn't have any, honest I didn't. They wouldn't let me in anyway, so I sat outside with Props all the time."

He nodded gravely and said, "Well, I'm certainly glad to hear that. It happens so often that whenever anyone comes into money they go hog wild and throw it recklessly away as fast as they can. I'm glad to see that you've been able to resist the temptation to go off on a wild spending spree, especially with company money. I'll just keep this document—*and* the sixty cents returnable—as a model for my other producers to follow."

I felt immensely relieved. Reprieved. I said humbly, "Yes, sir. Thank you, sir. Would there be anything else?"

"Mmmm, no, nothing in the production line just now. But have your mother come to see me at eleven tomorrow morning. Will you do that?"

"Yes, *sir!*"

"Don't forget, now."

"No, sir, I won't. I'll tell her the minute I get home."

And I did, too. She wanted to know what for, but I couldn't tell her because I didn't know. She seemed to worry about it. Probably something about one of the girls. She must have spent an uncomfortable night, but I didn't. I was happily counting my wins: peacock, spider, the shot where the horse kicked the magazines off my camera, and now this. But not the lily. I was still trying to live that down. But then, nobody can win them all, not even Griffith.

Eleven came the next morning, then eleven fifteen, then eleven thirty. I was a little worried about my mother, because she had been in Frank Woods' office an awfully long time, so it must have been something serious. But there was nothing I could do about it one way or the other, so I kept right on with my job, which was making a whole flock of new ground glasses for the Pathés. The cameramen kept cracking or dropping them (they're very fragile), so I was making up an ample supply to keep well ahead of the game.

She came in, her face very serious. She had a big, legal-looking document with a blue backing in her hand. "Know what this is?" she asked.

"I'll bite. What?" I answered, grinding away.

"It's your contract."

"My *what?*"

"It's your contract, a personal contract with Griffith himself. See? Here's his signature. He signed it before he left this morning. And here's mine, accepting it for you." She became a little apologetic as she continued, "Maybe I should have spoken to you first, but Banzhaf was there and Mr. Woods said it was all right, so I signed it for you. You see, before you're twenty-one you're an infant in the eyes of the law and a mother has to sign for her minor children, who can't sign anything at all until they reach their majority."

"Why not my father?" I demanded with some indignation. What was the world coming to, that a man can't sign for his own son? Are women taking over the world *entirely?*

She explained. My mother always explained everything. "You see, when a mother is going to have a baby, the fact becomes more and more apparent as the months go by. But as to who the father may be, everybody has to take her unsupported word for it, and that is hearsay, and hearsay is not admissible in a court of law. Anyway," she continued brightly, "here it is, all signed, sealed, and delivered. Four solid years; no options; no ifs, ands, or buts. The company itself may go under, but Griffith has obligated himself to pay you your salary each and every week for the next four years. You'll be twenty-one by then, and you'll be free to make your own decisions without anybody's say-so one way or the other. Isn't that fine?"

Fine? To be stuck with ten dollars a week for the next four years with no chance for advancement no matter *what* I did? I said as much, a little bitterly, with a broad hint that she had sold me down the river just because I was too young and helpless to defend myself, not legally, anyway.

"Ten dollars!" she exclaimed. "Do you think for one instant I'd do anything like that, especially to you? Look at these terms. Automatic raises on a sliding scale. They're starting you at forty a week as of right now this minute, then you jump to sixty-five, then eighty-five, then a hundred, and then —what's the matter?"

I was feeling a little sick, for some reason. I suppose I should have cheered or jumped or fainted or something, but I didn't. I just sat there, grinding away mechanically at those glasses, feeling numb and dumb and weak and sick. She must have sensed how I felt. She usually did. But then she had known me all my life.

She became suddenly very bright and cheerful. "Don't let it worry you. Everything's going to be fine, and to prove it we're going to let you take both of us to the Hoffman House for dinner tonight to celebrate."

"I'd better go see Mr. Woods and thank him."

"No. Not now. Tonight. You can buy him a drink. Not beer. A *drink!* Now, I'll go put this away in a safe place. 'Bye!" And she was gone.

I sat there, numbly grinding away at those glasses and wondering how and why things happen as they do. Hard work never got anyone any more than the chance to do more hard work. This was not cynicism. I was seeing it all around me. It's all a matter of how things happen to fall out.

That scene of the bombardment was a perfect illustration. The exact instant when the gray of my ships and the gray of the dying daylight matched to perfection couldn't have lasted more than two minutes. One hundred and twenty seconds to make or break a life. So it was all a matter of blind chance, of just happening to be in the right place at the right time with the right thing. Earnestness, ability, and even genius had nothing to do with it. Suppose Edison had been born an Eskimo? Or Henry Ford a Mexican peon? Or Griffith a Negro?

I snapped out of this gloomy brooding with an effort of will. There were things to be done. Taking my father and mother to the Hoffman House for a big celebration dinner meant that I'd have to go home and get all slicked up and put on my other suit and shine my shoes. Yes, and shave.

I rubbed my hand over my six or eight whiskers speculatively. It was true. They were getting out of hand again, and much as I hated it, I'd have to borrow my mother's manicure scissors and give myself a good, clean, extra-close shave for my first really big night on the town.

❧ 9 ❧

Kings Go Forth

*There were giants in the earth
in those days.*

GENESIS: VI, 4

THE year 1914 had been remarkable for the enormous changes it had brought to the slow, humdrum way of life for the common man. Things had been going along pretty much the same for fifty years or more. All society was divided into three parts: low, middle, and high. Then suddenly, for no apparent reason, Henry Ford celebrated the New Year by raising the pay of his workers from $2.40 for a nine-hour day to an even $5.00 for each eight-hour day, a move that shattered the financial structure from end to end and from top to bottom.

Everyone who hired help wondered what the world was coming to, with a madman like Henry Ford on the loose. It was a bitter day for all employers.

It was the same story everywhere. Everything was being blown up out of all proportion to its former self. Ziegfeld had glorified the old music hall into a super-elegant variety show that was so outrageously extravagant that he himself had named it the "Follies." Griffith had changed the cheap nickelodeon into a poor man's palace, and now everybody was going overboard for twelve-reelers in the grand manner.

Bigger and better, bigger and better became the constantly chanted watchword of the year. Soon the two words became one. Bigger meant better, and a sort of gigantism overwhelmed the world, especially the world of motion pictures. But to top all our relatively puny little efforts, Europe went to war with Europe. We had a terrible time trying to sort out who was at war with whom and why. According to reports reaching us through the newspapers, some student had shot some ruler in a place called Bosnia, wherever that was, and because of that everybody declared war on everybody else, and all Europe went up in flames.

The newspapers were confused as to what to title this war. Calling it "The Great War" seemed adequate, but for some reason it never quite caught on. Not big enough. Finally some unknown genius came up with a title that stuck, "The World War," and everybody settled back comfortably to watch the show and speculate on the outcome. There was no sense of danger to us. Not with the whole width of the Atlantic Ocean between us and an international quarrel in which we could not possibly become involved.

During all this frantic proliferation of everything everywhere, we at the studio were asking ourselves and one another what Griffith could possibly do to top *The Clansman*. The answer was soon forthcoming. He was going to make a *little* picture, another of the sort he had made for Biograph time and time again, a simple little thing called *The Mother and the Law,** all about a young man condemned to death for a crime he never committed and his young wife and baby who were left defenseless in their slum tenement, plus all sorts of frantic but fruitless appeals to the governor for clemency, ending with the usual last-second rescue. It was an awful comedown. Dreadful.

But I recalled a line from Gilbert's *Pinafore* in which Captain Corcoran sings, "Things are seldom what they seem," and with my misjudgment of the original *Clansman* story, not to mention *The Avenging Conscience* and *Home, Sweet Home,* still rankling, I displayed a hard-won restraint and said nothing, not even to myself. This was a good time to wait and see.

For the first time in my sketchy experience, Griffith not only rehearsed but did some on-the-spot personal research. Since Bobby Harron, playing the downtrodden hero, had to be shown in prison, it followed that we had to go and see what an actual prison looked like. But this wasn't good enough. We needed a really big prison where they had death houses and gallows and all the latest improvements. Nothing small about Griffith. When he did a thing, he really *did* it, in the grand manner, accepting nothing but the best.

So we all piled aboard a train named *The Owl,* which made a night run to San Francisco, where they had the best prisons this side of Sing Sing. As the junior member of the entourage, I was assigned an upper berth, and since my established duty of guarding Bitzer's camera at all times was very much in force, I had to take the camera to bed with me. I cannot recommend a Pathé camera as the best of bedfellows. Turn over in your sleep and bang goes the camera with a destructive crash to the aisle of the car. But I discovered that by putting the camera on the inside of the berth it would be quite safe, because if I rolled out it didn't count, and all would be well.

* *The Mother and the Law* was in production before the première of *The Clansman.*
KEVIN BROWNLOW

Our first visit was to the San Francisco city jail, and a more repulsively fascinating place I had never seen. It was not only damp, it was wet all the time, with slippery cement floors and cells made of flat, strapiron gratings and not the round iron bars so familiar to moviegoers. It was much too dark inside that jail to shoot anything without lights, so we had to pass it up so far as getting any film was concerned. But we did get indelible glimpses of haggard, unshaven faces peering out through the square gratings, of the slippery sliminess of the cement floorings, and of an all-pervading stench that seemed to compress all the horrors of incarceration into one grim statement. .

Next stop, San Quentin, which by contrast seemed to be a beautiful, airy, almost luxurious summer resort. The location of the prison was as fine as one could wish. Few last glimpses of the outside world are as lovely as those seen by condemned men going to their death in San Quentin.

There were only three in our little party: Griffith, Bitzer, and me. Griffith and Bitzer were guests. The warden himself greeted them warmly in his office, where the ceremony of the drink was solemnly enacted.

I watched with fascinated attention as the ritual was performed. I'd seen men drink ever since I could remember, but it had always been a sort of hail-fellow-well-met business with lots of laughter and jollity. This was not. The three gentlemen were seated. The warden produced a bottle from which he filled three small glasses. The three took up their glasses. No toasts, nothing. Each glass was carried to each respective mouth. Lower lips were projected as sort of funnels. Heads were tilted slightly backward, and the whiskey was allowed to glide down over the tongue, the mouth remaining open all the time. Each glass was emptied completely. Glasses returned to table. No words, no comments, nothing. The ceremony was over and now business could proceed.

I was not introduced, or invited to sit down. It was not even necessary to explain my presence. This was plain at a glance, because I was self-evidently an equipment caddy, with camera, tripod, and equipment cases hanging from every protuberance.

This condition was soon changed by the warden, who stated politely but firmly that although he had been authorized to show us everything relating to death by hanging, he could not allow us to photograph anything at all. Our equipment would have to remain impounded under guard right there in his office. He assured us that it would all be perfectly safe. He would appoint his own personal trusty, a murderer of the highest ethical standards, to guard our goods.

This man, a slender, silvery-haired gentleman of the gentlest of demeanor, was a model of courtly grace. He took his place, standing beside the pile of equipment. The warden led the way out of the office, followed by Griffith and Bitzer, while I brought up the rear.

I couldn't help casting backward glances at this aristocratic killer and wondering how one of such obviously gentle birth and breeding could come to such a pass. I caught snatches of the warden's explanation as he told Griffith all about it.

It appeared that this man, who was referred to by number and not by name, had been born and reared in one of the great houses of Nob Hill. His father had been an imported butler of the finest antecedents, his mother a lady's maid. Upon the death of the father, this man had succeeded to the important position of majordomo, where he served with distinguished success until a squabble occurred between him and the master over the favors of an exceedingly pretty and pliable upstairs maid. Whereupon, in a fit of pique, this man had doctored the master's *potage Mallarmé* with arsenic.

Ordinarily, poisoners are given no mercy. But this was a San Francisco jury; San Franciscans are famously fond of good living; good servants are hard to find and even harder to keep; it seemed a sin and a shame to destroy so splendid an exemplar of the art of elegance; and so they gave him life. And besides, who can really condemn a crime of passion? It could happen to anyone. Especially in San Francisco.

"And a damn good thing it was for me that it turned out as it did," continued the warden, as he led the way into one of the huge, steel-and-concrete cell blocks. "I never had it so good. Cook? That man's a wizard. Makes me the best meals I ever had. Got me so spoiled that I can't down the stuff they serve at Solari's or the Poodle Dog. And wines? I bet you that man knows every grape of every vineyard personally, year by year and month by month. And bossy? He won't let me touch so much as a ham sandwich without the wine of *his* choice on the side. I never used to go much for wines. I was always a whiskey man, myself. But he's got me so up on wines that if I ever lose my job here, I can go to work tomorrow morning as a *sommelier* in any great restaurant in the world—London, Paris, Rome, anywhere. Even in San Francisco."

"Aren't you afraid to eat his cooking?" asked Bitzer. "You know—after what he's done?"

"Hell, no," was the warden's honest response. "He's got nothing against *me*. Sure, I have to get tough once in a while. That's part of the job. But nobody holds it against me personally. I just work here."

That cell block, with its tiers of steel walkways, was as big as a convention hall. It somehow reminded me of what one of the big steamers would look like with one side sheared away. And clean, too; clean and airy and spotless in every detail, so vastly different from the city jail that we couldn't help remarking the contrast. The warden had an easy and obvious explanation. The city jail had a floating population, here today and gone tomorrow. But San Quentin had a stable clientele of something over five thousand, and it isn't too hard to keep a place tidy with a work force like that.

We passed out of the far end of the cell block into the open air. Flowers, flowers, flowers wherever a flower bed could be placed. Patches of velvet-smooth lawn. Everything perfectly tended and maintained. "You may not believe this," said the warden, "but we've had lots of men who have been released after ten or fifteen years who can't wait to get back inside again. Going is tough for an ex-con. They stand it just so long and no longer. Then they commit some harmless crime, like beating up a cop, so they can come back home where everybody understands them. Those buildings," continued the warden, "are where we keep the condemned men. They've been here for I don't know how many years, way back to the fifties, some of them. We've been trying to get new ones—these are simply firetraps. But Sacramento won't spend the money. Say they're only for temporary housing at best. Maybe they're right. Men are sent there to die, not to live."

We climbed some rickety outside stairs and entered a long, high room where a dozen or so thick ropes were hanging from an overhead beam, each holding a heavy sandbag. "Here's where we stretch our ropes," explained the warden. "These are 150-pound sandbags, average weight of a man. The standard hangman's noose is already tied, and you'll notice they're looped around a billet of wood the size of a man's neck. These are all old, well-seasoned ropes. New ropes are no good. Too much spring, jounce around. Takes six months to stretch the jounce out of a rope. We keep a dozen or so ahead, just in case. The gallows is right in the next room."

He led the way toward the door leading into the death chamber. I was all prepared for what I was to see because everyone knows that gallows are painted black and that there are thirteen steps.

To my astonished disbelief the gallows was painted a delicate baby blue. It was much bigger and higher than I had expected, all of twenty feet from the floor to the top crossbeam. There was only one drop, or trap door, where I had expected maybe three or four. I had seen pictures of multiple drop hangings, notably those made by Brady showing the hanging of Lincoln's assassination conspirators. But this had only one.

The warden took us underneath to explain the mechanism. "You can see that the drop is held by a pair of simple door hinges on one side, with an ordinary bolt or latch to hold it on the other. See these four cords? They're heavy, hundred-pound-test fishline and they run through a pulley to this fifty-pound sandbag. Cut the cords from above, the sandbag drops, and here —I'll show you."

He pulled the cords by hand. The latch released the trap, which was made of heavy, laminated wood. This let the trap swing heavily to the opposite side, where it clanged loudly into another spring latch. That sound, in that bare, echoing room, was ghastly. I had never heard death proclaim itself in such a loud, definitive way.

The warden continued in his calm, museum-guide tone. "That catch is so the trap won't swing back and bang into the man who is now hanging below. Not that he'd mind. Hanging is the swiftest, most merciful death now known with the possible exception of the guillotine. Neck breaks instantly and he can't feel a thing. Oh, he flops around a little, but that's nothing but muscular reflex, like a chicken with its head cut off."

"How do *you* know?" asked Griffith, with a note of challenge in his voice.

"Doctors all say so," replied the warden in a matter-of-fact tone. "Spinal cord carries all sensation, all consciousness. Snap spinal cord and that's the end of everything. The man feels the sensation of dropping and then it's instant oblivion forevermore."

The warden restored the drop to its original position and then led us up the steps to the top of the gallows. I was so unnerved by that dreadful sound that I forgot all about counting the steps and I don't know to this day whether there were thirteen or not.

The top of the platform was like any other: a flat area with the trap in the middle, wooden railings all around, but with a sort of partition six feet high built across the back. There was a crossbeam above, of course, for the rope. There was no rope. That would be brought in during the night before the hanging, a new rope every time. Everything was painted in that same unreasonable baby blue.

The warden led us around to the back of the partition. It was a narrow space, just wide enough to accommodate four men who would stand facing a narrow wooden shelf across which four of the heavy-test fishlines were already stretched, taut and ready and waiting. There were four razor-sharp, hawk-billed linoleum knives, obtainable in any hardware shop, on the shelf. The warden explained, "Of these four strings only one is 'live'—that is, connected to the trip weight you saw below. We have four men posted behind this wooden screen, each with one of these knives. They can't see the prisoner. Nobody can see them. I stand beside the trap. When the time comes I raise a white handkerchief high over my head. The instant they see that handkerchief they *cut,* hard, fast, and deep, as fast as they can. *One* of them springs the trap. They never know which one, which makes them feel better, for some reason."

"Who cuts these strings, prisoners?" asked Griffith.

"Never. We keep it out of the family, so to speak. We use deputies, mostly, or civilians, when we can get them. Notice how deep they cut."

We looked. The cuts were indeed deep, the cuts of overwrought, keyed-up men—dozens of cuts in the soft wood.

"How about religious matters, priests and the like?"

"We give them priests, rabbis, ministers, whoever they want. Even the atheists get someone to sustain them in that last moment. We've had a few who refused to have anyone at all, mostly out of bravado to show how tough they were. But we send the prison chaplain along with them, just in case. They might get a change of heart at the last instant, so we take no chances."

"How do they take it?"

"Now, that's a funny thing. They're usually the calmest ones in the room. They know it's all up with them for sure, and when there's no hope there's no fear, not that I could ever see, anyway. Something holds them together. Pride, maybe. Wants to die like a man no matter how he's lived. It's his one last chance to show the stuff he's made of. Might be bravado. I simply don't know. That's all here. Now I'll show you where the man spends his last night."

The warden led the way down the steps to a door opening into an adjoining room. This was a big square room with a high ceiling, bare except for four wooden kitchen chairs placed along all four walls and facing a wooden cage, painted that same baby blue, built in the middle of the room. The cage was about ten feet square; a cube, really, made of wooden bars about two inches square. A single bare electric light bulb hung from the ceiling directly over the barred top of the cage. The door, also of wood, was standing open. The only furniture was a single cot, neatly made up, army fashion, with smoothed gray blankets, as though ready for inspection.

"Here's where they spend their last twenty-four hours," explained the warden. "We place a guard in each of those four chairs, to watch him all the time from every angle. That's so that if one should doze off, there will always be three more left awake. But nobody sleeps much on those nights, me least of all. Might be a call from the governor. You never can tell."

This sparked a thought in Griffith's mind. "What about a last-second reprieve? I didn't see any phone on that gallows."

"You didn't because there isn't any. We wouldn't take a chance on not hearing the phone ring at a time like that. We have a direct line held open to the governor's mansion all during that last twenty-four hours; the instant a call comes through, the switchboard hits a big alarm bell that sounds all through the prison. The instant that bell sounds everything stops, and I can take my time answering the phone and above all, making sure it's on the level and not some joker tapping into the line with a phony reprieve. Way I look at it, it doesn't pay to go off half-cocked in a matter of life or death."

"What about this business of the condemned man walking down between rows of cells with all the prisoners yelling and reaching out to shake hands and all that?"

The warden shook his head. "I don't know. It might happen somewhere else but not here. As you've seen, our death house is far removed from the rest of the prison, so they couldn't even if they wanted to. His last walk is from here to the next room, with nobody around but the guards and the chaplain, or whoever else he has chosen for religious comfort. Want to look inside?"

We did. There wasn't much to see. The inner sides of the soft wooden walls were scratched with names, evidently made by thumbnails, since nothing sharp was allowed inside that cage. They were mostly names like "Red" and "Pete" and so on. But one man had scratched what appeared to be the word "erythrosine," vertically on one of the bars. Now why in the world would a condemned man want to spend his last hours scratching the name of a pink dye on the bars of his death cell?

On the drive back to San Francisco we paused on a high road overlooking the new San Francisco Exposition, where we stopped to shoot several angles of the broad expanse of the fanciful, glittering buildings that were to be thrown open to the public next year, in 1915. The Tower of Jewels was especially impressive, and Bitzer took a number of long shots of it, mostly matted in such a way as to show only in the upper corner of the frame. These shots were *not* to be developed but saved for some future ending of some future picture. For Griffith loved to end pictures with his lovers dreaming of a beautiful vision of castles in the air, and this called for double exposure in the camera, since there was no way of duping a negative without getting a lot of grain.

I remembered all too well one of these endings* in which Walthall and Miss Geeesh were seated on a high bluff overlooking the ocean, with the sunset sending a broad path of light down upon the waters below. In the upper left-hand corner was a double-exposed vision of towered and turreted castles. Griffith had conceived this as a roseate dream, so the dream had to

---

* This is the final image in *The Birth of a Nation.* GEORGE PRATT

be made roseate. To this end I was given the endless job of tinting the dream by hand with a fine brush and a solution of erythro . . . wait a minute! Erythrosine. The word I had read in the death cell. Could I have imagined it, through association? I asked Bitzer and he said no, he'd seen it, too. It was erythrosine, all right. It's strange how a thing like that can nag. This one tiny link, the name of a dye, had made me somehow a part of that unknown man who had fallen into the eternal dark.

Something of the same feeling seemed to have come over Griffith. Back in the studio, preparing to shoot the picture, he no longer sang from *Tosca* or *Pagliacci,* but he would declaim to the skies, over the noise of the construction crews, "For who can tell to what red hell his sightless soul may stray!" So Poe was out and Wilde was in for the duration of the picture.

It was a strange picture, one for which I was totally unprepared. It was completely serious in the manner of grand opera. It was as though he had declared, "I come no more to make you laugh," and that he was determined to sting some hard truths home to his audience. That visit to an actual prison inhabited by living dead men seemed to have worked a profound personality change in him.

The first set erected for the picture was a replica of a cell, not the clean and airy kind as in San Quentin but the slimy, stinking hogpens of that utterly repulsive city jail. Lillian Gish came on the set. Griffith asked her what she thought of it.

She looked at the cell with all its squalor, including the lidless china toilet bowl, which denied the men any chance of leaving their sties for any reason. The floors were wet and slimy smooth. It reeked of uttermost degradation. She said nothing but turned away, to bar it from her sight and memory. Griffith said gravely, "Well, that's life," and went about his business, which was the recitation of as much more of *The Ballad of Reading Gaol* as he could remember. (I scribbled swiftly and impulsively on a back page of my notebook, "It's hell to be a poet," and let it go at that.)

The rest of the picture was more of the same, only more so. Griffith was not content with calling a spade a spade. It had to be a damned dirty old filth-reeking shovel.

We went downtown to the Plaza area to search out life at its worst. Hidden between Main Street and the railroad tracks was a two-story, U-shaped brick building with the open end of the U facing the tracks, as though turning its back on the city. This building was designed for a special purpose. It was simply a series of cells, door-window, door-window, door-window, with just room enough inside each cubicle for a cot and a chair. It was exactly like the cell blocks we had seen in San Francisco, except for one distinctive difference. The doors were of wood instead of steel, and each door proclaimed the name of its occupant, painted in flamboyant letters: Frisco Kate, Minnesota Minnie, Rhode Island Red, French Fifi, and so on.

The action was clear enough. The place was being pinched, and the police were hustling the girls, all in various states of professional undress, into patrol wagons. The girls were protesting, some violently, others by speaking their minds in the most scurrilous of billingsgate, charging the cops with such things as invasion of privacy, restraint of trade, and whatever else occurred to them at the moment. It was a short, grim, hard-bitten social commentary told in terms of violence.

Even more violent was the sequence we shot just across the tracks in the warehouse district. Here we had no mere policemen but uniformed troops, barricaded and with machine guns, firing into a mob of charging strikers and mowing them down in droves. It was not merely violent, it was a brutal massacre, naked and unashamed.

Crowds of onlookers had been following us all day. Among these was a little Mexican woman wheeling her paralyzed child in a little home-contrived wheeled stretcher or bed. The wheels, evidently salvaged from the city dump, were wobbly, and the bed was made of scraps of lumber nailed together. The child, possibly seven or eight years old, was a helpless body under a white covering, with only her eyes moving as she followed all that was happening.

Griffith paid no attention to her, but he spoke privately to Siegmann, who hurried away, to return some minutes later with a small heavy canvas bag. Griffith took the bag, and at a time when he thought he was unobserved, he went to the little girl's cot and outlined her entire body with silver dollars taken from the bag, placing them carefully edge to edge all along her arms and legs, neck and head. When he had finished, there were more dollars left in the bag. He handed the bag to the mother and turned away. No words at any time. No explanation. Nothing. Griffith knew no Spanish, the mother no English. But the tears that overflowed her eyes were thanks enough and to spare. And the personal satisfaction for Griffith must have been equally gratifying. Nobody—that is, nobody who counted—saw it. I saw it because I was there guarding the camera. Everyone else was loudly busy shooing the crowd back to make room for the next setup. No; it was not for publication in any form. It was an act of impulse, born of his own long years of frustration, starvation, and despair. He was merely doing for that little girl what he had hoped somebody might have done for him back in the days when all the skies of his world were black.

The deeper we got into the picture, the more puzzling it became. Griffith seemed to be ignoring or kicking aside all the principles of filmmaking as he himself had established them. No light and shade, no comedy relief, no brilliance of characterization. Everything was dull, drab, grim, and gray. Even the photography. I don't know what discussions Griffith and Bitzer may have had or what decisions they may have made, but Bitzer's camera work, usually so characteristically outstanding, became one long gray series of pictures in unrelieved monotone.

Not that the result was weak or ineffective. The contrary. The constant and hammering insistence on the grim facts of life as it is lived, not as it is dreamed, carried the searing permanence of a Gorki or Dostoevsky, of Poe or Wilde. Injustice, forever injustice as an all-pervading force, ruled every scene. Villainy in the physical form of a stereotyped heavy went by the board, to be replaced by an abstraction of human intolerance in all its many forms.

One little sequence seemed to wrap the whole message in a single compact statement. Mae Marsh, bereft of her husband, who is being railroaded to the gallows, is trying to care for her baby, although she herself is weak with hunger and illness. She is living in the poorest of poor slum tenements. A kindly neighbor (the poor are always kind to the poor), played by little Max Davidson, brings her a little bit of whiskey, a few ounces in the bottom of a half-pint flask, for her cough. Social workers, reeking of yellow soap and Lysol, invade the place on a snooping expedition. They discover that little bit of whiskey, hold it up with cries of triumph, and take the baby away because the presence of that whiskey is proof positive that poor little starveling Mae Marsh, with her shivering body and her worn rag of a clutched shawl, is an unfit mother.

Cheap? Hokey? Not the way Griffith shot it. Few close-ups in the annals of screen photography can come even close to the quintessence of despair shown by Mae Marsh's face in those grayest of gray full-screen portraits that showed Bitzer at his best and Mae Marsh at her most effective, with each surpassing all previous triumphs by daring to be true to the subject itself, without so much as a fleeting hint of prettiness or conscious art or professional slickness. It takes more than art to achieve such results—it takes guts.

Although he changed the content, he could not change the framework of his picture. Certain well-worn clichés of picture making had to be included. There was a sequence aboard a train carrying the governor. This train had to be caught to reach the governor with the life-saving message. This called for a fast train chased by a fast car with time running out. Now it is a firmly established rule governing all picture making that when you have anything happening upon a train, you absolutely *must* have a close shot of the drive wheels and the connecting rods of the locomotive going as fast as possible (undercranking helps here). So we took the shot, clamping the camera to a broad beam that runs across the front of the engine. It didn't mean anything, not really, but it is a useful shot to cut to from time to time, and since everybody used such a shot as a sort of article of faith, without which salvation cannot be accomplished, we used it too, so as not to disappoint the audience. The gallows was black, not baby blue. Audiences would not understand or believe a gallows not painted black. And we had a priest, complete with an identifying biretta, so as not to confuse the audience. These were technical concessions, nothing more. The theme of the story, man's inhumanity to man, was straight out of Robert Burns, with additional details by Poe and Wilde and Griffith's own personal observations, both past and present.

In the due course of time, the picture was finished and Griffith once again took up semi-permanent quarters in the projection room, running, running, and rerunning the picture, changing this, changing that, taking stuff out, only to put it back in again—the usual thing for him, and for Jimmy, and for Rose Smith.

But there were no previews, sneak or otherwise. Nobody knew why. The general impression around the studio was that he wanted to keep the story under wraps so nobody could steal it. This was thought to be a wise precaution, because everybody stole stories as a matter of course.

For why buy stories when there were hundreds of them freely available everywhere in the spate of magazines that were flooding the newsstands? Frank Munsey, of the Munsey magazine empire, controlled dozens of publications from which one could pick and choose. True, they were copyrighted, but that meant nothing. All anyone had to do was to take the story of his choice, change the locale and the character names, and there you were: a new story costing nothing but the price of a hack writer who knew how to do such things.

And how would this about-face, absolutely reversed-values production do in the world of bigger and better? Nobody knew and nobody cared to guess. Its very difference might make it stand out as a great individual achievement in contrast with the flash and glitter of the usual Hollywood glamour film.

The last thing I scribbled on a reverse page of my notebook before turning it in was the observation, "You never know until later."

This would have to do.

All that remained for us now was to wait until later.

10

The Way of an Eagle

Mr. Finney had a turnip . . .
And it grew, and it grew . . .
LONGFELLOW'S FIRST POEM,
WRITTEN WHEN HE WAS A CHILD

WHAT happened later was nothing. Nothing at all. *The Mother and the Law* became a dead issue as far as anyone I knew around the studio was concerned. There was speculation that the picture had been shelved. This made sense. Good, or even inspired in many of its aspects, it was simply not the sort of picture everyone had come to expect of Griffith. I had thought of it at first as opera, grand opera, because of the seriousness of its subject matter. But it was a hybrid, a high tragedy up to the finish, where it ended with his trademarked nick-of-time rescue, with everyone living happily ever after. Well, more or less happily, the social conditions as he had described them being what they were.

In Los Angeles we had a little square-block park at Fifth and Hill called Central Park. Here soapbox orators held forth on all the evils they could think of. Our English actors told us that there was a similar place in London called Hyde Park, where anybody could work off his resentments by damning everybody and anything without let or hindrance, as a sort of emotional safety valve. They even had a story to go with it, about a wild-eyed, bewhiskered radical screaming invective about the King of England. A bobby stood placidly by, making no move to interfere. An American asked, "Do you allow them to *say* such things over here?" To which the bobby replied in slow, calm, measured tones, "Why not? His Majesty will never hear of this, so it will do him no harm. And it might do this poor devil some good—who knows?"

So maybe making *The Mother and the Law,* with its brutally effective excoriation of things as they are, was simply Griffith's way of blowing off long-pent-up steam. It would harm nobody, not even himself, so long as he did not release it to the general public. It had been an expensive way of relieving his inner pressures, but the cost of the picture compared with the seas of money that would soon inundate the studio from *The Clansman* was like dipping a cupful of water from the ocean and tossing it away. There was plenty more where that came from. Plenty, plenty, and plenty more.

Some of this flood of money went for more and more studio expansion. A department was created to do nothing but process still pictures of all kinds. Production stills for lobby displays and for publicity illustrations, portrait stills for distribution to the emerging class of movie fans who were writing in for pictures of their favorites, enlargements for lobby displays, blowups from 35 mm. frames for the set dressers, and even action stills made with small, high-speed cameras to catch our various stars in unconventional, off-scene, candid-camera shots.

This department was run by a highly educated but self-effacing scholar named Woodbury.* Woodbury was a spare, dry, quietly humorous man who sometimes, but not often, let drop an occasional Greek or Latin epigram in the original. He was also a lover of classical music, which his daughter, an accomplished pianist, played on a precious little Tony Weber piano in his modest, nearby home. But his real love was photography. He knew every process and every trick of the trade. He subscribed to every photographic magazine in current publication, and he had files of old magazines dating back fifty and sixty years, all dealing with the same subject: how to get the most out of a negative. From my seventeen-year-old point of view, he was quite elderly, probably forty-five or even fifty. Naturally, any poor old man of so advanced an age couldn't last long, so I hurried to glean as much as I could of his vast store of learning while he was still around.

This entailed a certain amount of love-me-love-my-dog admiration for his daughter's piano playing, which went very much against the grain. Not that she couldn't play. She could play altogether too well for comfort. It's all very well for a Paderewski or a Josef Hofmann to do miraculous stunts at the keyboard because that's their business. But when a middy-bloused high-school girl could ripple off light and pearly chromatic runs in thirds as though it were the easiest thing in the world, I felt it to be something not far from vulgar ostentation. I was of the firm opinion that the Dead March from *Saul* was plenty fast enough for anyone. Especially me.

My admiration for Woodbury might possibly have been influenced by the fact that he had lightened my workload by a considerable degree. I no

---

* James G. Woodbury operated a photographic studio in Los Angeles for many years and was an outstanding photographer. He made the celebrated still of the Babylon set of *Intolerance,* reproduced so often. GEORGE J. MITCHELL

longer had to develop and print stills, which was a time-consuming job that could not be hurried. Another load had been lifted from my back by the establishing of a title room, managed by a heavy, jowly, wonderfully mustached Russian named Lippin.

Lippin was given a small, unventilated hole-in-the-wall cubicle in which he lived, breathed, smoked, drank, and had his being. He worked the lantern-plate system, which we had found to be the best, and the combination of smells inside that black-painted cell, composed of acetic acid in the fixing solution, stale Russian cigarettes, vodka, and Lippin himself was something that protected his privacy absolutely. Everybody stood outside and handed things in. Lippin didn't mind. He had his world all to himself and he loved it, leading me to suppose that a person can get used to anything, even himself, in time.

With studio prosperity came private automobiles for the upper crust of our studio community. Griffith led the way by showing up in a Fiat so big that at first glance one would assume it had been made by the Baldwin Locomotive Works rather than in Turin. I was so deeply impressed by this monster that I asked Mac, Griffith's driver—no, correction—his chauffeur, uniform and all—what it was like to actually drive so magnificent a work of automotive art. "Damned old hunk of stove iron" was his disgusted reply. "Can't park this thing at all. Have to dock it, like a battleship."

Douglas Fairbanks had a Fiat, too, but his was a little two-seater, small but elegant and the pride of Fairbanks' heart. "Easy as an old shoe," he told us, as we crowded around to gape. "Runs like a dream." And he'd prove it, too, by getting into gear and scooting away like a scared cat.

There were other cars of varying degrees of elegance. I don't know how many makes of cars there were on the market. Fifty, seventy-five—there was no telling. Except for body design, most of the newcomers in the motor business were sisters under the skin, because they were assembled from parts bought from manufacturers who specialized in some one of the various components. The motor would be from Continental, the bearings from Timken, the electrical equipment from Bosch, and so on. They were called, aptly enough, assembly cars.

Now that my forty dollars a week had put me in the higher-earning brackets, I began to dream of owning a car myself someday. The trouble was that cars came high. To Griffith and Fairbanks that meant nothing, but I was neither Griffith nor Fairbanks, so I had to do some pencil work. Fords could be bought for around $400, but who wanted a Ford? (Practically everybody, to judge by the swarms of them cluttering up the roads.) I wanted something with class to it, something to proclaim to all the world that I was a person of substance and social significance. So I settled for a brand-new shiny Studebaker. It cost $850, which was a tremendous amount of money for just one car, but what's money for, if not to spend? So I bought it on time, a matter that called for a little maneuvering. I was not authorized to incur debts, since I was an infant in the eyes of the law, but I made a shrewd bargain with my father: he'd buy it and I'd pay for it. That seemed to be fair enough, so I was saddled with a car that I didn't know how to drive or take care of or do anything else to. However, the studio drivers took me in hand and I learned about driving from them.

During all this, Griffith was still in and out of town, managing the various business details of showing *The Clansman*. Too big and much too important to be handled through normal booking channels, *The Clansman* was peddled out to various moneyed men on a franchise basis, in which the purchaser got the right to exhibit the picture within certain defined territories, plus a percentage of the earnings over an agreed-upon ceiling. The New England rights went to a junk-dealer named Mayer, Louis B., who made a fortune out of his investment. How much our number-one money man, Harry Aitken, made from the picture was unknown, except that it could not help but be a huge amount. Bitzer too. He had thrown ten thousand into the picture when ten thousand meant all the difference between going ahead or folding up.

So Bitzer's offhand, what-the-hell investment made him a millionaire overnight. Not that he had as yet actually received that much in cash, but simply that he could have sold his share to any bank or investment house for at least a million and maybe a lot more. So it all came to the same thing. And Bitzer showed it, too. Not so much out of any weakness of character but more out of obedience to the long-standing tradition that millionaires have to behave like millionaires.

Millionaires were no novelty to me. They haunted every big musical or musical revue as stage-door Johnnies, all of them out mousing for showgirls. They owned flashy cars and had expensive apartments run by Oriental houseboys in white coats. They dined in lobster palaces, and they had a different girl every night. They could carouse all night and sleep all day, and it was nobody's business but their own. If you don't believe it, see any movie. Or any play. Or read any best-selling novel. The hero was always a man with nothing but money and with nothing to do but spend it.

Bitzer saw no reason why he should depart from so firmly rooted a tradition. He went all out for what was called hitting the high spots. He bought a champagne-colored Packard with a driver to match. He spent his nights in high wassail and his days in trying to get through the work by any means possible.

This called for a locked cabinet in the experiment room in which he kept an ample supply of restoratives known as the hair of the dog. There were times during the day when he had to run, not walk, to this cabinet for a swift slug of restorative to make it possible for him to function at all. This burning of the candle at both ends could not last for long and it didn't. Griffith suspended Bitzer and put Landers in his place.

Some inner pride, the slave driver of all true artists, compelled Bitzer to behave himself or he'd never be allowed to touch a camera again. The artist in him subdued the man, and Bitzer became a good boy and got his job back. Not that he became less fond of his luxuries. Merely that he became circumspect. Which, I suppose, is as much as can be expected of any man in his position.

Griffith seemed to be immune to this rich-man syndrome. What he may have done during the time he spent away from the studio was unknown, at least to me. Maybe he had his moments of relaxation. But if so, he did not flaunt them, while flaunting is the hallmark of any Good-Time Charlie I ever heard of.

Anyway, that little tempest in a teapot soon subsided and we went back to our usual preoccupation of wondering what Griffith would do next. Griffith had had his little spree of purging himself of all his long-festering resentments against the cruelties of the world through *The Mother and the Law,* in which Society was the blackhearted villain and Sacred Motherhood the heroine, and now the question was one of what he would *really* do to show up the imitators who were shooting the works to be bigger and better than Griffith at his best.

Strangely, he went all-out for a costume picture, a thing set in the time of Catherine de Médicis and her infamous massacre of the Huguenots way back in 1572 and froze to death.* This was more like it. Big sets, fine costumes, royalty, and lots and lots of action. Not that I knew this all at once. But the library was only a nickel's car ride away, so I buried myself in the sixteenth century and came up all primed and loaded with everything I wanted to know about what we were going to do. It all sounded fine to me. There had never been anything wrong with the works of Dumas or Hugo, or the swashbuckling adventures of the Three Musketeers, and the great James O'Neill hadn't shouted, "The world is mine!" from upstage center

---

* Old theatrical gag, meaning "Date not exact, but it will have to do." (Author)

over five thousand times to tumultuous applause without leaving an indelible impression upon the general public that *The Count of Monte Cristo* was probably the most satisfactory show ever played upon any stage.

Griffith's upcoming production was right out of the same box. A little more remote in period, but with plenty of big sets, skulduggery, and sword-play in it. This was all great stuff for the grandeur-conscious audiences of the new generation of moviegoers. We plunged into the picture with the sure confidence that we had something that would knock them for a loop.

So our crew of stage carpenters and set dressers built us a French street of the sixteenth century, more or less, from designs culled from old pictures in books in the public library. It was a beautiful set, all crooked and old and romantic. Here people ran and fought and had all sorts of trouble, dressed in the costumes of the period. There was no trouble about getting the costumes. Goldstein was ready and willing to turn out anything Griffith wanted, no matter how much trouble it might be.

There was one curious and baffling thing about this French picture. Griffith kept referring to it as *The Mother and the Law*. Furthermore, it was the same story, only in a different period. A lot of important people forever picking on a lot of unimportant people. In *The Clansman,* Joe Henabery, playing Lincoln, was shot in the back of the head with a derringer pistol. In this one Henabery, playing Admiral Coligny, was stabbed in the front of the throat with a sword. Same story, different period. It seemed odd. Others were copying Griffith all the time, but for Griffith to copy himself seemed to be a little out of keeping with one who had become known as the great originator.

No matter. We of the working crew had problems of our own to solve. How to tell the difference between two widely different pictures, both called *The Mother and the Law,* became a simple matter of giving the new picture a new number. *The Clansman* had been F (for "feature") 1. *The Mother and the Law* became F 2. This French thing became F 3. So now if he decided to make *The Mother and the Law* twenty times, we'd simply raise the F number to correspond.

There was always an interim between Griffith pictures. Time for him to think up what the next one was to be about. During these breaks I had been given any number of little special jobs that only the young and eager, with nothing to lose and everything to gain, would tackle.

There was a man named Victor Forsythe who had made quite a lot of money drawing a cartoon comic strip called Axel and Flooey. Vic had the idea that his cartoon characters could be animated by drawing a series of pictures in which the figures moved very slightly for each frame, thus giving the illusion of natural motion. This would call for stop-motion shooting, with the attendant problem of getting absolutely even exposures for each frame. It all turned out to be very easy. Rig a pendulum. Fit it with a broad piece of thin board covered with black velvet. Cut a slit in this board. Mount a hook to hold it to one side. Open the shutter. Release the pendulum. Let it swing back and forth just once. Those two glimpses of the cartoon made one complete exposure, always the same, never to be varied until or unless the law of the isochronization of the pendulum failed, which seemed unlikely.

It was all a very good try, but it didn't work out. The action was all right. Fine. But the lines wavered, because try as he would, Vic could never get the same weight of line for every drawing. It was used just once, in somebody's comedy. One of our comedians paused in front of a billboard advertising El Ropo cigars. The figure of Axel, the tall one, was shown on the billboard, smoking an El Ropo. As our live character pauses, the cartooned billboard character hauls off with one foot and kicks him in the rear, much to the live character's surprise. This was supposed to be suffocatingly funny, I never knew why.

Following Vic, another artist appeared, this one named Perley Poore Sheehan,* who had an idea that the titles could be enhanced by painting pictures on the title-card backgrounds. This idea worked beautifully and for the simplest of reasons. Varnish the picture and the blacks stay black, the grays gray, and the whites white, no matter how much light you poured onto the title card.

We tried everything, and everything worked. It worked so well that we began to wonder why this same principle couldn't be used for certain kinds of establishing long shots. We tried that, too. The scene: a farmhouse at night, with only one light showing in a dormer window. A big tree draping its foliage from one side, while distant fields receded under the light of a visible moon, hanging right there in the night sky. Fade in. Hold just long enough to establish, then dissolve to the interior of the farmhouse dormer bedroom to continue the action. Keep it short. Never give them a chance to figure out how it was done.

All of this took place in a crowded little corner of the general camera room, where most of our equipment was stored and which was used by our many cameramen, who were constantly coming and going, which was all right, or who were stopping to watch and make suggestions, which was not all right.

* Perley Poore Sheehan was also a writer; De Mille's *Whispering Chorus* was adapted from his novel. As a film writer, he wrote the scenario for *The Hunchback of Notre Dame* (1923). DEWITT BODEEN

I don't know how it came about, although I suspected the fine Ohioan hand of Frank Woods was somewhere back of it, but Griffith built me a splendid new playroom all of my own. There was one precious spot of open ground between the assembly room and the vault. Carpenters, electricians, and plumbers swarmed over this plot, building, wiring, installing pipes and sewer connections to the end that within a few weeks there was a fine, new, triple-strength unit known henceforth as the experimental laboratory. Triple strength because the flooring, mounted on concrete piers, ran in three directions for the ultimate in steadiness for multiple exposures. Heavy work benches, rock-solid. A complete darkroom with vertical tanks and racks for processing film right there in that unit, with no waiting for our regular laboratory. Everything had been planned, thought out, made ready for anything and everything that might work. As a final touch I was given a sheaf of requisition books that would be honored like checks drawn against an inexhaustible fund. It was no longer necessary to ask anybody for anything. Simply write out the order, charge it to Picture F 3, sign it, and that's all there was to it. No more running around, either. Whatever had been requisitioned would be delivered to the door as quickly as possible.

Now, you would think that all this would have filled me with a soaring sense of top-lofty superiority. Not so. For it was really Bitzer's room, not mine, and the requisitions had to be signed by Bitzer, not me. I was still the tail on his kite, and I was never allowed to forget it.

However, there were compensations. Bitzer was so preoccupied with his private life that he was seldom to be found around the studio, except when Griffith was actually shooting or rehearsing. So I was allowed to sign the requisitions, "G. W. Bitzer, per K.B.," which worked out very well as far as I was concerned. The fact that he was hardly ever in the room gave me perfect freedom to play around with any experiments that might or might not come to anything.

Slowly, and against my most stubborn opposition, the idea became firmly implanted in my mind that everything new grows out of something old, and that before you can achieve any significant advances in your chosen profession, you must dig back through the past until you come to fundamental bedrock, after which you build from there.

This was no sudden flash of dazzling inspiration. I had had it ground into me by that sternest of teachers, failure. I had wanted to play the piano, not merely well but brilliantly. So I took lessons. My teacher actually had the gall to expect me—*me!*—to waste my time on five-finger exercises instead of tossing off the Chopin Études with the easy confidence of a De Pachmann. So I abandoned the piano and took up the violin. Same thing. My teacher made me draw the bow over an open string as slowly as possible. Just that. Nothing more. When I got to the point where I was able to sound one string with the bow just barely moving, and this without the slightest variation of tone or volume, it would be time to take up the business of fingering out simple exercises. This was not what I had in mind. It was "Devil's Trill" or nothing, although in a pinch I would have settled for "Hora Staccato." So it was nothing.

Well, I now had four years of paid employment nailed down and I did not want it to come to nothing. So I tore up all my dreams of sudden glory and picked on Woodbury as my most likely source of the bedrock fundamentals of photography. He was loaded with them. He knew all about the earliest fumbling gropings toward what was to become the solid, worldwide profession of photography as we knew it. Seeing my confusion, he recommended a book for me to study: Cassell's *Encyclopedia of Photography*.

I bought the book, and by the mere turning of its pages, a whole new window on life was opened. How *old* everything was! Why, when Daguerre finally discovered that an image could be captured by a film of silver fumed by iodine, lenses and cameras and everything else needed to make daguerreotypes had been ready and waiting for centuries. And from the moment it had become established that an image could be captured and held by a silver salt —in Daguerre's case, silver iodide—improvements came tumbling head over heels into the world from dozens of investigators. Silver plates gave way to paper, and paper to collodion-coated glass. The cumbersome wet-plate process was superseded by the dry plate, which in turn gave way to the celluloid film base that made moving pictures possible.

Much of this I had known about for some time. What I had not known about was the almost infinite variety of printing processes that these old-timers had used to give variety and character to their pictures. Carbon; gum bichromate; a strange sort of thing called the dusting-on process, in which the printed image is represented by varying degrees of stickiness of the surface. Dust on powder of your choice, any color at all, and it will adhere to the sticky places and not at all where the light has hardened the surface. Then there was a swelled-gelatin process in which a glass plate is given a very heavy coat of gelatin sensitized with potassium bichromate. Expose under a negative, wash out the bichromate, and what remains is a low-relief picture in varying thicknesses of gelatin. The principle was that wherever the light had hit the bichromated gelatin, it had become hardened, tanned really, like leather. This tough, water-resistant gelatin would absorb nothing and it wouldn't melt, even in hot water. The unaffected gelatin would absorb water and swell, and it would melt and run away in hot or even warm water. This was the most important principle in all photography, since upon this single characteristic—the hardening of a base or ground by that action of light—all photoengraving processes depend, requiring only the interposition of a screen to convert masses into dots.

Even more exciting was the old news that these swelled-gelatin plates would absorb dyes as well as water. This opened a whole new field of inquiry. I was well informed about color separation. Wratten was marketing panchromatic plates. Why not make three plates with the three primary-color filters, print them on swelled gelatin, then dye these plates with the appropriate colors and press them, in register, upon an absorbent paper surface to get direct color prints? Why not indeed! I was busily and happily shooting and developing three-color shots of still-life subjects, such as brightly colored flowers, and messing up everything in sight with a weird conglomeration of colors that the rainbow had never heard of when Griffith interrupted my avid investigations by rudely and inconsiderately starting another picture. This meant time out to earn my salary. Too bad. A shame. But then, that's the way things happen.

This new one was a Biblical picture, called, for some eccentric reason, *The Mother and the Law.* I didn't know how he had ever become stuck in this rut of calling everything *The Mother and the Law,* but that's what he called it. Not that it mattered. We simply numbered it F 4 and let it go at that. For regardless of what it was eventually titled, the story was that of the Passion Play, dealing with the trial and crucifixion of Jesus Christ. Surefire, absolutely.

For the very first time I felt certain that Griffith was on safe, solid ground. He had an absolutely foolproof story written by a team named Matthew, Mark, Luke, and John. The story had been given the widest possible kind of publicity for going on two thousand years. It had been hammered into the heads of young and old and even babes in arms throughout the world, not in any hit-or-miss manner but every Sunday and every Sunday and every Sunday, with extra performances on Easter and Christmas. I mean no sacrilege. But a fact is a fact, and this one cannot be denied. Yes. He was on safe-enough ground. Even if the picture was *bad,* nobody would dare to dislike it, not in public, anyway. You can't *get* any safer than that.

It was widely believed throughout the picture world that Griffith never shot from a script. But this was one time when he most certainly did. It may not have been in the form of pages held in his hand, but he followed the script nevertheless, down to the finest detail. For once in his life he had no choice, no leeway, for if he had departed from the original by so much as one jot or one tittle, there would have been howls of protest from all over Christendom.

However, he could compress, and that is just what he did. It was a matter of picking key episodes of this best known of all biographies and playing them for all they were worth. We did the marriage at Cana with painstaking attention to detail.

I say "painstaking" because that was forced upon us by the confusions and contradictions of the four different versions by the four different writers. They were long on character but short on description. They told us all about who was who but nothing about what was what. How were we to know what Jerusalem, or the temple, or Golgotha, or the house at Cana actually looked like? Huck Wortman had to be given *some* idea so he'd know how to lay out the sets. Herbert Sutch had to know exactly how everybody dressed so he could plan costumes for Goldstein to make. What was the furniture like? Or, for that matter, what was the actual physical appearance of Christ during his life as a man on earth?

This called for research, so Joe Henabery became our one-man research department. The desks in Griffith's and Woods's office were piled high with books. It would take a full day for anyone to thumb through them even in the most cursory manner. So the significant pictures were cut out and mounted in a scrapbook for ready reference. Then there was another scrapbook, and another, full to the bulging point. No two authorities agreed about anything, but one book, Tissot's illustrated Bible, was set aside as a sort of standard reference, mostly because the illustrations seemed to be more humanly real than any of the others. The Old Masters were out; though very great works of art, no two pictured the same face with the same expression. They were artists' conceptions of what ought to have been and not what must have been.

Griffith cut the knot of bewilderment with a single decisive stroke. People believe only what they already know. They knew all about how people lived, dressed, and had their being in Biblical times because they had been brought up on Bible pictures, Bible calendars, Biblical magic-lantern shows, Christmas cards, Easter cards, pictures of every incident with which we were concerned. Never mind whether these pictures were accurate or not. Follow them in every detail because that's what the people believe to be true, and what the people believe to be true *is* true—for them—and there's no budging them.

From then on it was all plain sailing. No questions, no doubts. It was a real treat to watch Huck Wortman, with a big quid of tobacco bulging one cheek, and with a brightly colored Sunday-school card in his hand, profanely blistering some hapless carpenter with the most scurrilous of invective for stupidly placing the sacrificial altar of the temple too far downstage.

The marriage at Cana now went forward without a hitch. The set was built according to the specifications laid down by the Sunday-school pictures. The costumes were exactly what everybody had been taught to believe they would be. The wedding procedure was supervised by the highly respected Rabbi Myers,* while the equally highly respected Father Dodd, Episcopalian, stood by to make sure no Christian beliefs would be shaken by this purely Jewish ceremony.

It was apparently impossible for Griffith to shoot any sequence without at least some element of suspense. It opened on a note of tension. The bride, played by our lovely little Bessie Love, was nowhere to be seen. She was in an upper room, reached by a short flight of steps at the back of the set. Inside, fortunately out of sight, she was being examined to see if—to see if—well, to make *sure*. Tension among the assembled guests. Was she or wasn't she? The tension was broken by my father, made up as the master of the house, rushing out to exclaim joyously, "Everything is all right! Wonderful!" Out came Bessie, prettier than a picture in her wedding apparel, smiling and happy and blushing and proud because she had passed her physical with flying colors.

From then on everything went according to John, because Matthew, Mark, and Luke had skipped this sequence. Joy reigned everywhere around until, as has happened at more than one party, they ran out of wine. Then the miracle of turning water into wine, which was no ordinary wine but wine that was truly miraculous in more ways than one. The master was rebuked for serving his best wine last instead of first.

The picture ran its course along the inflexible lines fixed by tradition. The set for the Via Dolorosa was crooked, cobbled, arched, and beautiful. Each and every Station of the Cross was played out in careful detail. Father Dodd was right on the job every step of the way, making sure that nothing was missed. Griffith simply stood by, happy to leave such details to a qualified expert.

We were shooting out of sequence, as usual, with the order of shooting determined by the availability of sets, costumes, crowds, and in some cases, by Griffith's personal feelings of what he'd like to do next. The marriage at Cana came first because the set was ready first. The woman caught in adultery followed, because that was an easy and simple sequence to stage. The

---

* Father of Carmel Myers. KEVIN BROWNLOW

capture, trial, condemnation, and Stations of the Cross, followed by the crucifixion itself, were made in a series of crowd-filled days.

We had Roman soldiers all over the place, with swords, spears, and standards reading S.P.Q.R. I sort of half-remembered what those initials meant, but Woodbury knew offhand. Our working crew didn't know at all, so they translated them to read Supers Paid Quite Regularly. We also had Jews in great profusion. Not Jewish people. Jews. Real, old-time orthodox Jews from somewhere in the Boyle Heights district, who knew all the traditions handed down from father to son for five thousand years. Nobody had to supply them with beards. They had their own, home-grown. Nobody had to tell them how and where and when to wear phylacteries. They had their own, with Rabbi Myers on hand to make sure there were no mistakes.

In a sense we had three directors on the picture. Griffith was there to make his wants known and to pass on the results. Rabbi Myers was there to direct the Jewish details of this Christian drama, while Father Dodd was there to keep this event in Jewish history in line with Christian beliefs. And so, between them, the filming proceeded quite smoothly, except for us in the camera department.

The trouble was all with Howard Gaye and his makeup as Christ. He came out on the screen looking exactly like Howard Gaye in makeup, while Griffith wanted something that he described, with vague gestures, as "mysterious, mysterious." We knew what he meant, but the problem was how to get it. Soft focus was an old story with all our cameramen, and all kinds of fine silk net had been used to conceal the ravages of time on superannuated leading women who looked very well on the stage but who could not stand having a camera crowded in for a full-head close-up. We tried everything. Individually, the shots were passable, but when cut into the action, no. First you'd get a shot that was clear, sharp, and bright. Fine. Then you'd nip in a soft-focus close-up and everything seemed to be swimming in milk—clear, mushy, clear, mushy. It just wouldn't work, so we played Gaye in medium and long shots and hoped for the best. And with Griffith's close-clipped cutting, it might not be half bad at that.

We did the crucifixion last of all, hewing strictly to the line all the way, and then the picture was finished. Griffith disappeared into the projection room, Bitzer disappeared I know not where, while I disappeared into my long-neglected experiment room to see what I could get into that nobody had gotten into before.

Our failure to make the close-ups of Christ look like anything but Howard Gaye with long hair and a beard nagged at me. I studied the various pictures.

Some were woodcuts, some were steel engravings, while most were cheap lithographs. The figure and features of Christ were always sharp and clear. No soft focus there. Of course they could use halos, which helped. Helped? It made all the difference in the world.

I wandered over to Woodbury's department. He was in the enlarging room, making some enlargements of his stills of Christ. The problem of making him "mysterious, mysterious" wasn't bothering Woodbury at all. He had an assortment of pieces of cardboard of all different shapes that he waved over the projected image being printed on bromide paper, acting like a cross between an Egyptian dancer and a three-card-monte dealer.

"What are you doing?" I asked, with pardonable ignorance.

"Dodging," he explained, flipping the yellow filter over the projector lens to end the printing. He took the paper from the easel and slipped it into the developer. The image came up. "See? I've held back the places that I want kept light and I've darkened the places that I don't want to show up so strongly. See his face? Almost washed out, while everybody else is sort of murky. Makes him stand out. Different."

It was different, all right. Of course it wouldn't work with picture film because of the motion. And besides, how are you going to wave things between the printing light and the image in a Hausmann step printer? Impossible, of course. Forget it.

But I couldn't forget it. Those close-ups of Christ, which were now among the discards and out-takes, showed practically no body motion. Surely something could be done if I could only think of it. Why not play around with it for a while and see what happened? I could develop, print, and project my own tests without anyone being the wiser. Yes, print, because I could squeeze both the positive and negative films face to face into the Pathé gate and run them through in stop motion, using a light box for a printing light.

A week or so later I was beginning to see daylight. It was perfectly easy, with Woodbury's equipment, to blow a single frame up into an eight-by-ten negative that could be worked on the same as any other negative could be retouched. So I went to work on that enlarged negative with pen and pencil, brush, and even airbrush for the softest possible gradations. I even tried, very tentatively, to put a hint of halolike radiance around the head.

So now I had an eight-by-ten negative transparency that looked pretty fair, if you didn't examine it too closely. Next step, make up the old tried-and-true Farmer's reducing solution and take out the silver image entirely. I now had a plate of clear glass with a lot of meaningless marks, smudges, and smears on it. Dry. Mount the glass in the light box. Thread up the camera with the original negative and fresh raw positive stock face to face, the negative in printing position. Focus the camera on the plate, bringing the marks and smudges in register with the negative, which had been placed in the aperture gate under the ground glass. Remove ground glass. Put negative and positive face to face. Engage claws, being sure that the negative is in frame. Install pressure pad. Close camera. Begin turning, clocking off the stop-motion frames one by one.

Develop positive. Dark, too dark. Should have made light tests, but I was in too much of a hurry. Examine under magnification. Scratches, blobs, and pencil marks show up like sore thumb. Idea. Shoot them a little out of focus. And *this* time make light tests.

I did. The print looked fine. I took it to the little projection room we had installed high over the rehearsal hall and threaded it into the old Edison projector that was good enough for test runs. By golly, it *worked!* Woodbury's dodging technique *could* be carried over to motion-picture film after all.

I couldn't wait to show it to Griffith. "That is very fine" was his comment. "Who showed you how to do this? Billy?"

"No, sir. Woodbury."

"Who's Woodbury?"

"Our still man. It's called dodging."

"Hm." There was a pause. "Think you can do this with other shots?"

"Yes, sir. I think so. Depends on the shot. How much he moves around. Sitting or standing still would be all right. Moving across the screen, no. No way to follow action. Not yet, anyway."

He understood. "Is there any way you could make him more—more mysterious?" His waving hands expressed what his voice could not.

I thought fast and hard. "Well, maybe—just maybe—we could give it a texture—like canvas—an oil painting—"

He brought his hand down on the desk with a slap. "That's *it!*" he exclaimed. "That's what I have been trying to think of all along. They're used to seeing his face on *canvas!* Jimmy, give him the negative of all the close-up stuff."

Jimmy Smith was aghast. Negative was literally more precious than rubies, because rubies can be replaced, while negative cannot. "But, Mr. Griffith, that's *negative!* If anything happens to that negative—"

Griffith cut in to finish the sentence for him. "—I'll do it over. I might do a lot of this over anyway, with no advisers. Too many cooks. Give him the negative. Right away." Jimmy hurried off. Griffith spoke to me, "How soon do you think you can have more of this stuff for me to see?"

"Will tomorrow do?"

He smiled dryly and replied, "Tomorrow will be fine."

Jimmy came back with a can full of small rolls of negative. He gave them to me without a word, but with a sadness that made words unnecessary. I took the film and left.

I worked all night long and well into the following morning. Getting a canvas texture to the picture meant a second plate in the light box, this one a transparency shot of a piece of stretched canvas secured from Cash Shockey. It took time, and trial and error, to get the right weight of image to give just a hint of canvas texture to the picture, but it worked and that's what counted.

I managed to get four shots done by ten the following morning. I didn't even try to develop and dry the positive film myself. I sealed the four exposed positives in a can, gave them to Joe Aller, told him what they were, and left all the rest of it up to him.

Looking at the stuff in the projection room that afternoon, I came to a full realization of how little, how very little, I had actually done. That selective lightening and darkening of the picture through dodging and retouching had been an essential part of the theater's stock-in-trade for not only years but decades. To pick out a central character and give him a special lighting while holding the rest of the set in relative darkness was simply the ABC of theatrical lighting. That canvas was merely the old theatrical scrim that interposed a mysterious something between the audience and the scene on the stage. The character of the Ghost in *Hamlet* had actually *worn* a scrim to make him appear dim and mysterious and otherworldly, way back in the days of Booth and Barrett and even further back in theatrical history. Maybe Shakespeare himself wore a net when he played the Ghost in his own *Hamlet*. And so, although the shots were effective, I had not done a single thing but put old methods to a new use.

Griffith thought it was all "very fine," probably because it was what *he* was used to during his years on the stage. So his philosophy about audiences clinging to what they knew snapped right back and hit him, too.

"I'll use a lot of this," he said to Rose and Jimmy Smith. "I'll plan for it."

That was all. I left the dark projection room, squinted a little until my eyes became adjusted to the sun, and then made my way back to the experiment room, trying to get used to the feeling of being worthwhile for a change.

If I could have looked into the future to see what all this would mean, I might not have been so happy. Because for a long time to come, no matter how hard a day had been or how exhausting the work, whenever I came plodding wearily back to that room, there would be a big stack of bright film cans inside the room waiting for me.

For this bright idea of mine would work only on the positive prints. I tried to dupe negatives, but it was no go. Fine-grain stock did not exist, and dupes made on negative stock were impossibly grainy. So I had to process every scene of every release print separately, no matter how tired I was or how long it might take. There were times when I wished heartily from the depths of my soul that I had never started this thing in the first place. But . . . what's done is done, and I was stuck with it. As a modern philosopher has said, too smart is dumb. But that's something everybody has to learn for himself —the hard way . . .

❧ 11 ❧

The Towers of Babylon

And they climbed and they climbed
'Til they could climb no higher . . .
BARBARA ALLEN

THERE is a story that deserves to be true, even if it is not. Way back in the eighteen forties, the head of the Patent Office resigned his post, because there was nothing left to invent. That old fellow was more than half right, at that. Try as I would, I could find nothing to do that had not been done years and years ago. This was no snap judgment—it came of long, hard, frustrating experience, not unmixed with humiliation.

Griffith wanted a long shot of Jerusalem taken from the Mount of Olives. Fine. We had a moundlike hill covered with olive trees only a few hundred yards away. I got into my brand-new 1915 Studebaker and growled up to the top in low gear. The view was splendid. Only one thing wrong. It was of the Griffith studio, not Jerusalem.

However, that could be corrected. Simply mask out the studio and replace with a still of Jerusalem. Worked fine. I was very proud of myself until I discovered, by unhappy accident, that the old-time wet-plate boys had been making composite pictures as an important part of their bread-and-butter trade way back in the seventies.

Same thing with clouds. I saw no point in spending days up on a rooftop shooting clouds on film that could be double-exposed into a scene once and once only, when it was just as easy to shoot a lot of stills of a lot of clouds of all different types from lofty thunderheads to low-flying storm scud. These cloud shots could be blown up as transparencies, mounted in front of the light box, and shot at leisure whenever required. Furthermore, they could be made to move, simply by mounting the frame in which they were held on a screw-threaded rod that could be turned at any desired speed.

I was very proud of this discovery, which I wore closely concealed in my innermost heart as the most precious of jewels, until I found that the early pictorialists had been doing this not merely for years but for decades.

It was all very disheartening. No matter what I thought of or how brilliant the idea seemed at the time, it always turned out to be something old as the hills. I had not been pioneering at all; I had been stupidly hacking my way through the forest primeval, when there was a broad, clear, well-traveled road through that same forest, ready and waiting for anyone to use. Anyone, that is, except those too stupid or ignorant to know that there are books on almost everything.

So it was back to the library for more digging. About the first thing that dawned in my benighted mind was the clear and open—but unperceived —idea that people like pictures. Not just some people. All people of all ages, from the cavemen who drew pictures of animals and men on the walls of their caves to the Morgan Collection in the New York Metropolitan Museum. There were pictures, from the Sistine Chapel down to the latest graffiti in the men's room. Everything the mind of man could think of had to be expressed somehow in picture form. Even God Almighty, who was one of Michelangelo's favorite subjects.

Apparently people cannot or will not accept abstract ideas. Faith, Hope, and Charity turn out to be three rather handsome, if loosely clad, young women doing some sort of round dance hand in hand. All the emotions— love, hate, misery, gladness—have to be personalized and drawn, painted, or sculpted before people can believe in them.

No wonder moving pictures were being so eagerly swallowed by the people. For they filled the need for pictures, and added the mystery of how pictures can be made to move. And the love of mystery is second only to the need for pictures. This kept leaping out of the books I was searching for clues to what makes things work, especially in the field of photography.

Moving pictures *began* as magic shows, with Méliès as the principal trickster. Many of his pictures were hand-colored. Not that it made much difference. The people were not critical. If they saw pictures, and if the pictures moved, that satisfied them. And if the pictures showed things that were wondrous to behold, such as the devil appearing and disappearing in a puff of smoke, or people going to the moon, all the better. There was a one-reel film of the French Revolution that showed a man being guillotined. Well, almost guillotined. The knife descended, and just as the angled blade was about to touch the back of his neck—*flick!*—off went the picture just in the nick of time. (Nervous screams and laughter from the audience.)

There were more tricks in those pictures than you could shake a stick at, as the saying goes. There was one about Jesse James (somebody is always making a picture about Jesse James), in which the murder was shown with the screen quartered into sections, with separate actions shown in each corner. In the upper-left-hand corner Jesse is standing on a chair straightening a picture. In the upper-right corner the dirty little coward who shot Mr. Howard is seen drawing his gun and making ready to plug Jesse in the back. The lower right shows Mrs. James running to warn her husband, while the lower left shows a big crowd of ten or a dozen enraged townspeople running hell-bent for some reason or other that is never made clear. It was a good idea that didn't work out, because it was a four-ring circus with more going on than anyone could follow. Full attention can be given to only one thing at a time.

There was another picture that was run repeatedly because everybody had heard about *The Great Train Robbery* and wanted to see it again and again. I got to know the picture by heart. There was one scene in particular that fascinated me. There's an interior shot of a telegraph office with the usual observation bay window upstage. A train, a real train, goes thundering past this window. How in the world had they ever managed to get that effect?

The answer was clear enough to me now, in 1915, after three whole years of experience in the actual business of making motion pictures. It was a double exposure. A black backing in the window. A matte cut to fit the opening. Shoot the interior. Then fit the matte and shoot the train passing. Nothing to it. It was all in knowing how.

But where did that leave me? Just about everything anyone could imagine could be done in the camera, as Méliès had demonstrated. That the results were crude cannot be denied, but what was there that was so very refined about the early locomotives, such as Puffing Billy, or the railway cars, which were simply stagecoaches on iron wheels? Or for that matter, the high-wheeled, tiller-steered, horseless carriages as compared to my sleek and powerful new Studebaker with its four cylinders instead of one, and with a top speed of up to forty miles an hour?

It left me absolutely nowhere. I knew nothing but what had always existed within my lifetime. But then, where did that leave everyone else? For we were all in the same fix, each and every one of us. Even Griffith. And upon second thought, especially Griffith, because he was the big, the enormous, the overshadowing Colossus of the picture world.

Which opened a new line of thought. What had Griffith, the one-time grocery boy, elevator operator, bad actor, and worse poet, hop picker, ore shoveler and, worst of all, outstanding failure as a husband, done that had raised him to such dizzy heights of success?

The answer was as simple as the Columbus egg trick, which we all knew about from our schooldays and which punched home the simplest of morals: anything is simple if you know how.

Everything Griffith had been touted as having originated had been done time without number. And yet he must have done *something* to make him what he was today. And that something was to take the old tried-and-true gimmicks of the standard, workaday business of picture making and do them better than anyone had done before. And this simplifies itself into the single abstract term, Art.

What Griffith was doing at the moment was making ready for another picture, this one not merely big, but a fantastically huge thing all about ancient Babylon and called, naturally enough, *The Mother and the Law.*

First order of the day for me was to find out all about ancient Babylon. I was already somewhat informed about the period and its people and the principals in the drama because of the Sunday-school sessions I had been forced to attend back in Delta during school sessions. My grandparents, stern and rockbound Calvinists both, not only kept the Sabbath holy but went to some pains to see that I kept it holy too. Otherwise I would have been to some pains for not having done so. Anyway, I now headed straight for the library to bring myself up to date on the latest happenings in the b.c. years.

Luck was with me. There on the shelf was a brand-new, hot-from-the-press edition of a book by somebody named Breasted, *Ancient Times: A History of the Early World.* Publication date, 1916—this year—published by Ginn and Company, the people who printed most of our school books, so it was sure to be scholarly. This book was an eye-opener. I had no idea as to how *vast* the distances were in the ancient world; or of the immense stretches of time involved. At one time, Egypt owned all of this world. A map colored pink said so. Then the Assyrians came down like a wolf on the fold and took it all. And why did they go to all this trouble? Simple enough. The more land the more people; the more people the more taxes; the more taxes the richer the rulers. That was what our current war was all about. Maybe that's all any war has ever been about really. Armed robbery on a massive scale, made legal by solemn proclamations and sanctified by patriotic fervor. These old rulers did everything on the most enormous of scales. That bigger meant better was no new movie idea. The greater the ruler the bigger his statues, with seventy-five feet in height being about right for a man of Ramses's prestige. Nor would a single statue do. The more the merrier, so it was Ramses, Ramses, Ramses all over the Egyptian empire of three thousand years ago, just as it was Coca-Cola, Coca-Cola, Coca-Cola all over our present-day world. The supposedly modern advertising saying that repetition is reputation was an accepted article of faith more than a thousand years before Christ.

Their buildings were designed along heroic lines. The higher, the wider, and the handsomer the better. The great walls that surrounded the cities were great indeed: eighty feet high with towers of a hundred feet, wide enough for chariots to race across the top, and fitted with ramps so the king could ride his chariot anywhere along the walls without his sacred feet ever touching the profane earth. The great gates were so heavy that they had to be worked by machinery. Gangs of slaves strained at bars that turned cogs that worked gears that swung these ponderous gates open or closed.

The king's palace was in keeping with his magnificence. He'd build his own private mountain inside the city walls and perch his palace on the top, where he could look down on everybody. This called for more ramps, so the resulting structure was a sort of pyramid encircled by a roadway for the royal chariot. Not that the palace was in any way cramped by its tiptop position. The top was flattened so his great hall could be reckoned in acres rather than in feet, and there was no roof. Open to the sky. For nothing must be higher than the king of Babylon. Not even a roof beam.

And there must be ornaments everywhere—not common, ordinary, every-day ornaments such as the common rich men had. What were the most costly, the most hard-to-come-by materials? Gold, of course, and ivory and ebony and mother-of-pearl. And who designed all this magnificence and who brought it into being? Why, artists and artisans from wherever they could be found throughout the length and breadth of the Assyrian empire. The most important of these captives were the Jews, whose reputation for general all-around smartness had been earned the way all smartness is learned, through adversity. Originally a quiet, pastoral people they soon be-came tired of having their herds raided by their neighbors, the original cattle-rustlers.

The trouble with raising livestock is that there is no way you can keep them under lock and key. So the Jewish people began to turn their attention to articles of small bulk but high value, such as gold and diamonds and pearls, stuff that could be concealed. This worked for a while, but not for long, not as historians reckon time. It soon became known to the robber barons of that day that hidden wealth could be extracted from the jewelers and money-changers. So what was left? What thing of great value can be hidden in such a way that not even the cleverest or cruelest can steal it?

Knowledge. Of course! Put your wealth in your head, for knowledge is power, and that's all money can buy anyway—power. So the Jews became doctors, lawyers, musicians, artists, philosophers as a matter of ethnic pride.

Yes, and of profit, too, for they had skills that could be found nowhere else in the world. But there was a way to steal even this kind of wealth, and Nebuchadnezzar found it.

This king of Babylon came along in about 600 B.C. and took Jerusalem, stripped it of everything of value for his own private treasury, including the best of the Jews—"well favoured and skilful in all wisdom, and cunning in knowledge, and understanding science"*—housed them in princely luxury in the king's own palace for three years so they could learn to speak Chaldean, after which they were supposed to wise him up, as we would say in our crude modern way. Everything worked out according to plan. Daniel, who headed this captive brain-trust, performed well. He and his companions outshone the best magicians and soothsayers Assyria had on hand. Daniel could interpret the king's dreams, while his companions could survive the fiery furnace, and Daniel himself spent a quiet, harmless night with the lions that were supposed to have torn him to pieces. All this set them in solid, and all would have been well, except that Nebuchadnezzar became unreliable and had to be replaced by Belshazzar. Daniel and his friends got along fine with Belshazzar too, until that mysterious hand appeared to write on the wall. Just exactly what happened then was not too fully reported: "In that night was Belshazzar the king of the Chaldeans slain. And Darius the Medean took the kingdom, being about threescore and two years old." There can be such a thing as being *too* terse.

I knew that if Griffith was going to picture the fall of Babylon, he'd need a more detailed account than that. Breasted was not of much more help. ". . . Cyrus had no trouble in defeating the Chaldean army led by the young crown prince, Belshazzar . . . In spite of the vast walls erected by Nebuchadnezzar to protect Babylon, the Persians entered the great city in 583 B.C., seemingly without resistance." Hm. Thin, very thin. The king is simply "slain." No mention of how or by whom. And Cyrus had no trouble defeating the Chaldean army. Well, if he had no trouble, what happened? Did the Chaldeans turn tail and run or did they just give up without a struggle? Either way, you can't play that for thrills, and thrills are the lifeblood of anybody's motion picture. And I couldn't find out who the villain was, either, and you can't make a picture without a villain.

How was anyone to distinguish between Darius and Cyrus, or the Medes and the Persians, who were generally spoken of in one breath, like ham and eggs? So I asked my own private encyclopedia, Woodbury, about it. Woodbury scratched his chin thoughtfully and replied, "Well, I don't exactly

* Daniel 1, 4.

know. There is some confusion about that, because one man's Mede is another man's Persian." However, I was comforted by one cheering thought: Griffith would know because he had to stage it. All I had to do was wait, and I'd find out, too, in the course of time.

I wonder if anyone can realize how long "the course of time" can be in the making of a really big production? You start out all filled to the brim with vim and vinegar, ready to cope with anything that comes along. Christmas comes, and you're still plugging away at the same old job. Easter finds you at the same old task. Then it becomes summer, and the kids are all out of school, but you're not. You're still doing the same old thing the same old way. Autumn. The leaves turn on their annual grand display of silent fireworks. Winter comes, and another Christmas. Still at it. Another Easter and it's the same old thing. You wonder if it will ever end. Someone voiced this one afternoon when we were well into our second year of shooting *The Mother and the Law the Fourth.*

"I don't see why everybody is in such a hurry to get through," mused Griffith, half to himself. "We'd only start another one."

This had the reviving effect of a dash of cold water on our wearied spirits. For why should we, theatrical people all, complain because our show was having the longest run of all? We should be proud and happy, not bored and sated. And yet, somehow, in spite of all rationalization, we were becoming fed up with making the same old picture over and over again. For this *was The Mother and the Law,* because there was a big long painted sign on the back of a huge wall on Sunset Boulevard that said so.

The first thing to go up was the Walls of Babylon, which ran along the northwestern side of the Griffith lot. Every detail of this wall matched the descriptions of fortified cities of the third millennium B.C. Not Breasted alone but every other authority had been searched for the most meticulously accurate reproduction of those long-vanished structures. Most of these were highly educated guesses as to what ancient Babylon must have looked like, because Babylon itself had crumbled into dust, but from the bits and pieces unearthed by archaeologists it was possible to make pretty fair assumptions. So up went the walls, with towers that went higher yet. The great gate was worked by primitive, man-powered machinery exactly as Breasted had pictured it. It was a remarkable achievement, a project that called for swarms of carpenters and immense quantities of lumber. Our painters had to hang from the top on special rigs to paint and decorate these walls. A special building on Sunset Boulevard was the plaster shop, where Italian experts in staff work, as the casting and molding of plaster was called, worked day and night to perform their own special magic.

The work of these artists fascinated me. First, the original image was modeled in clay. Then these finished pieces were cut into convenient sizes for casting. A wire, strung between two heavy handles, would be drawn slowly and carefully back and forth by two men to force it slowly into the partially hardened clay. The sections were put aside with the greatest care. Drop one piece and the whole thing is ruined. They did not drop any pieces. Next step, coat each section with glue until a heavy coating, inches thick, has been built up. Let it set. Make sure it is good and firm. Then pull it off, slowly, carefully, with two or three men using strength to disengage the glue in a single unbroken mold from the original clay model or pattern. Now dust it all over inside with fine plaster of Paris. Now a very thin cream of plaster and water is to be poured into this mold, which is turned and rocked and worked until every smallest part of the mold is coated, with no air holes or bubbles. Let it set. No, it's not ready yet. This is only a surface shell, a mere eggshell, so to speak. Now fill the rest of the mold with good thick strong liquid plaster, and be sure to mix in as much plasterer's hair as it will take. This hair, so-called, came in bales and we must have used it in carload lots. Why? Because plaster alone will crack under the stress of the heat and cold, wetness and dryness of the open air. In very large castings, such as our upright elephants, it would actually collapse unless supported from within by these millions of fibers—the old story of Gulliver held bound and helpless by the many thin threads of the Lilliputian ropes.

Putting these sections together was an even more fascinating process. First, an armature was built of wood and wire and steel rods; then, beginning at the bottom, the proper sections were fitted into place and tied to the armature by thick, wet, loose strands of burlap sodden with plaster. This wet, soft, sloppy stuff did not have to be knotted. Simply flop one end over another and it will all harden into place so solidly that it would take a hammer and chisel to break it loose. Little cracks and crevices where the sections did not fit perfectly meant nothing. Paint them over with a thin mixture of plaster on a big brush, and the job is done.

The assembled pieces were then ready for the painters. Plaster is porous, so their first job was to coat every casting with clear shellac. After they were thoroughly dry, the actual painting and decorating could be done, and this, in some cases, required a great deal of expertise.

The Babylonians had no end of gods to worship, but the big, overriding god of them all was Bel. He was the god of earth and war, and since war was what had made all Assyria great, and Babylon greatest of all, he was the one to be treated with the greatest of respect. Bel had the body of a bull, and the head and face of a man. Not an ordinary man, but an old, square-bearded, crafty-wise man with cruel eyes, who wore the back-slanting high round crown of ancient Egypt as a symbol of supreme authority. This figure of the recumbent, man-faced bull was so huge that it required eight strong men to carry it in ceremonial parades, its weight being supported by carved and decorated poles borne on the shoulders of gigantic slaves. The figure itself was one great mass of glitter from its many-jeweled coating of gold.

And how did all these things—these walls, these gates, these decorations, these implements of ancient war, these fish-scaled coats of armor, these chariots—all happen to come together? Because of one short moment in time, seemingly so long ago, when we had left the prison at San Quentin during the making of *The Mother and the Law* (phase one). We had stopped the car to look down at the Tower of Jewels in the San Francisco Exposition—that was the moment. Here was magnificence, and below us were the workmen who had brought all this magnificence into being. Griffith, who had been penny-pinched by Biograph during his one previous attempt to reproduce Oriental grandeur in *Judith of Bethulia,* was now face to face with everything to make that early dream come true. He not only had the money, but a trained army of workmen, ready to do his bidding, now that the Fair had been built and finished and all these men were looking for jobs.

Griffith required a worthy organizer who could bring to full fruition all the grandiose dreams that were bursting for realization in his imagination. Huck Wortman was the best in his line, but there are limits to what even the best of stage carpenters can do. Somebody had to design the show, and this somebody had to be the very best of all. Griffith found him and his name was Hall.

I later heard that his full name was Walter L. Hall, but nobody around the lot knew it at the time. He was *Mr.* Hall, if you please, and he remained Mr. Hall until he had talked so interminably to everybody about perspective, perspective, perspective that everyone called him "Spec" Hall, and there was nothing he could do to change it.

Except for Griffith and Bitzer and Scholtz and Aller and Huck Wortman and Lillian and Dorothy Gish, Hall was in his own way the most remarkable person I had ever met. Oh yes, and Johnny Leezer and Al Wyckoff. And Frank Woods, of course. The Griffith lot was fairly crawling with geniuses, and it took all anybody could do just to keep up.

Hall is hard to describe physically. Let me try it this way: in the second year of the war Gallipoli was under attack by British forces, and the minister in charge was a round-faced, bulldoggish sort of person whose picture had appeared in the newspapers—Winston Churchill. His attack failed and he was set back hard. Except for that one dreadful reverse, he might have amounted to something. Anyway, Hall was a double for young Winston Churchill. Same face, same bodily structure, and he already had the accent.

Hall had two all-absorbing interests: the science of perspective and an alert fearfulness for the safety of his teenage daughter. I never saw much of young Miss Hall. She was not part of our stock company, so she never appeared before the cameras. I don't know where she kept herself, but during the few occasions she was on the lot, she was constantly under Hall's eye. I've never seen a man worry as much as he did about the safety of his darling daughter.

Hall's working-quarters was a long wide room built up on stilts at the east end of the lower stage. There were plenty of windows, placed so he could look down on the lower stage to watch his plans being put into execution. Hall would lean out from one of his windows, like a captain from his bridge, watching the workmen punch his designs into heavy paper. Suddenly he'd become wildly alarmed. Where was she? Then he'd discover her, sitting serenely alone in the sun, quietly resting. Then back to work. Then another alarm. She's gone! Oh-my-God, where? Down the steps at a dead run, a dash to where she was last seen, and another crisis ended when he discovered that she had merely moved into the shade, out of that hot sun, on the opposite side of the dressing-rooms. I don't know why he was so worried. She didn't look like the wild kind to me—more the milk-and-water type, but you never can tell.

My interest was strictly with Hall, because he was something entirely new in my experience. I had seen all kinds of theatrical sets, from the extravaganza of *Louisiana* to the unbelievably intricate mechanical marvel of the chariot race in the stage version of *Ben Hur,* with its moving background of the crowded Colosseum and its double-tracked treadmill for the two chariots driven by Ben Hur and Messala, with William S. Hart as Messala, as well as the onrushing locomotive that stopped inches short of the footlights. But I had never seen these things during the drawing-board stage. The designing of theatrical spectacles was Hall's life work. He could draw with superlative skill and paint better, or at least more accurately, than anyone I had ever seen work with paint and brush. Watching him work was like seeing one of the big, all-evening magic shows of Harry Kellar or Houdini. Things happened that you knew *couldn't* be happening and yet they did! There was always a perfectly logical explanation behind these illusions.

Hall combined the great gift of an imaginative creative artist with the needlepoint accuracy of a fine architect. His preliminary drawings were all done with pencil on specially surfaced heavy cardboard, like title cards. Correction: pencils, plural, because he had a whole spectrum of pencils always at hand, graded from 6 H to 6 B, from hardest to softest, but all of them kept as sharp as possible at all times. There was no tentative fiddling around; a bold stroke here, and half an arch was on the board; another stroke, and the entire arch was there, hard and clear and firm. Quick sleight-of-hand while he changed pencils. A zip here, another zip there, and a pair of pilasters framing the arch were right there looking at you. Another lightning change to another grade of pencil, another succession of swift sure strokes, and the leaves of the acanthus came to life on the capital.

Huck, who was waiting for the finished drawing so he could order material and assign men to the job, watched with as much open-mouthed amazement as I did. Huck's was tempered by the eminently practical consideration that he had to build whatever was being drawn, and he could not bring himself to believe that anything done so offhand and so freehand could be technically accurate. And Huck *had* to have accuracy, or how could he measure and cut lumber to fit?

"That all looks mighty pretty, Mr. Hall," he said, as a detail of the great gate took form under Hall's flying hand. "But how do I know how *big* everything is?"

"You want a scale?" Hall drew a swift, straight line at the bottom of the design. (He never used a straight-edge or T-square or compass.) He ticked off sections of this line with pencil strokes. "There. That's your scale. In feet."

Huck scratched the back of his grizzled round head dubiously. "You sure?" he asked.

Hall was annoyed. He snatched a scrap of paper from the wastebasket, drew a swift, short line on it, and then with a needle-sharp 6 H pencil he drew two all but invisible fine lines exactly perpendicular to the horizontal black line. "That's an inch," he said. "Measure it."

Huck drew a fine steel scale from his pocket and put it over the drawing. I leaned over to watch. It was not only an inch but it was a finer, closer inch than the one shown on the steel scale. For the scale's markings had definite width, while Hall's hairline limiting marks split these widths exactly in the middle. Huck shook his head and sighed. "All right, Mr. Hall. I'll set her up just like she's drawn."

"You do that" was Hall's answer. "And start the staff men on the lions. I want to see the clay models before they start casting. Might want to make some changes in case they don't get the expression just right."

Hall's attention to the minutest of details was phenomenal. Nothing escaped his eye, even in the dimmest of blurred half-tone pictures printed when photoengraving was still a young and somewhat smeary process. He could look at a pictured fragment of a recently unearthed archaeological find and from it reconstruct the entire subject, whatever it might have been. A partial remnant of a stairway at Persepolis became the entire great stairway to the great palace of Belshazzar. Dim and weatherworn wall paintings became clear and bright and new under his magic pencils.

If he could work in small, so to speak, he could also work in large. Some of his sketches of Babylon at the moment of its greatest glory were breathtaking. I say "sketches" because of the swiftness with which they were done, but the results were far from sketchy. They looked like studies, and very good studies at that, for a tremendous panorama. Best of all, everything was so *solid*. Everything sat firmly on the ground. These pencil drawings might have been copied from an actual photograph of Babylon.

Needless to say, these drawings delighted Griffith. His characteristic "That is very fine" took on a tinge of deep respect that drew nothing but a "Humpf!" and a nod from Hall. Of *course* they were very fine! Hall's head would go up and his eyes would dart around as though seeking anyone impudent enough to disbelieve so obvious a truth. And then he'd remember that he hadn't seen his daughter for at least five minutes, so he'd dash to the window, look frantically around, murmur a hasty "Excuse me," and go rushing down the steps. That poor girl never had the slightest chance, not with Hall around.

What was his secret? Perspective, always perspective. His one criterion for the judgment of any masterpiece was the correctness of its perspective. "Corot!" he'd snap. "Ever see a Corot? Especially that thing of his called 'The Dance of the Nymphs'? Humpf! Those damned nymphs are dancing *five feet off the ground!* If you don't believe me, look at it, see for yourself. Corot! Humph!" We didn't happen to have the original Corot hanging on our living-room wall, but there were plenty of reproductions in the library. I looked. It was true: they're a good five feet off the ground.

He must have had a hundred or more pencils within easy reach, but not one eraser. Not even a piece of masticated rubber or art gum. He could *not* make a mistake. It was beyond his power.

"How'd you learn all this?" I asked one day.

"Learn? *Learn?* Learn *this?*" You'd think I had insulted him, from his tone of outrage. "Nobody can learn this. It's something you *have* to *do*. My father was the same way. If he wanted a thing, he had to have it, no matter what. I remember one Christmas he wanted fresh grapes. Fresh, mind you, from the vine, not this miserable stuff they pack in sawdust. He didn't care if they cost five pounds a grape. And he got them, too. I don't know how much they cost or where they came from, but he had his grapes. Like father, like son. I wanted to draw. So I drew, and I kept on drawing until I got so I could *really* draw. I didn't care whether I ever made a sou markee out of my drawing in my life. I didn't care then and I don't care now. Drawing, to me, is like my father's grapes. He wanted them so he got them."

"It must give you a great deal of satisfaction to be able to do anything so wonderful so easily," I remarked enviously.

"Satisfaction? Humpf! Chained to a drawing board hand and foot, day in and day out, when I ought to be out looking after my daughter? It's a dog's life, Brown—a dog's life."

"Then why do you do it?"

"Because I must, can't you see that? Because I *must!*"

"Don't you *like* drawing?"

"I hate it," he said vehemently. "It's the most demanding, the most merciless work a man can do."

A great deal of this work was the making of stencils for the guidance of our painters, who had somehow to put Hall's pictures on the great walls. There were also friezes that had to run here, there, and everywhere along the walls, high and low—some of them eighty or ninety feet above the ground.

Hall's pictures or designs were first covered with small squares, like the squares of graph paper. The lines of each square were faithfully copied on much larger squares of tough, parchmentlike paper that would not flutter or tear in the strong winds of high places. These lines were then punched through with sharp points. A phonograph needle mounted in a pencil-thick dowel stick was about right. These punched holes were quite close together, about four to the inch. Laboriously and dangerously, these squares were fastened, in proper sequence, to the walls. Then workmen armed with what were called pounce bags—large cheesecloth bags filled with fine-ground charcoal—banged and pounded these bags against the perforations in the paper, with the result that the charcoal went through the holes to become attached to the wall itself. Once all this was done—and it took a long time— the painters could move in and follow the dotted lines with their brushes and paints until the original small drawing that could be held in the hand had become a winged god forty feet high on the great back wall. The friezes ran everywhere, and the many-branched Tree of Life stated its ancient message on wall after wall, a reminder that all life, however varied, grows from one single sacred Source.

The original studio, as distinct from the lot where the big Babylon set was being erected, was packed to its smallest crevice with people working at all sorts of unimaginable tasks. The big stage, which had been built for that abortive shot of a sky full of angels flying to the rescue, was simply a large oblong platform on stilts. No land had ever been leveled for building anything, so there were high and low places under the big stage, according to the rise and fall of the natural contours of the ground. This provided space where people could work, and so the underpart of the big stage became a series of workrooms, mostly for wardrobe people who were sewing metal scales on knitted garments to simulate armor. At another place painters would be decorating chariots with gold, or a fair imitation called Dutch metal. It came in books, like gold leaf, and it had to be applied as carefully as gold leaf itself, handled with a camel's-hair brush and never touched by hand. This was a skill known only to sign painters, so we captured all the sign painters running loose in the Los Angeles area and put them to work gilding.

The old original lot consisting of two houses, two stages, and a few accessory shacks had grown to the bursting point. Thoren, the owner, had been moved out of his own house to make room for progress. Griffith now occupied the lower floor of the Thoren house for his office and dining room. Here he entertained the dignitaries who had money to invest. The upper floor, consisting mostly of bedrooms, was now a chemical laboratory run by a man named Bloom. Bloom was a smooth-faced, smooth-spoken man of medium build and of medium age who seemed to know everything about everything. I asked him, once, what he had done before turning to pictures. "Made and lost five fortunes" was his laconic reply. I questioned him no further, because there was one thing I was sure he didn't know: how to hang on to money.

Bloom's job was to find some way to make the basic developing agent used by our laboratory. This was metol, or monomethylparamidophenol sulphate, once supplied by Bayer in Germany but now denied us by the war blockade. He was succeeding, too, after a fashion. He was producing a dark and messy sort of substance that looked awful and smelled worse. It *could* be used as a developer, but just barely. Anyway, it enabled us to get by, and that was what counted.

Out of all this vast and varied series of preparations the first of the great Babylon sets took form and finish and became ready to use. This was the exterior of the Babylon wall, and around this a battle was to swirl.

That it was to be a big battle that would dwarf all previous picture battles was self-evident. Great attack towers had been built and they were now ready for action. They were square in section at the bottom, and this square tapered to the top, which was the height of the main wall of Babylon. They looked like oil-well derricks boarded up and armored, only they were much broader and heavier. No human power could move them, so we brought in elephants to shove them into battle: big, full-grown elephants to lower their heads and nudge these monstrous towers forward, a few feet at a time. Bridges, or gangways, were hinged at the top. These were to form a bridge over which fighting men could swarm onto the walls. Maybe. Meanwhile, gangs of men with battering rams were to attack the great bronze gates, in spite of the rocks and boiling oil poured down upon them from above.

The more I saw of these preparations for an all-out attack on a walled and defended city, the more I was glad that I had not been born a soldier in that era. Swarm over those teetery planks ninety feet above ground into the teeth of a horde of defenders armed with spears and bows and swords, ready and waiting and eager to do you in. I'd be more likely to sit down on my hunkers and inch over, holding on with both hands and being extra careful not to look down. And as for working a battering ram under a rain of scalding oil and hundred-pound rocks, I think I would have regretfully tendered my resignation, mailing it in from far Cathay.

Well, now, we had the set; we had the equipment; Siegmann had lined up the men—a couple of thousand of them—you'd be surprised how a really big set can eat up people; the costumes were ready; the dressing tents, the size of circus tents, were ready; and even the latrines had been dug, not silly little privies such as we used in Delta but big, majestic twenty-holers as befit the majesty and dignity of our production. The cameras were ready. We had film, carefully ordered from Eastman so as to have but one emulsion number to shoot on. This film had been tested for sensitivity, gradation, and how it would work in our now makeshift developing solutions. We were as ready as we would ever be.

All that remained to be done was to do it.

Karl Brown on the running board of his brand-new 1915 Studebaker. He took the photo with a self-timing device. His mother is resting on the grass and his father in the back seat

KARL BROWN: "This is the only picture (1912–13) I have of a Kinemacolor set. That's David Niles, the director, with his hands on the chair; my father, arms akimbo, is beside him. You can tell by the chairs it's a 'rich' interior. Over the top of the set can be seen the chimneys and roof of one of the houses that remained as part of the Griffith Fine Arts studio-to-be. The open field is now (1973) crowded with apartments and the low hill (Olive Hill) is now the site of a museum"

KARL BROWN: "This photo of my father as a comedy cop shows the 'California construction' of studio buildings: first a framework; then upright boards; then redwood battens nailed over the cracks. The open wiring was standard. It was also called 'board-and-bat construction.' Nobody thought pictures would last, so why waste good money on elaborate buildings?"

KARL BROWN: "This shot of Arrowhead shows what our very good roads were like in 1915. My father at the left is playing Pooh-Bah as usual, while my mother is looking into my camera from the car"

Billy Bitzer's shot of Henry Walthall and Blanche Sweet in *Judith of Bethulia*, which the author asked Bitzer about at their first meeting (see page 12)

Billy Bitzer, right, in 1914 relaxing on *The Clansman* set with Tom Wilson in blackface. *George Mitchell Collection*

Karl Brown as he appeared playing the theme music of Griffith's *Home, Sweet Home* (1914). *Museum of Modern Art*

D. W. Griffith, Douglas Fairbanks, J. A. Barry, and Billy Bitzer (in striped shirt) in 1916. *George Mitchell Collection*

Griffith, with megaphone, directing the strike sequence of *Intolerance*. Karl Brown at right, holding slate, with Bitzer hidden by the camera. *George Mitchell Collection*

Another shot of the same scene, with Bitzer next to camera at far left and Karl Brown (in cap) holding slate. The plate camera above the Pathé is for stills. *George Mitchell Collection*

D. W. Griffith in coolie hat directing *Intolerance*. Karl Brown at extreme right in shirt sleeves, with Bitzer (face hidden) cranking the Pathé camera. *National Film Archive*

The Griffith-Bitzer-Brown trio, with Brown on the far right recording the scene, during the filming of *Intolerance*. The smiling woman directly behind Griffith is Karl Brown's mother. The boy at the left is Ben Alexander

The Babylonian set of *Intolerance* seen from the corner of Talmadge Street and Prospect Avenue in 1915. The ABC-TV studio now (1973) stands at this spot

One of the elephant columns of *Intolerance* under construction. *George Mitchell Collection*

The bacchanal and orgy scene of *Intolerance*. *Paul Ballard Collection*

Workers cleaning the Babylonian set between takes. The lettered sign obscured

ing at upper right reads: D. W. GRIFFITH. *Museum of Modern Art*

ND THE

D. W. Griffith in a posed shot in a balloon on the *Intolerance* set. The words on the banner at the left are part of THE MOTHER AND THE LAW, the original title of the modern sequence of *Intolerance*. *Academy of Motion Picture Arts and Sciences*

Another rare photo of the *Intolerance* set, showing the balloon used for publicity purposes. KARL BROWN: "That figure in the center, facing you, is your author at seventeen going on eighteen." Bitzer's head can be seen behind the camera tripod in center. K.B.: "I designed that special tripod—no pan or tilt. I made all the special effects and multiple exposures and needed rock-steadiness to keep the images from 'weaving.' " Griffith is standing at right beside chair. K.B.: "That's Elmer Clifton under and a little to the right of Griffith's left foot." *Academy of Motion Picture Arts and Sciences*

The *Intolerance* sets crumbling. A move in 1919 to preserve the set as a Hollywood monument got nowhere. *National Film Archive*

D. W. Griffith in 1914. *George Mitchell Collection*

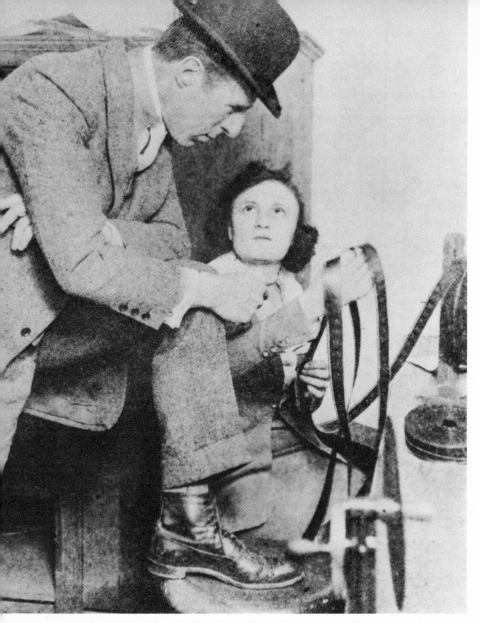

Griffith with Rose Smith, film editor. *Kevin Brownlow Collection*

Griffith at left (his head under the cap appears to be shaven) with Harry E. Aitken, president of Mutual Films. *George Mitchell Collection*

Griffith, center, with Sir Herbert Beerbohm Tree at right and Frank E. Woods at left, on the ballroom set of *Intolerance*. *George Mitchell Collection*

A Griffith portrait by Hendrik Sartov. *Kevin Brownlow Collection*

Rare photo of the Fine Arts studio taken by Karl Brown in 1919 "from what was left of the great wall of Babylon during demolition. The facings had already been taken down, leaving only the skeleton timbers. So I climbed up through these timbers and shot the scene, standing on the boards visible in left foreground. As far as I know, no similar picture can be in existence. At far right that square

black building is the lower stage, roofed in to protect the big sets from weather. The long building with all the windows is the laboratory." Karl Brown took this photo after Griffith "had deserted California for Mamaroneck. All that empty land in the background has since been covered with hospitals. The dimly seen row of eucalyptus trees in right background marks the future site of Paramount"

A traveling shot from the modern sequence of *Intolerance*. Griffith on platform at right, beside Bitzer. Tom Wilson at rear, Miriam Cooper in black hat, Mae Marsh in front seat with driver

Dorothy Gish, Frank Bennett, director Edward Morrissey, George Larsen, and (at far right) Karl Brown shooting the Triangle–Fine Arts film *Stagestruck* at the old Arcade Station in downtown Los Angeles, 1917. *George Mitchell Collection*

Dorothy Gish, director Elmer Clifton, Karl Brown (behind camera) and his assistant George Larsen, and an unknown reporter on a set of *Her Official Father,* Triangle–Fine Arts, 1917. K.B.: "Note Clifton's hat. He's imitating Griffith's freakhat habit, as many others did, notably William de Mille." *George Mitchell Collection*

Elmer Clifton (hatless this time) directing taxicab-fight scene in *Her Official Father*. Karl Brown, wearing hat, at the Pathé camera, and Dorothy Gish, with megaphone, as back-up director on Clifton's first film. *George Mitchell Collection*

SCENE	PRODUCTION NO. F2 DIR. D.W.G. CAMERA, G.W.B.	X	I	E
387	Marsh in past camera, pauses, looks back, sees Gus o.s. runs away through woods 18 ft	✓		
388	Same setup, Gus in, running same, lost, loses sight of Marsh, looks around, sees her and rushes after her, running very fast, 16 ft.			
389	Reverse angle same location, Marsh in from b.g., very scared, looks back, sees Gus, panics, runs out past camera, 15 ft.	✓		
390	Repeat action of Gus in 388 from reverse angle, 16 ft.	✓		
391	Forest, big dead log in f.g., Marsh in from b.g., scrambles over log, tries to find place to hide, sees Gus o.s. Runs out camera left, 20 ft.	✓		
392	Same as 391 except exits to camera right, 20 ft.	✓		
393	Same setup as 391-2, Gus in from b.g., stops at log, looks for hiding place, hears noise o.s., sees Marsh, runs after her, camera left, 18 ft.	✓		
394	Same as 393 except exit camera right, 18 ft.	✓		

Rough sketch, drawn by Karl Brown, of a typical page from his slate, the closest thing to a script in use by Griffith for *The Birth of a Nation* and later films. The first column gives the number of the scene; "Production No. F2" was first called *The Clansman;* "Dir. D.W.G." and "Camera G.W.B." refer to Griffith and Bitzer; "X" means *Exterior,* "I" means *Interior,* and "E" means *Electric* (Cooper-Hewitts, kliegs, and spots). Scene 387 reads: "Marsh (i.e. Mae Marsh) in past camera, pauses, looks back, sees Gus o.s. (off scene), runs away through woods. 18 ft." Thus each scene filmed was recorded on the spot by Karl Brown

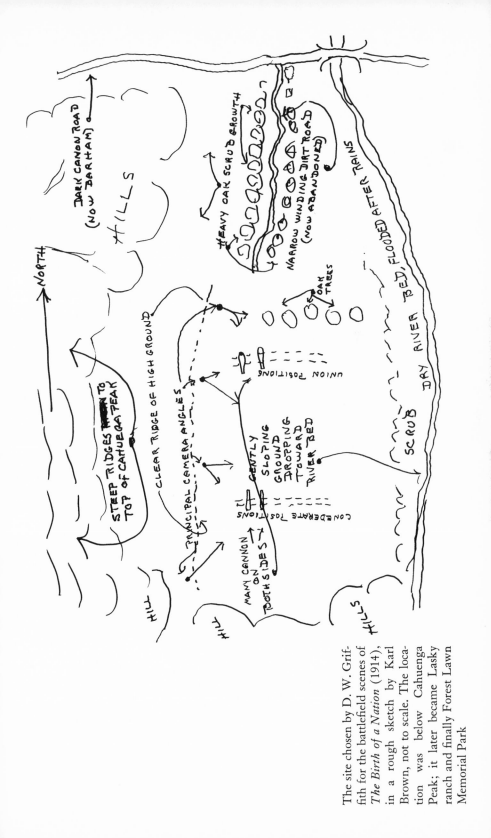

The site chosen by D. W. Griffith for the battlefield scenes of *The Birth of a Nation* (1914), in a rough sketch by Karl Brown. The location was below Cahuenga Peak; it later became Lasky ranch and finally Forest Lawn Memorial Park

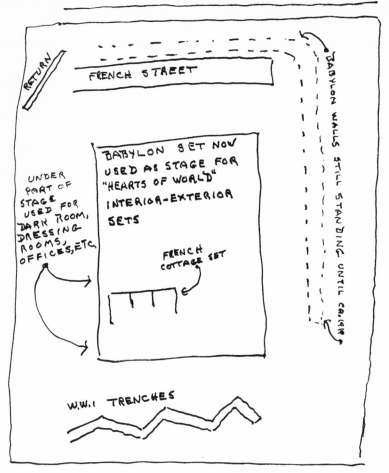

The following labels appear in the drawing:

RETURN

FRENCH STREET

BABYLON WALLS STILL STANDING UNTIL CA. 1919

UNDER PART OF STAGE USED FOR DARK ROOM, DRESSING ROOMS, OFFICES, ETC.

BABYLON SET NOW USED AS STAGE FOR "HEARTS OF WORLD" INTERIOR-EXTERIOR SETS

FRENCH COTTAGE SET

W.W.1 TRENCHES

The Griffith exterior lot, across from the Fine Arts studio, shown in a drawing by Karl Brown (not to scale). The period is 1917–18, during the filming of *Hearts of the World*. The old Babylonian set of *Intolerance* (1915), whose walls remained standing until 1919, was converted into the interior and exterior scenes of the World War I film, for which other footage had been filmed abroad by Griffith

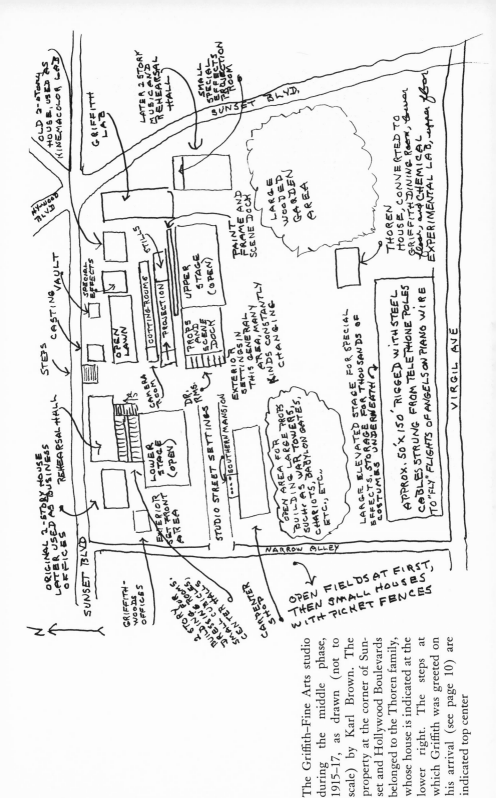

The Griffith–Fine Arts studio during the middle phase, 1915–17, as drawn (not to scale) by Karl Brown. The property at the corner of Sunset and Hollywood Boulevards belonged to the Thoren family, whose house is indicated at the lower right. The steps at which Griffith was greeted on his arrival (see page 10) are indicated top center

Karl Brown in Los Angeles in 1971. *Photo by David Thaxton*

❧ 12 ❧

Babylon, Babylon,
That Mighty City, Babylon

*For in one hour so great
riches is come to nought.*
REVELATION 18, 17

A GREAT wind came howling down out of a cloudless sky to the north, bringing a sandstorm of flying grit from the barren waste that was the San Fernando Valley.

People walked bent over, eyes almost closed, and holding hard to their hats as they made their way along Sunset Boulevard. Signs collapsed, trees were downed, and garbage cans went rattling and leaping along the street with the high spirits of puppies let out to play. For this was a full gale of wind, as the sailors say, and the walls of Babylon swayed and buckled under the onslaught. It appeared to be highly probable that these walls, which had been built at so much cost of time and money, might very well be reduced to splinters before a single inch of film had been made of them.

We all stood around, our clothes whipping in the wind, watching helplessly. All except Huck Wortman, who said, "Well, it ain't going to do no good standing watching. Come on, you fellows. Get some lines on her."

Picks rose and fell as small graves were dug for railroad ties. Heavy ropes —hawsers, really—were attached to the key timbers at the tops. These lines were carried to the railroad ties, made fast, after which the ties were put into their graves and covered over. "Dead men," they were called, and in this case the dead saved our lives, or at least our picture, because the walls held, the wind subsided, and the day was saved. All of which showed that there was more to making a picture than assembling a camera and crew and shooting some actors going through their motions.

The wind, known locally as a Santa Ana, seemed to feel that it had done its full duty by California and moved eastward. The days were clear, calm, and perfect for photography. The soldiers, most of whom had been recruited from the great army of the unemployed, arrived to do battle. Costumed as Assyrians or Babylonians, they were herded through their paces by everyone we had who could handle a group of untrained, and in most cases, unwilling workers.

Griffith used dozens of assistants, each in charge of this unit or that. There was a man named Van Dyke, who must have had a first name but nobody used it. He was called Woody, for some reason. Then there was Monte Blue, who stuck close to Griffith through all the battle, because Monte gave the signals to the various unit directors scattered through the crowds. Crowds, plural, because we had one attacking crowd on the ground to storm the walls and another on the walls to defend them. Monte presented a very war-like appearance because he wore two heavy .45 revolvers, one on each hip, with a number of different-colored flags under one arm. The revolvers were loaded with blanks, and they were for signaling purposes only. A yellow flag meant one thing, a red one another, a green something else. Monte was a very busy man. And of course, down in the crowd or up on the walls, we had our tried-and-true actor-assistants, all in costume, leading their various groups in whatever maneuvers the shots or flags called for. Elmer Clifton, George Siegmann, Joe Henabery, and even Spec Hall had been pressed into service.

So the battle was on, with everybody yelling, throwing things, and being as obnoxious to one another as possible. The towers, pushed by elephants, advanced toward the walls. Then the towers stopped, and there was a lot of commotion and trumpeting of elephants around the towers. Monte Blue blasted a series of shots into the air to signal a halt until someone could find out what was happening.

Siegmann came running to the bottom of the twenty-foot platform from which we were shooting and called up to Griffith, "It's the elephants, sir. They won't mix."

Griffith's answer was nothing if not simple: "Find out what's wrong and fix it."

"Yes, sir."

Siegmann hurried back to where there was quite a bit of turmoil going on around the base of the towers. The elephant men were having a lot of trouble with their elephants. I climbed down with my camera and hurried over to grab any shots that might be of use. I met Hall, whose eyes were dancing with high excitement. From him I learned that there were two kinds of elephants in the group we had ordered, boy elephants and girl elephants, and that the boy elephants saw no point in pushing these silly towers around when there were girl elephants to be courted. The keepers could not control them, so we had to get rid of the boy elephants and let the girls take over the tower-pushing chores. This took time, so it wasn't until after a late lunch hour that we were able to get our first and only shot for the day, that of a general advance by the attacking party on the walls of Babylon.

I don't know how many days we spent shooting that attack from every possible angle. Every time we thought we were all through, Griffith would think of something more to try, so that ran into another day. He even wanted a night shot of the battle, which I thought was an impossibility because there wasn't enough electricity in our studio to even begin to light that vast area.

But it didn't bother Bitzer in the least. He had old Fireworks Wilson come out with all the three-minute magnesium flares he could find. They spent most of the afternoon climbing over the walls and placing these flares in improvised holders. The flares were built on handles, and there were holes bored into each of these handles. These could be slipped over large nails. Huck built a special arrangement by which a horizontal beam held between two uprights could be raised to any position. The flares were mounted on these beams.

Bitzer placed these flare holders himself, always with an eye to having the flares themselves hidden from the camera by some portion of the set. Six flares in one position, four in another, eight at yet another place. And all of this in broad daylight. He couldn't see what the effect would be. He had to know in advance how much light would be needed to cover a given area and set the flares accordingly. This came about as close to dead reckoning as anything in photography could.

The night came. The forces were placed, including our all-girl band of elephants. The warriors were ready on the ground and on the walls and towers.

"Ready, Billy?" asked Griffith.

"Yes, sir. Ready."

Griffith nodded to Monte Blue, who fired one shot into the air. That was the signal to light the fuses, the hissing firesticks that would light the flares. The night was dark, very dark. But we could see the light from the fuses glowing from the various emplacements. Another nod from Griffith. This time Monte let go with two shots, the signal to light all the flares. They came on slowly, because you can't light a bank of eight flares instantly. But when they were all going, it was really a sight to behold. Never was any set so beautifully lit, purely by theory. Bitzer was indeed the master of them all.

Three blasts from Monte's revolver and the action began. The elephants, the men, the towers, all moved forward. There was the din of battle. Everything we had done in the day long-shot was being done even better in this night shot because by now everybody knew from experience what *not* to do.

The flares lasted three minutes. When they went out, the darkness was more than mere blackness. Something of the dazzle of those flares remained in our eyes and made us blinder than blind. But Griffith said, "That's all for tonight," and groped his way to the railed ladder leading twenty feet to the ground. Everybody was dismissed. The camera gear was packed up and taken to the studio. I developed a test end, dried it in alcohol, and blew it up to about sixteen-by-twenty with Woodbury's equipment. It was beautiful.

The film on the screen was beautiful, too. But it drew no "That is very fine" from Griffith. Not that he was unappreciative. But he expected everything from Bitzer to be very fine, so why make a big thing of the obvious?

That battle went on and on, seemingly without purpose or end. I knew that a lot of men on the ground were attacking a lot of men on the walls, but I didn't know why. Nobody that I could talk to seemed to know, either. And nobody seemed to care. After all, it was a Griffith picture, and it was big, very big indeed, and everybody was being paid, so that seemed to satisfy everyone.

The king had to ride his golden chariot along the top of the city wall to direct the battle from above. Fine. So the horses were led up the zigzag ramp at the back of the set, one at a time, while the chariot was brought up by hand, with as many men straining at the tongue and wheels as could get around it. Our cameras (I was running the second camera) were set up on one of the towers, shooting down on the top of the wall below us, with the battle going on way down below on the ground.

Somehow the men who were handling the horses, experienced cowhands all, managed to hitch the horses to the chariot. This took some doing because the horses had horse sense and the footing underneath was anything but firm. Anyway, they were hitched and headed toward us. The signal was given. The soldiers far below, with Siegmann in charge, began to fight. Griffith called, "Fade in," and we faded in. Another signal, and the horses were driven forward at a dead run, straight toward our cameras, while that structure beneath us, weakened by the wind, swayed like grandma's worn-out wicker rocking chair.

I was not the least bit frightened. With careless, almost ostentatious ease, I asked Bitzer, "Wh-wh-what s-s-stop are you u-u-using?"

To which he replied, with perfect *sang-froid,* "F-f-f-eight, or maybe e-e-leven. L-l-look around and s-s-see."

This required leaning out over the edge of the tower. I was sorry I'd asked. But I did so because I had to show that I had nerves of steel. "Ha-ha-halfway between e-e-eight and 'leven," I replied.

He didn't answer. His cigar had become suddenly distasteful, so he flung it over the side. I set my stop to match his. It was hard to do because the ring controlling the stop seemed to be unaccountably wobbly. Strange. It had never behaved that way before.

Huck Wortman came charging up the ramp, red-faced and out of breath. "Mr. Griffith, you can't run horses up here! She ain't built for it!"

Griffith ignored him. He spoke to the horse handlers in a casual tone, "Let's try it again. A little faster, if you can."

Huck was not to be ignored. "And besides, that wind's weakened her I don't know how much. She's liable to collapse on us if we ain't careful!"

Griffith paid not the slightest attention. The horsemen, tough Western wranglers all, would have died rather than let any effete Easterner surpass them in nerve. They unhitched the chariot, ran it back by hand, coaxed and cajoled the trembling horses back to their original positions, and hitched them up.

I studied Griffith as though I had never seen him before. He was leaning casually against a parapet, his cheap straw hat shoved back on his head, his mouth slightly open in a grin of purest delight. The man was actually *enjoying* the situation. Then I happened to remember. This, in principle, was what he had been doing in one way or another as far back as I could remember, betting everything he had, including his life, on an all-or-nothing gamble. A Kentucky aristocrat, scornful of fate.

The horses came charging forward at a runaway, scared-to-death pace. The walls wavered correspondingly. "That was very fine" was his comment. "Did you get it, Billy?"

"Y-y-yes, sir," replied Bitzer instantly, adding with unnecessarily firm emphasis, "I-I s-sure *did!*"

I didn't know how he could be so sure because he hadn't even opened his camera to check for scratches. I opened mine and looked. You don't look at the film, you look at the aperture plate. If there's the slightest speck on that polished steel plate, or on the black-satin covering of the pressure pad, you've got a scratch and that means do it again. Mine were both clean, so we had the scene.

That was all for up there on the wall, at least for the time being. There was no guessing how much more he might think of later on. The horses were led, trembling and snorting, down the ramp. The chariot was taken down next. We went down last. I never knew the earth could feel so solidly good before. No wonder the old Romans called it *terra firma*.

Then there was that business of the toppling tower. Griffith had decided that it would be very fine to have one of those big towers totter and fall right into the camera. How any such thing could possibly have happened in real life was more than I could understand. Because the towers were outside, on the attack, and the defenders were inside the walled city, beating off the enemy. How the people on the *inside* could make a tower on the *outside* fall over was beyond my comprehension. However, that was what Griffith wanted, and it goes without saying that that was what he got.

But not without difficulty. Those eighty-foot-high towers were heavy. Ask any of our elephants. But Huck and his gang of experts figured it out and made all sorts of arrangements to make the tower fall into the camera. They measured and remeasured everything with the greatest of care. I wondered why. I asked and found out that their problem was not so much tipping the tower over but doing so in such a manner as not to kill the cameraman.

This gave me pause, because I had been promoted to second-unit camera, and it was up to me to shoot all the scenes that did not involve the principals, small stuff involving only three or four hundred extras, mere inserts, so to speak. Siegmann could handle these as well as anyone. This meant that I was the cameraman that they were trying not to kill. It was important, too, because if they miscalculated they would have to build another tower and get another cameraman, which would run into time and money, which would probably annoy Griffith.

After much running of tapes and making figures on paper, they showed me exactly where to set up the camera. It wouldn't have been so bad if they'd let it go at that. But Huck told me it would be perfectly safe, nothing to worry about. Then Siegmann told me it would be perfectly safe, nothing to worry about. After five or six had told me it was perfectly safe, nothing to worry about, I began to wonder.

We had lots of cameramen on the lot, and they all had assistants who were young and eager and anxious for advancement. Why not be generous and let one of these—Phil DuBois, for example—share the signal honor of having actually shot a scene for a Griffith picture? They'd jump at the chance, and besides, it would prove to all that I was not the selfish type greedily gobbling up all the glory for myself.

But before I could put this noble thought into action, the men were ready and so, unhappily, was I. I started to turn. Siegmann called, "Let 'er go!"

The tower teetered, leaned, and came down straight at me. It crashed with a totally unnecessary amount of noise. Splinters flew and timbers scattered. I kept on turning. After Siegmann had yelled *"Cut!"* three times, I remembered to stop. But then, it must be remembered that Siegmann was new at directing and that he didn't realize the necessity for taking a good long test at the end of each scene. This particular scene ran about fifteen feet, the test something over forty. Nobody could say I hadn't been thorough.

We were forever going back to take more scenes of action that had been overlooked the first time around or had been thought up overnight. We had any number of long and medium and medium-close shots of Assyrians assaulting the Babylonian defenders from the tops of the towers. But that wasn't good enough. We had to have more really close stuff to get the expressions in full-head close-ups. So we did, endlessly and apparently pointlessly, because we didn't know which side to cheer for or which side to hiss. There was an awful lot of swordplay. In one scene an Assyrian's head was cut clean off by a single slash of a sword—a dummy head, of course.

Somehow we all got so accustomed to working on the heights of those walls and towers that it didn't mean a thing. In some of these attack scenes on the top of the wall, our people took fearful chances without realizing that they were taking any chances at all. I suppose the same thing must be true of topmast hands on sailing vessels or steel workers erecting the framework of a skyscraper or linemen stringing high-tension wires. It is not only conscience that makes cowards of us all; it is also imagination.

Eventually—and it was a long eventuality—we either got through with all that battle stuff or Griffith ran out of ideas. Anyway, we quit all that fighting and moved out to shoot endless scenes of the Assyrian army, under Cyrus or Darius (we were never sure which), advancing along the waters of Babylon to attack the city.

By this time, say about at the end of the first year of shooting, we were all becoming fairly well acquainted with the history of the thing we were trying to approximate. We knew the general geography of Babylonia and how two great rivers, the Euphrates and the Tigris, ran down along roughly parallel courses to empty jointly into the Persian Gulf. This meant that the advancing armies had rivers, big rivers, to contend with. And where do you find rivers of any kind in the Los Angeles area? The answer was plain and clear. You don't.

However, there was a stretch of land between Los Angeles and the sea where there were bodies of water called sloughs. These were shallow depressions in the almost flat coastal plain that had sunk beneath the level of the water table underlying the land and thus were in effect vast open-air wells of fresh water. The sloughs were irregular in shape, so we could choose our waterways at will, anything from a small creek to a mile-wide river. There was no current, so the water did not flow as a river properly should, but there was wind, and the wind set up ripples that gave the appearance of motion, which would have to do. Also, there were wild fowl in great profusion, flying, floating, diving for fish, and enjoying life thoroughly because nobody ever thought of shooting them.

The largest of these was called Dominguez Slough, so the trip there became part of our daily life. Up early, before dawn. Into the studio cars, bag and baggage, cameras, tripods, and film. Plenty of film. More film than we had magazines to hold. Canning exposed film and reloading with raw stock had become an old story by now. Simply find a sheltered spot and go to work with a changing bag, a strange contraption of triple-thick black cloth, a bag with sleeve holes secured with rubber elastic sewn into the armholes. One end was wide open but made to fold over to be secured by strong snaps. Put the magazine into the bag, along with an empty film can to receive the exposed negative and a full can of fresh film. Close snaps, roll up sleeves, insert arms, and then go to work by sense of feel. It was a weird-looking operation to those who didn't know what was happening. A person sitting on the ground with a black bag between his knees, groping at some unseen task.

I was always that person. I never quite trusted that bag to be light-safe, so I always covered it with a lap robe borrowed from one of the drivers. Sometimes it was quite hot in the sun, and with that heavy woolen lap robe over my widespread legs I necessarily perspired quite freely. Certain strangers, coming upon me sitting and working intently at some mysterious but all-absorbing business between my legs, which were covered by the lap robe, would stop momentarily, watch for a while, and then go away making smirking comments. But this also was something I had to get used to.

The trip from the studio to Dominguez Slough became a well-worn path: down Sunset Boulevard to the Plaza, then straight south on Main Street, which soon thinned out into open, rolling country thick with long wind-breaking rows of eucalyptus trees. At a small rise traversed by the narrow road was a big sign advertising acreage for sale at a development called, incongruously, Athens on the Hill. There was a real-estate office but no buyers. But that was nothing unusual. There were real-estate offices with no buyers all over Southern California, especially in the cactus-strewn wastes of the San Fernando Valley.

A few more miles and there was the slough, generally blanketed with fog and calling for a dead halt until the sun burned through. This might take until noon. Sometimes it didn't burn through at all, and that was a day wasted, with our attacking army loafing around, enjoying getting their three dollars a day for nothing, and a free lunch thrown in.

How Siegmann managed to move all this army from the studio to the location, costumed and ready for action upon arrival, was something I was never quite able to understand. It seemed easy enough in theory, because the Pacific Electric trains ran everywhere, up to the top of Mount Lowe, to the Cawston Ostrich farm, to the various beaches, and of course to San Pedro, our port of entry. This line to San Pedro ran close beside our location, so it was a mere matter of loading the men aboard the trains at Sunset and Hollywood and routing them to the Watts–San Pedro line and unloading them practically on the location itself. Sounds easy. But getting all these two or three thousand men out of the holes and warrens in which they lived, getting them costumed and armed and herded into the cars in reasonably sober condition was something altogether else again. For they *would* wander off, and they *would not* stay put, and how Siegmann ever managed to deliver them all on time, morning after morning, to the location must have taken some superhuman doing. I suppose he must have managed them the way they were handled in the battle scenes, in groups. A hundred to Clifton, another hundred to von Stroheim, another to Woody Van Dyke, more to George Hill, Vic Fleming, and so on. These shots of the approaching army were really nothing much more than what we called run-bys. There isn't really very much dramatic conflict to be developed from scenes of men marching. All we could get out of them was scenes of men marching.

However, we *did* get certain scenes that seemed to punch home Griffith's own personal belief in physical fitness. His rule that a man must perspire every day was made part of the Assyrian army routine. We showed them running, wrestling, fencing, sitting around eating voraciously, and bragging with vividly indecent gestures of their short swords as to just what they were going to do with these swords once they caught up with a Babylonian. These scenes delighted Griffith.

More and more people came into the picture. *Cabiria* had been released and we had all seen how eagerly audiences enjoyed the exploits of Maciste, a very big, very strong character who was a modern Hercules in physical prowess. So we had to have a big man or two of our own. One was named Elmo Lincoln, and he was big all over, exactly right. Another was named Milos, and although he was not big all over, he was very big straight up and down, so very tall that he really belonged in a circus sideshow. Milos used to come over to where we were shooting from a six-foot parallel and lean one elbow comfortably on the top to watch the scene. At one time I had to get down to pick up an accessory case. I started toward the ladder, but Milos simply reached up and took me by the waist with both hands and set me down on the ground without the slightest effort. I felt like Gulliver in Brobdingnag.

Constance Talmadge, who had played a fancy dressed-up part in the French episode, was playing a rough, tough, onion-chewing hoyden in this one. She was so wonderfully well liked that nobody ever thought of calling her Miss Talmadge. She was Connie, and she loved it. Connie had to drive her chariot all over everywhere in a wild ride to the rescue of someone, somewhere, who seemed to be in a lot of trouble, nobody knew just what. Anyway, we got the rides to the rescue all safely on film and maybe later Griffith would come up with someone in dire need of rescuing.

We ran the Assyrian army forward, backward, sideways, and crosswise. We shot them in close-ups and long shots, on the land and splashing through the water. I even took a chance on shooting one onrushing scene with a K-3, or deep-yellow filter, and then double-exposing a crescent moon into the resultantly dark sky, together with a wisp of cloud moving over the moon. Luckily everything balanced out and the shot went into the picture.

When we ran out of things to do with the Assyrian army, we went back to the studio and did some shots of Lillian Gish rocking a cradle, all to the tune of Walt Whitman's poetry, which Griffith recited with great feeling and surprisingly good delivery, considering how outstandingly lousy he was as an actor. It must have been one of his good days.

Then we did shots of the Three Fates, hooded old women sitting in a row. One spins a web of yarn from a whirling distaff, the second measures it out more or less at random, while the third snips the cord with a pair of sheep shears. This was Life itself, in the making, the living, and the ending. Woodbury knew the names of all three, but I could remember only the name of the third, which was Atropos, whose snipping shears made such a gruesome sound that Griffith exclaimed, "Gahhhd! If we could only get that *sound!*" He had said that very same thing once before, when the cross was lying flat on the ground in the Biblical story, and the Nazarene, spread-eagled, was being nailed with heavy spikes driven by a heavy hammer into the solid timbers, which gave out a deep-ringing sound that still makes my flesh crawl whenever I remember that moment. "Gahhhd! If we could only get that *sound!*" Well, he could have had it. Everyone could have had it. Sound came first, with the Edison phonograph. Pictures with sound came second when Edison tried, unsuccessfully, to coordinate the two. The two had been joined by others, and the sound-and-picture combination had been demonstrated many years earlier. Yes, and color, too. But nobody wanted it. Pictures were selling well as they were. Let well enough alone . . .

It must not be imagined that because we were in the toils of this monster picture the rest of the studio was idle. Quite the contrary. We had more companies, more directors, more cameramen, and more actors turning out good sensible money-making short and simple pictures, mostly comedies and Westerns. Arthur Mackley took care of the Westerns. Dressed always in the same clothes which, after months of hard use, took on the patina of sweat-soaked age, and wearing the sort of thick, curly-tipped mustache that can be raised only by daily applications of six-shooter smoke, Mackley was so perfect a type as the old-school Western sheriff that he became Sheriff Mackley on and off screen. He was a very good, very conservative director of the sort of Westerns moviegoers love with an intensity of devotion comparable only to small girls' love of old, torn, rag dolls.

The other pictures being turned out on a production-line system ran mostly to comedies and small-town, just-folks sorts of things, all about the trifling troubles of everyday life among the unpretentious. The outright comedies followed the Sennett pattern. Charles Parrott, a pleasant young man who looked like a juvenile lead in anybody's stock company, changed his name to Chase and attained a temporarily solid following of his Charley Chase comedies. Tod Browning used a cane as his trademark and spent most of his time thinking up new ways to get tangled up in it. Eddie Dillon turned out to be an adept director of all sorts of comedies, as did Lloyd Ingraham, who was portly and lovable and innocently but vividly off-color in his speech, especially when he was directing. I remember one time when I was crossing one of the stages as he was directing Dorothy Gish in a light comedy. He was saying, with the most fatherly of earnestness, "Now, honey, when you open that telegram and learn that he's coming back to you, you get so excited that you pee a ring around yourself." This may not have been the purest of polite English, but I doubt if it could have been topped as stage direction. I watched the scene. Dorothy did not follow the instructions to the letter, but she did become very deliciously excited and she did dance around in a whirl of delight that no lesser directorial instruction could have achieved. And besides, Ingraham was developing Dorothy into a very fine young comedienne.

In the meantime, the big set, the really big set, was going up on the lot across the tracks. The building of this set had to wait until we were through with the battle stuff around the walls, because we needed all the room we could get to maneuver our armies and towers and elephants. Now that this was finished, we could clear the land and have room to build. The French set had been struck to make way for the walls and towers. Now the Jerusalem street went the way of all things and so did Golgotha.

As in the case of the big stage, the ground was a gently rolling terrain. Nobody thought of leveling it. It was quicker and easier to build the set on upright timbers, which was just what Huck did.

Naturally enough, it had to be built from the ground up. First the grand stairway, then the flooring. After that, the great swelling columns, designed by Hall after no architectural model I had ever heard of. How he ever managed to hoist those trunk-raised elephants into place was something I never knew because I was busy elsewhere on about as silly a set of errands as one could imagine.

For some reason I had become known and accepted as a musician, which I was not in the accepted understanding of the term. I couldn't play anything. But I could read music, not only well but easily as you can read the printed words that are before you. Griffith was deep in the rehearsing of the various dances to be done at the great feast of Belshazzar and I was tabbed to find the right kind of authentic Oriental music—on records, mind you—and bring it back to the rehearsal hall so our girls could perfect their dances to the sounds of what had to pass for Babylonian music.

So while Huck was building the great hall of the king of Babylon, I was scouring the music shops for anything that could be played on a phonograph for the girls to use for dancing purposes. Of all the stacks of records I brought to the rehearsal room, only one survived to go into the picture as underscoring: the "Bacchanale" from Saint-Saëns' *Samson and Delilah*.

Then Griffith sent for some real Oriental musicians, who brought their ancient instruments to the studio and played all the traditional music they could remember. But most of it was dull, reedy, and to our ears, out of tune. It might have done very well as music to charm cobras with, but it did not fit in with Griffith's ideas of lushly luxurious sensuality. Amy Woodford Finden was going great guns at the time with her make-believe Oriental music, mostly set in the idiom of her famous songs, such as "The Kashmiri Song." These held his attention for quite some time, because they were so popular, these songs about being less than the dust beneath thy chariot wheel, or those pale hands I loved beside the Shalimar. Griffith's instinct was absolutely correct and he should have followed it. If the people—the audience, not the critics—believed this to be the true feeling of the mystic East, then you'd better concur with their beliefs. But he didn't. After trying everything else, he finally sent for Carl Breil and put him to work on the job of thinking up main themes for the main action of the four different pictures all called *The Mother and the Law*. Breil chose to bite into the Biblical picture first, sent for some gray-bearded Hebrew musicologists, and the sounds of the Hebrew wedding-dance and of "Mazel Tov" echoed through the studio for days to come, with Breil striving valiantly to adjust his musical thinking from the diatonic scale he was trained to use to the altogether different scale of Orthodox Judaism, which is neither major nor minor but an entity in itself, like the whole-tone scale of the early Greeks, which was also being explored by daring young moderns like Debussy and Satie.

Time passed and the big set was finally ready. There it stood in all its glory, the bulging pillars surmounted by trumpeting elephants, while at one side sat the great goddess Ishtar nursing a figure of a full-grown man at her enormous breasts. The set glittered with gold and glowed with color. Everything everywhere was richly carved, richly decorated, richly draped. It almost cried aloud for a Kinemacolor camera, so much so that I rigged a Pathé with an extra shutter wheel so as to shoot alternate pictures on red and green filters, did the same thing with a projector, and showed Griffith exactly what color would do for his set. It was no go. He was not a man to do anything by half measures. It had to be all color or no color at all, and he couldn't see retaking over a year's work for the addition of color alone. If he had known in time . . . but he hadn't. Too bad. Sorry.

The problem of shooting this enormous set was solved very simply. A two-level elevator of standard design was built into a tower that rolled on wide-spaced steel mining rails. The track was built at an exact water level, and the flanged steel trucks, four of them, were so exactly fitted and balanced that half-a-dozen men could push them back and forth without trouble. Dead-end stops were fitted at the ends so this rolling platform could not possibly get out of hand or run off the rails. The elevator permitted any camera height from ground level to fifty feet high. It was a beautiful piece of mechanism constructed by backstage experts who had been "flying" whole sets for years, building revolving stages, and installing rising and falling orchestra pits as a matter of routine. There was nothing new or difficult about it, not to them. They looked upon it as a simple matter of flying a couple of cameras and six or eight men, merely a matter of a thousand pounds at the very most, while they had flown literally tons of dead weight in the cramped quarters of the limited space of a stage. And besides, having all this open space to work in, without the need for concealing anything from an audience, and with plenty of counterweights to balance everything out, they found it all so easy that they marveled we should think it so marvelous.

The big day came. The dancers were assembled. People by the thousands, all in gorgeous costumes, were packed everywhere people could be placed, even along the top of the great back wall with its winged god and its twin Trees of Life.

We mounted in the elevator. Bitzer and Griffith were on the top level, and I was beside them with my camera. We had visitors with us; DeWolf Hopper and Douglas Fairbanks went along for the ride. On the second, or lower, level was Woodbury with his still camera, along with men to work the elevator. Monte Blue sat on a topmost beam with his pistols and flags.

The idea of a run-through for rehearsal was discussed and discarded. Might as well shoot it. A final checkup with all the various on-the-set costumed directors: Siegmann, von Stroheim, Woody Van Dyke, George Hill, Vic Fleming. They were ready, the dancing girls were ready, the light was brilliantly good.

Griffith nodded to Monte Blue, who fired a blast from one of his .45's. The action began, with the bacchanale in full swing as the tower glided slowly forward and sank at the same time. The action was beautiful. Everything worked to perfection. The scene had started with a full shot of the entire set, and it continued inward and downward, until it ended with a close-up of the king and his Princess Beloved admiring one another to the rhythm of our great crowd of dancing girls, dancing without music but in perfect cadence.

We ran the big rolling platform-elevator back and forth until we had taken all the long shots we could of the big set. I managed to get some fairly close shots of people on the elephant towers by using a six-inch lens that I had had fitted to my camera. With this much-modified camera I was able to range over the whole set, so to speak, with close-ups that nobody knew anything about, especially the characters in the picture. I got one particularly good shot of a group of people on the top platform of one of the big, swelled-out columns, just under one of the elephants. It was just right. Composition, lighting, everything. It was "very fine," except for one minor detail. One of the gorgeously robed men was having trouble with his underpants, which were too loose or something of the sort. So he hiked up his robe and corrected the trouble with a safety pin. He did this with such earnest concentration that you couldn't see anything else. Which was unfortunate. Not for him, for me. Because the technique of softening, subduing, or even blacking out portions of the printed film was old stuff by now, and it was just another arrow in Griffith's bulging quiver. So that scene became one of the many that I used to find waiting for me at the end of a day's work, carefully numbered as a positive print for me to work over with light box and camera. There were many nights when I regretted ever having thought of that business of reworking the positive release prints. And the fact that I had brought it all upon myself didn't make it one bit easier. That unknown man with his breakaway underbritches could never know how much night work that simple repair cost me.

So we got close-up action, and more and more close-up action. It didn't seem to mean much as far as I could see. A couple of high priests plotted to betray Babylon for reasons of their own. It appeared that Alfred Paget— pardon me, King Belshazzar—should have worshipped the ancient sun god instead of Ishtar, the most female of all possible female goddesses, whose seated image was forever before his eyes and whose precepts he followed with the greatest of pleasure. So the priests plotted, in good old reliable melodramatic whispers, to open the water gate so that Cyrus or Darius could sweep into the city and take it without a struggle.

This was all good plotting of the sort I could understand, but if that was what was to happen, why all that battling at the walls? There was so much about the picture that didn't hang together that I soon stopped trying to understand any of it.

Here we had a set that alone must have cost more than the entire production of *The Clansman*. And what was the big moment of this big set with its big everything? Why, the king sends a message from his side of the table to the princess at the other side, with the equivalent of an early-day greeting card drawn in a tiny golden cart by a pair of harnessed white doves. Talk of the mountain laboring and bringing forth a mouse! Even Woodbury commented on it, saying that it was like piling Pelion on Ossa, only in reverse, whatever he may have meant by that.

Then came what was to me, at that time, the greatest injustice ever to be inflicted upon me at any time in my whole life, absolutely without exception. Let me explain it to you carefully so there can be no mistake: Belshazzar worshipped female flesh, as represented by the huge nude figure of Ishtar, which was forever before his eyes. In doing so he was breaking no new ground; it was right there in the Bible, plain as print could make it, that Solomon had one thousand wives. (One of the favorite pastimes of the back-of-the-camera crew was figuring out his schedule, or how long it took him to get around to wife number one thousand, assuming that he was in good working condition all the time.)

Well, like Solomon, Belshazzar had his wives and lots of them, and they were all beautiful, the best the empire could provide. There had to be a scene in which King B. picked out his wife for the night. It was to be like any other beauty contest, with the eligibles draped around the throne but otherwise not draped at all, so he could make an intelligent choice unhampered by concealing clothing.

Our girls, beauties all, were to play the wives. Good! For time had been creeping up on me and I was now eighteen going on nineteen and of the age when I felt it to be a grownup dignity to complain about the nuisance of having to shave all the time. Naturally, I would be right there with Griffith and Bitzer shooting this scene. That goes without saying. And when my mother came home for dinner the night before this scene was to be shot, and complained that she had had a hard day getting the girls—*all* the girls— ready for this scene, and that the credit title would probably have to read, "Razors by Gillette," my anticipation knew no bounds.

Oh sure, I had been taking these girls out to dinner and whatever shows were playing at the Mason Opera House as a matter of natural course. Why not? I had had a couple of the raises called for by the contract and my worn-out old Studebaker had been replaced by a Graham-Paige, advertised as the most beautiful car in America, so my invitations were never refused. I had taken them more or less in rotation because—well, if you must know the truth—I would in all probability consider the matter of marriage in the not-too-distant future, and I felt it not unwise to survey the field and check them out, more or less, before making a final decision. So I never took the same girl out twice for, like Solomon, I had a lot of ground to cover, if that is the phrase.

But now I was to have the finest possible chance to do a bit of, shall we say, window-shopping or perhaps comparison-shopping, all together. How could such an opportunity occur again? I counted myself so blessed that I could hardly sleep that night, thinking of the boon that was to be mine the following day.

And can you guess what happened? They actually barred me from the set. And for the flimsiest of reasons. Said I was too young. Can you imagine any injustice so crass? Bitzer was allowed in, but what possible good could that do him? He was already married. Griffith also was married, or had been. Everybody allowed inside that closely guarded set had nothing to learn, while I, with everything to find out about, was excluded. Injustice, that's what it was.

I managed to dredge up one small bit of comfort for my stricken soul: eventually I'd see that scene on screen.

But it wouldn't be the same, at all.

Damnit!

ℒ 13 ℒ

The Perilous Edge

Awake, arise, or be forever fallen!
MILTON, "PARADISE LOST"

AND so, after spending something like $2 million and close to a year and a half out of our lives, Griffith shuffled all four versions of *The Mother and the Law* together like a pack of cards, and called the resulting four-ply story *Intolerance*.

It was a big picture in every possible respect. Furthermore, it was designed to be shown as a great theatrical spectacle in full-sized theaters at advanced prices. It required a full orchestra of symphonic proportions and a backstage crew of sound-effects men to build up the hullabaloo and clamor of battle. It also required packed houses to pay for the cost of showing the film—and it didn't get them.

It was, in short, a flop.

Not that it dropped dead—*boom!*—like that. No, it was a lingering death, and all the more distressing, because the issue was never in doubt. There was never a question of if, but only of when, it would die of box-office malnutrition.

Our publicity department, headed by Frank Woods, worked valiantly to save the day. It was no go, and for the simplest of reasons.

I had always admired Griffith for the plain, simple, common-sense way in which he had regarded his audiences as his Supreme Court sitting in continuous judgment on all things that he did, thought, or hoped for. What had happened to throw him so tragically off from his previously infallible sense of audience acceptance?

I heard many explanations. Too many. And too complex. And by far much too learned. And yet to me the answer seemed to be perfectly obvious.

We had a saying, "Keep your eye on the ball." Well, Griffith had taken his eye from the ball, not momentarily but for eighteen months, a year and a half. There was a war on, remember? And when we started this very long picture, people were determined to have no part of the war. Our politicians kept reminding us that George Washington himself, the Father of his Country and revered as a demigod, had warned us against becoming embroiled in any foreign entanglements. And our current President, Woodrow Wilson, had been swept into a second term with a whoop and a hurrah for his campaign slogan, "He kept us out of war." That was the mood of the country when we started the picture eventually known as *Intolerance*. A song that was sweeping the country was, "I Didn't Raise My Boy to Be a Soldier, to Kill Some Other Mother's Darling Boy." Everybody was for Peace at any Price—another hard-hitting slogan—together with the reasonable conclusion that there never had been a good war or a bad peace.

So it took Griffith a year and a half to build his tremendous indictment of man's inhumanity to man, together with a quadruple statement to the effect that this had always been so, and the implied warning that we'd better quit all this sort of nonsense before it's forever too late. *Intolerance* was nothing more or less than a good old-fashioned pulpit-pounding hell-fire sermon preaching peace on earth, good will to men as the only alternative to the hatred and bloodshed that comes of greed and intolerance.

I saw the picture more than once, mostly to try to find out what all these various critics were writing about. One of them called it "Griffith's crazy quilt."

It was nothing of the sort. During the shooting of the picture I had never been able to make much story sense of what was being played before the cameras, but once assembled and once its theme had been clearly stated in tones of brass from Breil's great orchestra, everything fit together. What if he did switch from period to period and back and forth, playing all four stories in parallel action? How else could anyone punch home the universality of the twin monsters of the world, intolerance and greed, except through showing this recurring nightmare of the ages through the history of man's life on earth?

And how could anyone glorify the rewards of peace more effectively than by showing innocent little children playing in a beautiful, flowery field where all was as lovely as nature could make it? I remember the shooting of that final scene well. The setting was an open, unspoiled natural garden that stretched between the railroad tracks and the mountains of Griffith Park, just to the north of a narrow asphalted road that someone had flattered by calling it Los Feliz Boulevard. There was nothing there to break the pure beauty of the picture: no houses, utility poles, nothing.

We assembled the children and let them play in this idyllic setting. What touched me most deeply was nothing that Griffith said. It came from Bitzer, of all people, when he looked longingly at a beautiful child and growled softly with an infinity of regret in his voice, "That's the only thing worth living for. Yes, damnit! The only thing!" Well, he should know. He'd tried everything else and now he had come full circle, back to the beginning of all things.

I was now able to see what all the fighting was about in the Babylonian period of the picture. It was simple enough once it was all put together. Belshazzar had something the Persians wanted: culture, beauty, peace. So they took it by a combination of force of arms and treachery. The history of the world packed into a few thousand feet of film.

Griffith had succeeded, not only well but brilliantly so. But he had succeeded with the wrong thing at the wrong time, for the world had changed. People who had been singing about not wanting their boy to be a soldier were now hot for war. The Germans had been sinking our ships and all the other shipping they could hit with their unrestricted submarine warfare. Never mind whether our ships had been carrying munitions to the Allies; they were our ships and our men were being killed. And that was one thing we would *not* stand for, no-sir-ree, sir! They torpedoed the *Lusitania,* which went down with the loss of over a hundred American lives, kindling the war fever to an even higher pitch. The newspapers were filled with more and more stories of German atrocities: little Belgian children with their hands cut off at the wrists; nurse Edith Cavell shot by a German firing-squad for helping British prisoners to escape.

America awoke with a start to the realization that we had no standing army worthy of the name. Well, the way things had been going from bad to worse with the Allies, we'd better build one and in a hurry, too. Yes, and a navy, too.

Preparedness became the one and only thing our people cared about. Broomstick-armed civilians were marching and countermarching in vacant fields all across the country. Some who could not wait for an actual declaration of war to get into the fight managed to join English and Canadian and Italian forces in any capacity. Ambulance driving, flying, anything at all.

There was a Preparedness Parade in San Francisco. A bomb was thrown, people killed, and the culprits captured. They were members of the hated I.W.W., the Industrial Workers of the World, whose belief was that since labor produced all the wealth, all the wealth should belong to labor. The initials were soon read as I Won't Work, which somehow became shortened to Wobblies, a term of utter contempt.

More things kept piling up. There was a huge explosion in Jersey City's

"Black Tom" depot. Forty million dollars' loss of munitions intended for the Allies, the work of German saboteurs working undercover right here in our own country. Less spectacular but more frightening was the silent visit of a German submarine to one of our harbors, bringing a full load of drugs and dyes. It was all done so swiftly and so secretly that it was all over with long before the people were even dimly aware of what had happened. The shock was profound, for if the U-boats could slip into one harbor with nobody the wiser, what was to stop them from entering New York harbor to torpedo warships in the Brooklyn Navy Yard, or from hitting us anywhere else? What had been an emotional reaction to the crimes committed against the people of other countries now became a very real fear of what might happen to us if we didn't move fast to jump into this fight with both feet. The fear became something close to mob hysteria. Anything and everything German or even German-sounding was hated. Nobody would touch sauerkraut until some genius renamed it Liberty Cabbage. Frankfurters and wienerwurst became hot dogs.

It was into this hate-poisoned atmosphere that Griffith launched his filmed diatribe against intolerance and greed. Naturally it failed. It could do nothing else in a world that wanted nothing but war.

Meanwhile, other companies had been rushing out quickies damning the Germans from hell to breakfast. The Kaiser became officially the Beast of Berlin. One of our assistants, Erich von Stroheim, became a blazing star overnight because he could portray the stiff-necked, shaven-headed, monocle-wearing, scar-faced, evil-leering Prussian officer—overeducated, overpolite, and sneeringly overcruel—so that he was eventually billed as the Man You Love to Hate.

The picture business was booming. Everybody was making money except Griffith, who was losing it hand over fist. There was no doubt in the picture colony of Griffith's personal situation. He had been knocked flat to the canvas and the referee was counting. It was questionable whether he could ever get to his feet in time to save himself from being counted out: out of the fight, out of the ring, out of the business.

We saw nothing of Griffith around the studio during these worst of bad days for him. He was in New York for a long time getting ready for his grand New York opening. Then we heard that he had gone to London with his picture, to try his luck there. From then on everything we learned of him came through hearsay. Fortunately, our hearsay was pretty reliable, because it came from Grace Kingsley, a remarkable character in her own right.

Grace—everybody called her Grace—was a maiden lady of uncertain years much given to flowered prints and the latest gossip. She went everywhere in town, saw and knew what everybody was doing, and she reported it faithfully in the Los Angeles *Times*. Grace was welcome everywhere because she not only collected news but she also spread it. She never had to pump news out of people. She exchanged confidences with them on a friend-to-friend basis. Nobody held back anything, because Grace was not only virginal in her personal life but even more so in her reporting. She would not touch scandal in any way, no matter how juicy it might be. She reported picture doings only, not bedroom escapades, brawls, separations, or desertions. Her idea of picture news was to tell who was doing what, where, when, and for how long. This sort of information was vital to free-lance actors, cameramen, and technicians. It gave them a daily guide to where jobs were open or were about to open. Her section of the *Times* was a sort of trade paper, read by everyone in the business as the first thing to do every morning.

I had seen a lot of Grace during the shooting of all the Griffith pictures. I saw even more of her during this fallow time when Griffith was away and there was nothing much for me to do. I had a car and Grace did not. So I drove her around from studio to studio as a sort of privilege because she was as concerned about Griffith's apparent downfall as I was, and she gave me whatever little bits and scraps of information about Griffith she could glean from the *Times* news wires.

Fitted together, these bits and pieces built a sort of grim picture of the merciless persistence with which the worst of bad luck had been dogging Griffith across the Atlantic. He prepared for the London opening with the most elaborate of expensive ballyhoo, only to have the picture open on the very day that the United States declared war on Germany. How could Griffith have foreseen such destructive timing? His Evil Genius knew, and it was on this fateful day of April 6, 1917, that he made his last desperate effort to achieve recognition for his masterpiece.

In the face of such a tremendous break in the deadlocked war, nobody in London had the slightest interest in the troubles of ancient Babylon, medieval France, or in the Passion they already knew by heart, while they cared nothing for the miseries of lower-class American working people.* I couldn't help thinking how Griffith must have felt on that electrifying night. For here was *his* story, the story he had used so effectively time and time again, played right out before his eyes: his famous run to the rescue. Only this time it was not a handful of desperate people but a typical Griffith production on the most gigantic scale: all Europe under the iron heel of a monstrous

---

* *Intolerance* was seen by English audiences as supporting their fight against Prussian intolerance and was actually better received than in America. KEVIN BROWNLOW

enemy, with the rescue now coming from the massed might of the United States of America. What a picture he could have made of this instead of *Intolerance,* if he could have foreseen! But he couldn't. Nobody could.

Life at the studio went on much as it had before. Elmer Clifton was promoted to director and I was his cameraman. Without realizing it, I had become a true cameraman in the sense that all my interest was brought to a sharp focus toward getting the best pictures I possibly could of what was before the camera. Stories were not in my department; I ignored them. One had Bobby Harron as an inventor, driving himself far into the night to perfect whatever it was he was working on. Another had Dorothy Gish in a strange sort of comedy in which she was pursued by a lover who had been deliberately chosen from the crowd of extras because he was the most ungainly, awkward, hopelessly inept actor anyone had ever seen. Apparently it was thought that he would be so bad he would be good, in the Cherry Sisters tradition. He wasn't, he was merely bad. We did a third picture in which Dorothy rode a bicycle all over the countryside, going from town to town selling Liberty Bonds. This went better, because nothing having to do with arming for war could fail at that particular time.

Then Grace came in with news that sent all our hearts soaring. Griffith had found a backer. No, correction; a backer had found Griffith, and that backer was the *British Government!* It wanted him to do a picture dealing with the Allied cause. He could do it his own way. Carte blanche absolutely. They'd furnish everything. Just name it. Battles? They had miles of film of real battle scenes, with real men being killed by real bullets, shells, explosions. Ruined villages? They had them in great profusion, from the Channel to the Alps. Airplanes? All freely his to use as he saw fit, except when they were needed for actual combat. Actors? Choose from the best, in or out of uniform. It was all in his hands. No interference, and preferential treatment from all the Allied governments, which now included the United States, headed by Woodrow Wilson, who was a confirmed movie fan and a great admirer of Griffith.

Now time began to crawl as we waited for news of Griffith's safe return to America. There was no shipping news of any kind. Sailings had been kept under the strictest of censorship since the beginning of submarine warfare. But news of sinkings could not be hidden, because the German press and radio news dispatches boasted of these sinkings with triumphant glee, usually before the Allied governments knew they had happened. These German broadcasts of German victories were shot out from their most powerful radio transmitter at Nauheim, to be received by our equally powerful station at Bound Brook. They were in Morse, of course, and our newspapers were quick to make use of them as news of the very first importance.

We searched every newspaper for the sinkings and the lists of the lost and the saved. Griffith's name did not appear on any of them. Then we learned, with great relief, that he had not left England at all but had cabled for his own contract people to join him in London to make the new picture.

Contract people? I was one of his contract people!

For a few delirious days I was walking on air. London, Paris, the battlefront, the trenches. I had always dreamed of travel and adventure and now here it was, all to be mine. Yes, I was well aware that there would be danger and lots of it: submarine wolf packs lying in wait, zeppelins over London, Paris being bombed by a long-range German gun that nobody could locate or silence. These considerations gave me pause, but not for long. For Lillian and Dorothy Gish were going, and if these *girls* could stand it, I'd be damned if I'd show the white feather, even if it killed me. And besides, if I had to be killed, wouldn't it be better to go out in a blaze of glory?

And then again, what if something happened to Bitzer? I would naturally step into his place. Not that I exactly hoped that any such dreadful fate would befall Bitzer, but as a poet has said, hope springs eternal in the—I mean, it's just as well to be prepared for any contingency by having a back-up man in reserve. There was not the faintest doubt in my mind that I could handle Bitzer's job, not only well but brilliantly. After all, if I could make a spider look good, what *couldn't* I do with Lillian Gish?

I had no sooner screwed my courage up to the sticking point than I was informed that I couldn't go because I was too old. Too *old!* What irony. Here I had been yearning for the time when I'd be twenty-one and become my own man, only to learn that I couldn't leave the country under any conditions because we were at war and I would soon be eligible for military service under the new draft law. There was nothing Griffith or anyone else could do about it. And so all the rest of the Griffith people went, leaving me a forlorn orphan of the storm of war.

The shock of bleak despair was followed by a fierce upsurge of outrage. Leave *me*, would they? Well, I'd show 'em. I'd get myself another job, that's what I'd do. There were plenty of studios in town and I'd pick the best one, dig in, and when they got back they'd find me well established in my own right and beholden to nobody.

But when I announced my determination at the dinner table that night, my father and mother both jumped on me with both feet. What about my contract? My mother rummaged and found it and showed me where it said

I could work for Griffith only, nobody else. So I was stuck, frozen, unable to move. I left the table—illegally, without first saying "Excuse me"—and stamped out into the garden to play ball.

Then suddenly, out of nowhere, came a bright ray of dazzling hope into my black-clouded life. It appeared that the passport people had to know everything about everybody, including proof that they had actually been born. And it further appeared that Billy Bitzer, whose official signature was G. W. Bitzer, was actually Gottlob Wilhelm Bitzer, than which no name could possibly be more German. Everything had to stop while Bitzer was investigated. For this was war, and American-born Germans *must* have engineered that Black Tom explosion and set up that secret visit of the U-boat.

Anyway, my dreams soared. If they nailed Bitzer, well . . . I had been second in command, so to speak. Why shouldn't I step naturally and easily into his place? Inexperienced? Nonsense! During the early exploitation of *Intolerance,* I had shot three pictures all by myself, with Elmer Clifton directing Dorothy Gish. They hadn't amounted to much as pictures, but I had shot them and there had been no retakes. So I was a full-fledged cameraman in my own right and I could prove it, too.

Grace Kingsley herself had used those very words, "full-fledged cameraman in his own right," in an article in the Los Angeles *Times.* I will not pretend that she did it without help. I will not pretend that I had in any way understated the importance of my promotion during one of our trips from studio to studio. The printed result occupied only three short lines near the bottom of her next day's story, but I felt at the time that although it was disappointingly terse, it was not Grace's fault. It was right there, in imperishable print, and if you can't believe the Los Angeles *Times,* what can you believe?

The bubble of future glory grew bigger and bigger, taking on more and more glorious colors, until I went to the studio one morning to discover that the entire Griffith contingent had left the night before, including Bitzer. And without so much as a single word to me.

Next morning I set out to see what I could to drive dull care away. I got into the car and drove out over Cahuenga Pass to see what was what at Universal City, an adventure all in itself. The Pacific Electric cars ran over a shelf cut into the east side of the pass, while the road ran over a similar shelf gouged out of the west side, with a rocky ravine between and below. The road was never intended for automobile traffic and it proved it by twisting and turning and climbing in short, sharp pitches that became worse and worse as it climbed, until the crest was reached over a series of potholes and bumps that forced all but the most powerful cars to drop back all the way into low gear. There were a few drivers who boasted that they could sail over the Pass without shifting gears. But then you will find liars wherever you go.

Once over the top it was an easy downgrade to the bottom, where a turn to the right brought Universal City into immediate view. It was really a city, too, incorporated as one, with its own post office. And it was owned, lock, stock, and barrel, by paunchy little Carl Laemmle, who was forever smiling and who had a face almost exactly like the Billiken dolls they sold in amusement parks. He was so beamingly pleasant that he was known affectionately as Uncle Carl. The studio frontage was set well back from the road, and it was all done in mission style, with lots of curves and plenty of empty bell openings. The open area was guarded by great eucalyptus trees, five feet thick at the base and towering eighty or more feet into the air.

This area was the assembling place of all the extra people who hung around waiting for the crook of an assistant's finger that would get them a day's work. It was also a great hangout for Western types, who showed up in boots and spurs, gun belts and guns, some of them with cow ponies and ropes, ready to take a shortcut over the hill and head 'em off at the pass at a moment's notice. For Universal was dedicated mostly to Westerns. It made other kinds of pictures, too, but they ran from bad to awful to simply terrible. It made its money on Westerns and lost it on dramas.

There was always a free show going on outside the studio entrance. Stunt riders did all sorts of fancy horsemanship: flying mounts, grabbing handkerchiefs from the ground at a dead run, and of course making all the different kinds of falls any director might be able to use. Fast-draw techniques were argued, and knife throwing from all positions from upright to rolling on the ground was demonstrated. It was all for a purpose. Someone might see them from a front-office window—even Uncle Carl himself—after which a bored assistant might step out, crook his finger at the lucky one, say, "You," and that lucky someone would be sure of a day's work and a free lunch and a little something at the end of the day to pay toward his arrears in rent.

The men were usually active, showing off, hoping someone would notice them. The women kept to themselves, at one side, exchanging gossip. I didn't know any of these people, but nearly all of them knew me. Not that I was famous or anything like that. Simply because Griffith had used all the extras in town at one time or another on *The Clansman* (as I couldn't help remembering it) or on *Intolerance;* they had seen me on the camera platforms, heard me called by name repeatedly, and so it was a totally one-sided introduction. But that's the fate of all cameramen. During the course of a few years, thousands of picture people see and come to know the cameraman, while the cameraman sees all these people merely as a swarm of shifting faces and bodies in ever-changing crowds, as thousands of indistinguishable individuals melted into a mass.

I turned around and drove back over the pass, being careful to go down the Hollywood side in second gear on compression, letting the engine brake the car. The rear-wheel brakes, which were collars clamped to the outside brake drums and operated through iron rods and toggles connected to the brake pedal, were always a problem. They were almost never in balance, and when one held better than the other, the car would slew around. It was better to let the engine do the braking, because that way the power would be equal for both wheels. The rule, observed by all but those dead to caution, was to descend a grade in the same gear used to get up.

The walls of the canyon forming the pass squeezed together and flattened out on the Hollywood side. The Pacific Electric car tracks and the roadway came together at the head of Highland Avenue. This left a little triangle of level land just before they joined, and it formed the site of a busy and prosperous repair shop for cars with burned-out clutches, stripped gears, and other casualties of the Pass, including total wrecks waiting to be towed away for salvage.

Coast down Highland to the Hollywood Hotel, which sat on the corner of Hollywood and Highland like a setting hen, spreading its broad verandas all around to shelter the harried city dwellers of Los Angeles who came all the way out here to restore their shattered nerves in the peace and quiet of rural Hollywood.

Turn left and go east on Hollywood, past elegant residences set well back from the road and approached by curving driveways. No business, of course, for this was strictly a residential district. Towering palms, fifty or sixty feet high, lined both sides of the roadway. There was a little cluster of necessary stores at Hollywood and Cahuenga (which was pronounced Co-*wen*-ga and which nobody could spell. Nobody could spell or pronounce Figueroa, either, so they ducked the issue by calling it Fig). There were a grocery store, a drugstore, a cigar store, and a brand-new bank of modest proportions located on the four corners of the intersection. These were allowed as necessities. Other stores were feeling for a foothold around this little cluster, but the going was hard. The residents didn't want their peace and quiet broken by a lot of cheap tradesmen and the riffraff they'd attract.

Continue to Vine Street, then turn right. Down Vine. And there, at the left-hand side of the street, stretched the block-long Famous Players–Lasky studio, a solid frontage of gray-painted, two-story wooden buildings extending all the way down to Sunset Boulevard. Big-boled, broad-branching pepper trees hung their lacy leaves and clusters of red berries all along the front of the studio, which, like all the established studios, had only a single entrance around which more crowds of extras were waiting to be noticed.

The studio had started in the same year and in the same manner that Griffith had started his studio, from scratch. We had perhaps a shade the better of it. We had two houses and two open stages and some scene docks and dressing rooms left over from the defunct Kinemacolor Company. They had only an old barn. We had grown, they had grown, and by now the Lasky studio covered all of the square block bounded by Vine Street, Sunset, Argyle, and Selma, along with a second square block to the east, always called the Argyle lot, for standing sets such as the New York Street, the Slum Street, an Elegant Mansion or two, all left standing and ready to be redressed by the art department to become anything a director might desire. Anything could become anything else provided the walls and braces were in place, and it was no trick at all for the art department of any studio to turn Hogan's Alley into a Norman Village.

I knew some people in that studio quite well. The head cameraman was Al Wyckoff, who shot the De Mille pictures and had the hire and fire over everybody in the camera department. Frank Woods had moved in as general supervisor of all story properties. One of our actors in *The Clansman,* known as Wally Reid, who played the part of a strong young blacksmith and made his entrance with a full-sized anvil cradled in his forearms, was now *Wallace* Reid, if you please, and a Big Name in his own right. Strange are the ways of pictures. Yesterday's blacksmith was now Don José, playing opposite Geraldine Farrar in *Carmen.* Even stranger to me was the idea of hiring a top-flight opera singer to appear in silent pictures.

Inside this studio was a girl who had also set her heart on becoming a famous player. I met her by sheerest accident. I was going into the Bimini baths, a very large indoor set of swimming pools or plunges located over a never-failing spring of artesian water at Third and Vermont. As I was passing one of the plunges, a face popped up from below and said, "Hello." It was a very nice face, what I could see of it. It belonged to nobody I knew, so I said, "Hello," and went on into the dressing rooms.

In the pool this girl swam over to talk with me. She had worked on some retakes on *Intolerance* so of course she knew me well, while I didn't know her at all. She was learning to swim to get ready for an upcoming part, so

I very naturally did what I could to help her learn. If there is any better way to become acquainted quickly, I've never heard of it.

Her name was Edna Mae Cooper. I took her to her home, where she lived with her widowed mother. She was buying it, a little down and a little whenever the payments were due. A solid, far-seeing girl. I was impressed. Well, one thing led to another. I discovered that she liked to eat, so I took her out to dinner. Her mother liked to eat, so she went along, too.

From one point of view it was all to the good. Since the dissolution of the Griffith stock company had left my father and mother without jobs, I didn't feel that I was in any position to support more than one family, including Ida Belle, our maid. But from another point of view it had drawbacks. Edna loved to ride, and on days when she was not working and on many evenings, we rode here, there, and everywhere, to see the country by day and the moon by night. All S.O.P., or would have been, except for Jack.

Jack was a dog. Not an ordinary house dog but a professional, hard-working sheepdog whose regular line of work had been to manage herds of hundreds of sheep. For the Hollywood that used to be had been a great sheep-raising country, so much so that the residents had a law on the books forbidding the driving of more than a limited number of sheep down Hollywood Boulevard. Jack had been injured in some way, and his owner had left him with Edna for rest and recuperation. The owner reclaimed his dog and tried to put him back to work. But Jack had other ideas. To his limited intelligence it was much easier to herd one girl than five hundred sheep, so he ran away and found his way back to his beloved Edna. The owner came and took Jack away again, and once again Jack ran away and was found waiting at Edna's door, tired, hungry, footsore, and thirsty, but happy. This time the owner gave Jack up. Being wise in the ways of the animal world, he knew that you can't argue with a dog in love.

Jack dearly loved to ride. Covering miles and miles of territory without doing it on his own four feet was a luxury new to him and he treasured it beyond measure. He needed no invitation. He was always the first one into the car, leaping easily over the closed door and claiming the back seat as his own.

One night when we had paused to see if the moon was still there, Edna said, from the far side of the front seat, "Put your arm around me."

"Huh!?"

She repeated, very calmly, "I said, put your arm around me."

Well, I had been told that no gentleman ever refuses any reasonable or even unreasonable request by a lady, so I slid swiftly over to oblige—when all hell broke loose from that back seat. Jack was up and snarling, teeth bared and clashing like castanets, hackles raised and eyes glowing in such a manner as to put the Hound of the Baskervilles to shame. I wasn't at all scared, though. Just petrified.

Not so Edna. She spoke, with unnecessary calm and deliberation, "No, Jack. It's all right. I asked him."

Whereupon Jack's fury subsided to a low-muttering growl. He remained poised for instant attack, his eyes never leaving me for an instant. Edna explained very casually, "Jack thinks that I'm a sheep and everybody else is a wolf. He won't let anyone so much as shake hands with me. I thought you'd like to know. Now why don't you move back to your own side? It'll make Jack feel better."

I did. Jack eased down onto the back seat. The rumbling in his throat stopped. But he never took his eyes off me. He now knew me for what I was and he was taking no chances.

A poet has written that the course of true love never did run smooth. Mine never had a chance to get started. I once drove Winifred Westover to San Francisco to see the Fair. Mamma Westover was planted inexorably in the back seat all the way there and back. In San Francisco Winifred Westover's father took charge of me. Clyde Westover was a newspaper man and president of the Press Club. He put me up at the club, while poor Winifred had to live at home with her ever-vigilant mother, way over in Piedmont across the bay. These things have a way of working themselves out. I became discouraged and quit, so she had to settle for Bill Hart instead of me.

Same way with Mildred Harris. She, along with twenty or thirty other girls of the Griffith stock company, was being mother-henned by my mother, who also kept an experienced eye on me. If one of her girls went astray after business hours, it could not be charged to my mother, because she could not be everywhere always, while the girls not only could be but were. I was under the Searching Eye *all* the time, because if I ever became involved in any sort of scandal, people would begin to wonder how she could supervise the behavior of all these girls when she couldn't manage her own son. After a few tentative dates, I lost interest in Mildred and she was reduced to marrying Charlie Chaplin.

Except for some widely scattered big houses here and there, the area surrounding the Famous Players–Lasky studio was given over to orange groves. Many orange trees had to be uprooted to make space for the studio stages and buildings. The local people objected loudly. It had taken years to bring these trees to bearing, while in their view the movies were a thing of the moment, soon to pass. This protest didn't change anything. The Lasky company owned the land, and down went the orange trees. But not the peppers. They furnished welcome shade to the western side of the studio, shielding it from a sun that could get very hot indeed when it warmed up to its work.

Most of the new studios were little concerns that could be built on an ordinary lot anywhere out of the high-priced district. All that was needed was a platform big enough for a small set, some diffusers and flats for reflectors, some thrown-together dressing rooms and offices, and that was it. Actors were no problem. There were thousands of them, mostly out of work and more coming in every day. There were also cameramen of sorts, and stage directors from small-town rep companies, together with grips and prop men and anyone else who had had anything to do with the theater.

The war was increasing in ferocity, and it seemed to me that the U-boats were everywhere, sinking everything from a rowboat on up to the proudest battleships. Crossing the Atlantic was not so much an ocean voyage as a running of the gantlet. Would Griffith ever be able to make it back home? The tension grew with every passing day. This was a cliff-hanger for sure, to use a term derived from the widely popular serials. Another word had also crept into the language of the street: *spurlos versenkt,* sunk without a trace. So maybe Griffith and all his little group were already dead. We could never know; only guess.

I tried to divert myself by coming to grips with the only phase of music left open to me. Performance was clearly not for me. I could play the piano, yes, but not in such manner as to impair the appetite of Josef Hofmann or to cause Sergei Rachmaninoff to be plunged into despair. So I went to Blanchard Hall, our music center of the time, and began to butt my head against the unyielding walls of harmony, theory, and composition. No go. I could never understand the why of using a double sharp or a double flat to move a note one whole tone up or down. Why not just move it up or down? But that would never do, because chords have to be spelled, like words. Why go through all that hullabaloosh, anyway? The real secret of success in music is to get a catchy tune and then hire an arranger. That's what Irving Berlin and Georgie Cohan had done, and nobody was complaining about *their* music.

Then the word was flashed that Griffith had arrived safe in New York with his little group. I stood not upon the order of my going but got out of Blanchard Hall fast, trailing no clouds of glory but leaving a lot of misspelled enharmonic changes and unresolved dominant ninths in my wake. The hell with music, Griffith was back!

We knew the exact hour of his expected time of arrival and I was right there at the Arcade station, motor tuned and tank filled, ready and waiting in case nobody else should be there to meet the train. I couldn't have been more mistaken. Mac was there with Griffith's big blue Fiat, along with Charlie Muth and his Packard, Eddie Hungerford with his Pierce-Arrow. There were a lot of other people there, too, among them Frank Woods, Harry Carr, and Grace Kingsley and a covey of news cameramen. Yes, and little Bennie Ziedman, Jack Lloyd, and I don't know how many other publicity men.

The train came clanking solemnly in, to come to rest with a relieved s-s-sigh. And there was Griffith, grinning and waving from the end of a middle car, while Lillian and Dorothy Gish, with their mother, descended to be swallowed up by the waiting crowd of question-laden reporters. Griffith came down. To my astonishment, he was smoking a cigarette. I had never seen him smoke at all before. Then back of him came Bitzer, looking drawn and tense, tired and discouraged. Bitzer also was smoking a cigarette. I had never seen him smoke anything but cigars before.

Bitzer saw me from the top of the train platform and motioned to me to stay put. He pushed through the crowd and came straight to where I was waiting beside my car. "Let's get out of here," he said. "Get away from this mob."

As soon as he was in beside me, I whipped the car around and darted away to be ahead of the rest of the cars. Bitzer cried out, "Easy! Take it easy! Think I want to be killed ... *now?*"

I slowed down and moved smoothly through town, headed for Sunset Boulevard. Bitzer found a box of cigarettes in his pocket. It was a cardboard box with a picture of a sailor and the word "Players" across the top. He lit one from the stub of the cigarette in his mouth. His hands were shaky.

"Pretty tough, huh?" I asked.

He nodded. "It was the gas, mostly. Turns your water into lungs—I mean, your lungs into water. Terrible."

There were a lot of things I wanted to ask him, but I felt that this was no time to probe into the gory details of what he must have seen. We rode along in silence together, with Bitzer lighting fresh cigarettes from the stubs of the old ones.

"What do you do when you want a smoke and don't have one to light from?" I asked, feeling that to be a neutral subject.

"Use this," he answered, drawing half a yard of bright yellow, loosely woven cord from his pocket. It had a wheel-like gadget at one end. "Trench lighter," he explained. "Flip this little wheel with your thumb and it throws sparks. Cord glows. No flame to draw enemy fire. Pull back. Little metal ball cuts off air, douses fire. Everybody uses them. Never run out of matches. Can't use matches anyway. Too wet in those trenches. Full of mud and rain. Mud and duckboards and rats. Hope I never live to see those red rat eyes glowing in the dark again. Horrible. And that *smell* . . ."

He fell silent. I did not urge him to continue. It was all too clear why all those rats were there. The dead. Out in all that barbed wire.

As we came to the old familiar sights of Hollywood, his mood seemed to brighten. He began to tell about some of the good things that had happened. An elegant dinner at Simpson's, but with the beef weighed out on scales because of wartime rationing. Plenty of Brussels sprouts, though. "To help the suffering Belgians," he added, with a flicker of his old-time gallows-wit. Of a brilliant musical extravaganza that was playing to packed houses, war or no war, *Chu Chin Chow*. Gay, bright, wonderful.

We soon pulled up in front of his home, a big, broad, low-nestling house guarded by towering, ragged deodars. The lawn had been cut that morning and the air was full of the sweet aroma of new-cut grass. Mockingbirds were yelling from the trees, and somewhere up the street someone, probably a school-girl, was playing Nevin's "A Day in Venice" very haltingly.

Bitzer was home, really home, and his face showed it. "Thanks for the ride. See you at the studio later on."

"Hey! What about your luggage?"

"Left it with the porter, to be checked. Pick it up later, soon as I know where I'm going to live."

I waited while he walked up to the front door. He opened it with his key and went inside. The door closed. There were no raised voices or crashes of any kind, so I drove away, reflecting that journeys end in lovers meeting. Sometimes.

The next days were some of the strangest I had ever spent in any studio. Confusion, dismay, rumors, and an awful lot of red-faced people I had never seen before shouting at one another. "All right, all right, dammit! We'll just *see* about that!" seemed to be the favorite line of dialogue. Those of us who had been with Griffith during his great days could only stand around and wonder what it was all about. We were all there: Abe Scholtz and Joe Aller, Cash Shockey and Huck Wortman, and even the phenomenally profane Polish stage carpenter known only as Max (pronounced Mocks), who had a last name that didn't do him or us any good because it could not be pronounced even by victims of hay fever. Rose and Jimmy Smith, of course. All the Old Guard on hand, and all of us helpless in the grip of these officious strangers.

The result of this day's turmoil was that Griffith was barred from his own studio. A concession was granted. He could use the *Intolerance* lot, where the big set was still standing, but not the main studio. Not even the projection-room, or cutting rooms, or anything else. Film? Not an inch. Credit? The very mention of that word brought an infuriated response, "Credit, schmedit, what do you take us for, schnooks? We gave him credit once before and what did he do? Lost us a million dollars and that ain't hay!"

"But he's accepted that debt upon himself. He'll pay it back, every penny of it."

"Yes, but *when?* Answer us that—when? Nah! We've heard that before."

The emergence of the lowly nickelodeon from a smelly storeroom to a grand enterprise making millions upon millions of dollars had attracted what was known as the fast-money crowd. They worked a dog-eat-dog system described by a writer named Lawson in a book called *Frenzied Finance,* which was much in the news. The picture business was no longer a business but a crap game, in which the dice were rolling all the time at several million dollars a throw. Crooked dice were part of the game, and the operator who could get away with them was known admiringly as a smart operator. The Wolf of Wall Street was the hero of their world, in which no mercy was ever shown to anyone, while the losers were simply obliterated.

This whole situation reminded me of the familiar old school-taught thing about what can happen for the want of a horseshoe nail. The nail in this instance was Frank Woods, who was now a prize captive of the Famous Players–Lasky company. Frank Woods may not have been the most infallible of judges of story properties, but as a pourer of oil on troubled waters he was without doubt the best pourer of oil in the business. He could have smoothed out everything in half a day. But he wasn't there, so we of the Griffith company moved across the street to the triangular lot where the Babylon set was still standing, to work with whatever we could find.

Griffith arrived, his big blue Fiat bumping and rocking over the uneven ground. He got out, as tall, straight, and immaculately tailored and groomed as ever. He was smiling and confident. With him was a shabbily dressed little man in baggy tweeds and wearing a cap. He had a curly mustache, apparently made of fine strands of copper wire.

Huck Wortman was the first to speak to Griffith. "What kind of sets do you want, Mr. Griffith, and where do you want 'em?"

"Mr. Baker here will tell you all about it. Mr. Baker, this is Frank Wortman, our master builder."

They shook hands. Griffith continued, "Mr. Baker will draw the pictures and you'll take it from there. Good enough?"

"Yes, *sir!*" Huck and Charlie Baker walked away together, talking earnestly.

Bitzer stepped in to ask, "What about film?"

Griffith's eyes were wandering all over the Belshazzar set, surveying the elephants, the statue of Ishtar, the great swelling columns, the immense back wall. Days of glory remembered in the hour of sorrow. There was a long pause. Then, suddenly snapping back to the present, he said, "Film? Oh, I arranged all that last night with Mr. Woods. Go out to the Lasky studio. They'll give us all we want."

Bitzer turned to me and spoke in a swift undertone, "Better scramble out there fast and get all you can. Go on. Scat!"

I scatted. I shot out Sunset Boulevard, turned up Argyle, and drove through the Argyle gate of the Lasky Studio, jumped out, and rushed into Al Wyckoff's office. Wyckoff looked up from his desk, recognized me, and rose with both hands extended. Remembered me instantly, although we hadn't worked together for a long, long time; five years, anyway.

"I'm here to pick up some film for Mr. Griffith," I began breathlessly.

"Yes, I know. How much do you want?"

I didn't know how much Griffith might need. He was indifferent, even wasteful of film. So I played it safe by saying, "All you've got."

Wyckoff smiled dryly. "Well, we do have quite a lot in our vaults, but I'd hate to part with all of it in case one of our own companies might want to shoot a scene or two. How about twenty thousand feet for a starter? If you use that up, you can always come back for more later in the day."

I said that would be fine, so he got into the car with me and helped me load cases of film into the back seat. I didn't have to sign anything. Everything had been taken care of in the front office.

By the time I got back to the *Intolerance* lot, Huck and his carpenters were already putting up the first set, guided by a drawing done on the spot by Charlie Baker. I looked at the drawing, which had been placed to one side on a sawhorse. It was not really a drawing at all but a fine watercolor done in the style of Arthur Rackham, with strong lines filled in with color. It was of the interior of a French farmhouse, complete to the finest detail. Not a matter of walls and doors and windows but a completely furnished set with chairs and tables and even flowers in the big bow window upstage. He had not only designed and drawn the set but he had dressed it, down to the texture of the floors and the aging of the worn furniture.

This fellow Baker would very obviously be worth cultivating. He reminded me of Hall, because he was so different. Hall had been a precisionist, Baker was an impressionist. One gave the facts, the other the effect of the facts. It was not until the set was up and ready to shoot that I realized how very much difference there could be between the two methods. The set had not only been designed, it had been *lighted*. Shaded corners were painted darker than the open areas that caught the light from the big upstage window. The farther from the window, the darker the walls. Shockey claimed no credit for this. "Just painted her like she was in the picture," he said. "That's what the boss said to do and that's what I done."

Strange. Here we were at a time when the neutral light of diffused daylight was about at an end, superseded by the unlimited flexibility of a wide variety of electrical lights. And only now, at this very late date, were we to learn that light can be painted *into* a set.

The day for shooting came. The set was ready, we were ready and waiting. A lot of other people were waiting, too. People who had worked with Griffith in the past, many of them, a crowd. Even Fairbanks was there, grinning and joking with Bobby Harron in his French, buttoned-back uniform coat, calling it a coat d'amour, whatever he meant by that.

Griffith arrived. He walked up the Babylon steps to the French farmhouse interior set, sprawled back in his usual kitchen chair, and began to rehearse a scene in which Bobby Harron enters from the outside to speak excitedly to Lillian, in English. Griffith halted him. "Speak French, both of you. Always French. Too many lip-readers know the difference. Go out and come in again."

He did. This time he came in and poured out a stream of meaningless French-sounding syllables that sounded like *"B'jou, b'jou, b'jou . . ."* However, the difference in his manner was astonishing. Apparently there is something about even *trying* to speak French that brings forth a whole new set of facial expressions and Gallic gestures.

And so the day went. Their child, in the picture, was an adorable little angel named Ben Alexander. He was absolutely charming. Dorothy Gish, as the German-hating French spitfire, was in her element and giving her finest performance. She could distill more venom into the word *Boche* than you'd believe possible.

We worked for days on the palace floor that had become our stage. Griffith thought of more and more things to do, which required more and more rooms of different kinds to be added to the original layout. Charlie Baker drew them all, perched comfortably on the temple steps with his pad of Whatman's watercolor paper on his lap, drawing and coloring and singing to himself as a matter of habit.

Charlie Baker was the most persistently pleasant human being I have ever met. He was his own best company, and he liked being who and what he was very much indeed. If there was anything highbrow about him it never showed. He was forever singing his favorite, "Knocked 'em in the Old Kent Road," using a dialect that defied all description and that he evidently relished.

Charlie would finish a sketch, tear it from the block, and show it to Griffith, who would always say it was very fine, after which it was passed on to Huck Wortman, who would now treat it as Holy Writ.

One day I found Huck and Max and some of the other help scratching their heads over a rough floor plan of what had started out as a single room. The additions went this way and that way until at least two of the rooms occupied the space of the original one. But nobody cared, a matter of curiosity only.

At some time during our first days of shooting on the *Intolerance* lot, we learned that the whole studio was now free and open to Griffith and our credit was unlimited. No more borrowing film, no more makeshift quarters. Nobody really knew what had happened, but the general guess was that word of these little money-lenders hampering a government project had reached up to where the big power lay, and that the word that had come back down had been more emphatic than polite. In any case, from then on it was "Yes, Mr. Griffith! Immediately, Mr. Griffith! Anything you say, Mr. Griffith!"

No wonder Griffith was so utterly devoted to his last-minute rescue. It had been happening to him repeatedly and infallibly ever since he had abandoned the play-it-safe idea of serving under others and had taken the long chance, way back in 1908, by making pictures *his* way, despite anything his bosses tried to make him do. *Intolerance* had *not* been a failure; it had merely failed to make money for the moneymen. Someday it would come into its own. And that's all that matters to any artist worthy of the name.

He was sure of this current picture, as yet unnamed. I could see why as the scenes were being played before the cameras. He was doing everything that had ever worked for him before. The only difference was that he was doing it better. And his confidence was unlimited. Never an instant of doubt or irresolution. He had his own story to show in his own way, he had his own people whom he trusted absolutely, and he had absolute freedom. What more could anyone want?

He had made mistakes in the past. Many of them. But these mistakes had been made through trying to show too much too quickly for his type of audience to grasp. He would not make this mistake again.

With unlimited backing and with armies at his command, he chose the simplest human story he could devise, the tragedy of one little group of ordinary people caught in the grip of a war they never wanted and could not understand. Where he could have had a cast of thousands, he concentrated on a few little people of no national or international significance or grandeur to tell a story of a small town overrun by tragedy, a town inhabited by people everybody could know and understand and take into their hearts.

Yes, there were big scenes, too. But these were merely to emphasize the massiveness of the juggernaut that was rolling over France and Belgium. Griffith was like a champion who had once been floored and who was now fighting his way out of a corner. He was using nothing but his best blows, delivered with all the power he could put behind them.

The thought of being called old hat never entered his mind, or if it did, he never betrayed it. There is always a gay dance before a great battle. He had one in *The Clansman* and he had one in this,* one in which I came within an ace of burning down the dance hall and everyone in it.

It was a big dance hall located downtown on Grand Avenue. It was gay with buntings and flags and draperies. Everything went fine until I was called in to make a still. This called for a flashlight picture. So I placed a cap under the hammer of as big a flash tray as I could find, loaded it high with as much flash powder as it would hold, set the shutter on bulb, called, "Still!" and when the dancers were still, I opened the shutter and tripped the flash, releasing an enormous billow of fire that surged up and sent all those folds of bunting and streamers billowing to the ceiling. Bitzer looked at me and winced. My invisible Guardian Angel unquestionably mopped his cosmic forehead with one wing. Griffith never even looked around. These things happen.

This same Guardian Angel was given a very good workout through much of the rest of the shooting. I was sent out to where the National Guard was to fire shrapnel at a target. Griffith wanted a close-up of a shrapnel shell bursting in air. I found the target and set up so as to cover the area just in front of the target, for this was where the shell should burst.

The gun was located quite far away. I could barely see it. But at the flash of fire I began to turn. The shell burst some fifty feet behind me. I might have stayed for another try, but some soldiers came tearing up in a car and grabbed me and the camera, and hustled me out of the target area. I never felt so lucky in my life.

At another time I was sent aloft to get some air-to-air shots of a plane painted with the black cross of Germany coming in to bomb or strafe the village. It didn't make much difference which because he already had the bomb-

---

* There is a betrothal party, before war is declared, and a dance involving Germans, subtitled: "Von Strohm and others demonstrate the harshness of trench life." KEVIN BROWNLOW

ing (real) and the strafing (real), but he needed a close-up of the plane with the black crosses. Besides, the actual bombing might look silly and get a laugh, because all the pilot could do was to heave a bomb over the side and hope it would hit something important. And there were no planes fitted with machine guns that were available to us. Our entire air force had only about fifty planes, with thirty or forty officers to fly them, and they were all more than busy elsewhere.

So we got a couple of stunt fliers who had been barnstorming county fairs for a living and painted one of the planes with black crosses, while they tied me into the back cockpit of the other with clothesline so I wouldn't fall out if the plane turned upside down. The camera was lashed by the tripod to the side of the camera plane by the same clothesline. The Pathé would never stand the prop wash with those big flat wooden magazines, so I used the nice little compact Debrie that Bitzer had brought back with him.

Everything was ready. We took off and sailed back and forth and around and about over the same Dominguez Slough we had used in *Intolerance*, trying to maneuver the planes close enough together to get the shot without tangling wings. It was all very awkward. I had to stand up to the limit of my tether to work the camera handle and the pan and tilt cranks, and I was working mostly with my back to the pilot. I had been given a flying helmet of leather, with ear flaps pointing backward so as to keep the propwash out of my ears. With my back to the wash, they worked like funnels, giving me the full benefit of the breeze boring into my ears.

I shot as much as I could, as often as I could, before running out of film. Reloading was out of the question. You have to unlock the Debrie and lift the entire front end and open both sides to get at the magazines, and that was no job to be attempted aboard a bucking airplane, leaning over the side to get at the camera. I motioned to the pilot to go down.

It so happened that I had theater tickets for a play at the Mason Opera House for that night. I took Edna. She enjoyed the play very much. I enjoyed it, too, the visible part. I had to take the dialogue on faith, because the wash from that propeller, funneled into my ears by the flaps of the helmet, had made me stone deaf. Couldn't hear a thing. It was the first silent stage play I had ever seen.

But I was happy. I'd had a nice free airplane ride and I was sure the shots were good because we had come close to brushing wings more than once. I couldn't possibly know at the time that Griffith would drop the entire sequence out of the picture or that my pilot would be killed within the next few weeks, losing control of his plane and falling into a deadly spin. Blessed are the ignorant . . .

The filming moved right along on schedule. We built a French street, behind the *Intolerance* set, and blew it to flinders by shellfire coming from real guns shown in close-up, stubby, vicious, short-barreled things with a big recoil mechanism mounted on the outside. They fired from camouflage, and at every blast leaves came snowing down from the concealing foliage spread over nets. Shot in France, of course, at the actual battlefront, but because of the way the film was cut, you'd swear they were just outside the village.

We cut zigzag trenches in front of the temple set and rigged rainpipes overhead. We had duckboards and mud and sandbags and incoming shellfire sending the men scurrying to dugouts when they weren't going over the top, yelling their lungs out. We had men wounded, men dying, men being carried to the rear to be tended (in real England) by Lady Diana Manners and her bevy of nurse-clad beauties. The film was continually switching from Hollywood to France to England and back to Hollywood, all within seconds of running time. A gun was fired in France and its shell shattered a wall on the *Intolerance* lot. The falling debris caught actor Adolphe Lestina, and after the dust had cleared, all we could see of him was one hand reaching up out of that pile of rubble, clutching, clutching . . .

All very easy, nothing to it. All you have to do is memorize every frame of every foot of fifty reels of footage supplied by the War office and then nip out bits from here and there to flow into your live action. Three feet here, a foot there, ten frames somewhere else, and it's done. Anybody could do it. That is, anybody who had learned how through making upward of four hundred pictures to get the hang of it. Not everybody had been willing or able to go through such heroic educational drudgery. And that, perhaps, was why there was only one Griffith.

The picture was finally all on film. A title was selected: *Hearts of the World*. Pretty silly, if you'd asked me. But nobody asked me.

A date was set for the opening at Clune's Auditorium. The place was packed to the rafters for the opening. We were all there, for the fate of Griffith and all of us who were with him would be decided within the next two hours.

It began slowly. That was typical of all of Griffith's pictures. There was a lot of stuff that people already knew about from the newspaper headlines about the war. Then there was all that cute stuff that some people said marred all the Griffith pictures, with coy dimpling and fluttering and even the orchestra playing a peek-a-boo song for that stuff with little Bennie Alexander.

But when the war rumbled into this idyllic world, what a difference. Here was the sheer brutality of the mailed fist smashing everyone's lives and hopes. George Siegmann was superb. No smirking von Stroheim he, but a slobbering swine who opened bottles by smashing the necks across the nearest table or chair, and he drank from the jagged edges, letting the overflow spill down his chin and onto his uniform. When he gave an order to one of his own German soldiers, he smacked the man across the face with the barrel of his pistol to get his attention. Then he gave him the order. This was not an officer at all but a Beast of the Apocalypse.

For his story, Griffith stuck doggedly to the simple lives of his simple people caught in the tide of hate and brutality, helpless and hopeless and yet clinging to what seemed to be hope in spite of all. In a world where there was no comfort, they comforted one another. It was all they could give because it was all they had.

Just as all possible hope had flickered out, and our poor, pitiable, but dearly beloved innocent people were huddled together near that big bay window in the farmhouse, Griffith threw away the book and *played his silent picture climax in terms of sound and sound alone!* No cutting back and forth at ever-increasing speed to whip up emotion. No. An offstage sound, very faint. Tramp, tramp, tramp. Our people stared, wondering if they had heard right. Stared in breathless suspense. Tramp, tramp, tramp, louder and nearer. The thin reedy sound of a distant band. And still nothing on the screen but those faces, reflecting the hope that was rising as they strained to see whether this was life or death. The sound came closer and louder, yet there was nothing on the screen but the faces filling with joy that overflowed into tears as *they* knew who were coming, if we did not.

The tramping, now very loud, was shaking the floor of the theater. The orchestra threw away all ideas of symphony and became a brass band, and a military band at that, joined by the great power of the auditorium organ as the head of the column of marching men passed that window close enough that one could reach out and touch them. And they were *Americans!*

The colors passed with a mighty ruffle of drums, and then the band, visually on the screen but actually in the orchestra, blared out Georgie Cohan's one great contribution to the war, his bugle-call song, "Over There!" The soldiers kept marching past that window, young and clean and incredibly fine after what we had seen of Siegmann and his hoglike Huns, and there seemed to be no end to them. On they came, more and more and more of them, and still more and more as the curtains closed and the picture was at an end.

There had been no applause, no cheering. The audience had picked up that marching rhythm and their feet were hammering the floor in cadence with the music, which by now was at its peak.

The lights came up. The people simply stared at one another, stunned by the experience. No elation. More of a grim setting of jaws and squaring of shoulders. They began to stream out, a sober and a determined crowd, unlike any I had ever seen before. Their blood was up and they didn't care who knew it.

There was only one mistake made in the staging of that picture. Nobody foresaw the mood of that audience. Otherwise they'd have had a recruiting station set up in the lobby. And they'd have signed up every man-jack.

Including me.

⚮ 14 ⚮

If at First You Don't Succeed, Try Something Else

Freedom lies in being bold.
ROBERT FROST

I CAN'T remember when the grapes were quite so sour as they were after the release of *Hearts of the World*. The general opinion, expressed in terms of hurt indignation, was that Griffith had botched his picture abominably. Made a mess of it. And what was it, after all? A made-to-order, government-sponsored, paid-in-advance *propaganda* picture! Horrible.

And I can't remember when our publicity department was ever quite so delighted as sour criticism after sourer criticism came in. Bennie Ziedman, Bill Keefe, and Jack Lloyd, all proud to be back with Griffith, collected these as treasured trophies and pasted them into a big album that they called a press book. They let me thumb through this book because I was by now an established old-timer of almost twenty-one, and they pointed out some of the more delicious tidbits, especially those by the critics who had moved the once despised nickelodeon into the class of a fit subject for their Olympian notice.

According to these erudite gentlemen, the old gray mare she ain't what she used to be. They harked back to the good old days when Griffith handled point-counterpoint with the most exquisite of skill as compared with this latest rabble-rousing exercise in blatancy. Once a master of the *épée*, he had now degenerated to a wielder of the meat ax. Griffith had sold out. No longer an artist, he was now a mere hireling grinding out propaganda to order, without honesty, integrity, or even the slightest shadow of the former greatness he had shown in his twin masterpieces, *The Birth of a Nation* and *Intolerance*.

Strange. When these now-revered pictures had appeared, the same exquisite essayists had slashed at him with every verbal weapon in their literary armories.* That which they had formerly scorned was now excellence beyond compare, while this latest offering was just so much thrown-together *blague.* The reason for all the deep chuckles by our publicity men was the smashing success of *Hearts of the World* wherever it was shown. Here was one picture that did not have to be sold to the exhibitors. They were all begging to get it, but with no luck. If anyone wanted to see the picture, they could go to where it was being shown, properly, with full orchestra and a busy crew of backstage sound-effects men.

Perhaps the greatest source of delight among the Griffith people was the heart-chewing remorse of the moneymen who had refused to put so much as one penny into the picture. I know that I was personally overjoyed by the thought of what they must have been going through. Not that I was particularly vindictive, but these men had put a few thousand into *The Birth of a Nation* and had taken out millions, with which they had bought chains of theaters and founded studios and had become extravagantly rich. Then they had put a few more thousand into *Intolerance,* cannily spreading the risk among themselves, gambling what had become to them small change from the money Griffith had made for them. When they lost their piffling investment, they set out to murder Griffith professionally, denying him even the use of his own studio. They snapped up his offer of full recompense, which he did not really owe in any legal or moral sense. And now that he had swept on to another victory, despite all they could do to destroy him, I could not help dancing inwardly, because they had been shown in their true light as the proverbial rats that desert a sinking ship.

If any of this had affected Griffith in an essential way, I most certainly could not see it. The only visible change in him was that he seemed to be more relaxed, and to smile and laugh more easily than before. Not that he ever laughed easily. The Griffith laugh was more on the order of a sudden and alarming seizure of some sort. I can't possibly describe it, but you can find out what it was like if you are willing to risk a chancy experiment. Find a secluded place, the more secluded the better; look around carefully to be sure nobody can see or overhear; then laugh backward. Yes, I said backward. Laugh by drawing your breath in, not out. Make it as loud as possible, only with indrawn breath. This will produce a strangling sound that will bring people running if they chance to overhear it. I tried it just once and somebody called the doctor. But with Griffith it sounded fine, because it meant that all was well, and that's what mattered to us.

* Though there was a great deal of criticism about the racial aspect of *The Birth of a Nation,* little evidence survives of a systematic denigration of Griffith's films. KEVIN BROWNLOW

Griffith never talked about the war or of his war experiences, except to remark with an air of betrayal that it was not at all dramatic. But then, how could it be otherwise? For unless you know the people involved in a life-and-death struggle, there isn't much you can feel about it other than a vague sorrow that such things can be.

Add the fact that these men are in gas masks, which dehumanize them, and that the air is full of blinding smoke, which turns them into wraiths, and it all becomes a mechanical monstrosity. I know. I saw miles of the real war stuff he brought back and it was—I hate to say this, but it's true—boring. So I suppose drama can come only through your own emotional involvement with the people or things that you cherish.

I did not know Griffith, not really, even though I had always been within sight and sound of him every working day of his Hollywood life, except for the times when I was on some special assignment elsewhere. His head was longer and his nose more beaklike than that of any man I ever knew. His personal peculiarities were there for all to see, because he made not the slightest effort to be other than what he naturally was, like it or not. When he wanted exercise he exercised, regardless of the size of the set or how many people, important or unimportant, were there. He had his little fears, one of which was loss of hair. At one time, during the shooting of *The Clansman,* he heard or read that shaving the head would encourage hair growth. No sooner said than done. He appeared next morning on the battlefield set during a scalding heat wave bald as an ostrich egg. The blazing sun soon reminded him that a hat would be a good idea, so he found a cheap straw hat of the sort generally put on horses. But this let in no air, so he borrowed Bitzer's scissors and cut four large holes around the top and sides of the hat for ventilation. The sun was very hot and his scalp quite bare, so he came on the set for the next day's shooting with four large, red, angry blisters on his scalp. Did this bother him or make him shy or apologetic? Not at all. Such things happen, and what about it, anyway?

He kept changing hats, trying to find one that would protect his head and yet let in the air. He finally found one, an Oriental contrivance that was a mere hatband holding a dish-shaped sunshade of yellow straw. He wore this all through the summer he was shooting *Intolerance,* and he liked it very much indeed. He wore it everywhere, regardless of the occasion. After all, what is clothing for except for comfort and protection? As for his other clothing, such as suits, shirts, shoes, and so on, he adopted the eminently sensible method of letting the best tailors and haberdashers fit him with the best money could buy and of employing an experienced valet to see that he was properly turned out each day—except for the hats. As for food, he had his own chef prepare his meals in the kitchen of the Thoren house, right there on the lot, so that no time would be lost away from the work on hand. This was a sensible luxury that gave him just that much more time to do what he was cut out for.

I had known Griffith for—let's see, now—from 1913 to 1918—five years. And he was always so different and yet the same that he reminded me of a river, sometimes swollen to flood proportions by success, as when he did *Intolerance* following the inundation of money from *The Clansman,* and sometimes dried down to not much more than a trickle because of lack of money. It seemed to make no difference to Griffith, either way. He was an infinitely adaptable artist, able to make beauty of whatever came to hand.

People not connected with the business side of filmmaking do not realize that it takes time, sometimes a long time, for a picture to earn its cost, let alone return a substantial profit. *Hearts of the World* was a smash hit, but it would be a long time before it returned enough money to Griffith to enable him to follow it with another big one.

So it astonished none of us when he turned this in-between time to use by making a nasty little offbeat melodrama in which Henry Walthall, known to all as the very Bayard of chivalry, up to and including *sans peur et sans reproche,* was cast as about as despicable a cowardly turncoat as one could imagine, in a picture with a typically bad title, *The Great Love.*

In this one Walthall played the dirtiest kind of scoundrel possible, a man who could smile and smile and yet be a villain.* He was a respected, honored Briton by day, but by night he drove his expensive car to the target areas the Germans wanted to destroy and shone his spotlight upward to show the Zeps where to drop their bombs. The fact that Henry couldn't drive a car at all made no difference to Griffith. We'd think of something. We always had, so Griffith never gave the matter a second thought.

Our crew fastened a camera platform to the back of Eddie Hungerford's big Pierce-Arrow, and they attached an ingenious towing arrangement of steel rods to the front of the foreign car in which Walthall was to speed all over the highways and byways of Griffith Park. I was elected to do the shooting because without panchromatic film (no German dyes) we could not shoot by daylight with filters, so we had to shoot our night scenes at dusk. Besides, I had shot dusk scenes before. Selah.

It worked fine: that towing rig was so arranged that wherever Eddie went, Henry was sure to go. So we skidded and swerved around the narrow,

* Walthall played Sir Roger Brighton, a character suggested by Sir Roger Casement.
KEVIN BROWNLOW

one-lane, heavily wooded, and bumpy service roads of the park, with Walthall driving furiously and spinning the steering wheel this way and that, wickedly intent upon his villainy, with one eye on the road and the other cocked up, looking for his friend the Zep somewhere up there in the dark.

Shooting from the back of the Pierce to get a full shot of Walthall driving hell-for-leather necessarily placed me so that I couldn't see where we were going, although I had an excellent view of where we had been. Walthall's reckless twisting of the wheel didn't worry me a bit: we had disconnected the steering gear so that, no matter what he did, it could have no possible effect.

What did worry me was the time when I had to shoot a downshot, supposedly from the Zep, of the Walthall car far below flashing its deadly signals to the sky. By this time I had scrambled all over Griffith Park and knew it well from top to bottom. There was one particular rock, called Bee Rock, that rose as a sharp, high tooth from the northern side of the mountains. It was a dangerous climb, at least for me, although it would probably be a mere walkup for an experienced, skilled cragsman. I had been up there once before, just to see if I could do it. It had been quite an adventure, because the rock was of weathered shale or decomposed granite that crumbled easily underfoot.

But there was a road almost directly below, so that was the place for the shot. Naturally, the job of taking the shot was given to me. Griffith always trusted me with such risky things, which I took as a great compliment, not knowing any better.*

So I took the Debrie, for lightness, and a baby tripod, for more lightness, and up I went. I'd made the climb before, so I knew the footholds and handholds, the traverses that were reasonably safe and those that were not safe at all; along with the most valuable knowledge of all, the resting places, to relax the quivering muscles.

Once up, and with the camera set and focused, there was nothing to do but wait for that moment between daylight and dark when the car would be just visible and no more. The car had been put back in shape with Eddie driving, doubling for Walthall. I had a flashlight for signaling, and at my flash Eddie would come hurtling furiously along the road, blinking his spotlight at the sky.

I waited and waited, checking the light for exposure. The moment came. I gave the signal and began to turn. Eddie came tearing by, far below, his

---

* Youths have been getting themselves killed almost every year trying to climb the steep face of Bee Rock. There is now a fine, well-engineered trail winding around to the top, but that's for sissies and little old ladies with canes. The youths simply *must* risk the climb to show, in their own phrase, that they ain't a-scared of nuthin'. (Author)

spotlight spearing a wand of light into the slightly misty, darkling air. Nothing could be better. Everything worked perfectly. To be safe, I shot it twice. Now I knew I had it, and when Eddie flashed the letter Q for question (we all knew a little Morse), I answered K, for the universally understood O.K.

It was a fine moment. I felt proud and happy. This was one shot Griffith would say was very fine. And he'd have to use it, too. No cutting out for this one, because this was a key scene of his picture.

Then I realized that while I had been congratulating myself so heartily, it had become quite dark and I had to get down off that mountain. Theoretically this presented no difficulty at all, because I could always *fall* down, but somehow this idea did not appeal to me. I could also sit up there all night until it became light enough to see what I was doing, but that light mist had turned into a clammy fog and I was afraid I might catch cold. Besides, Eddie was waiting for me and he hated to be kept waiting.

So I loaded myself up with camera and tripod and groped my way down. Yes, I made it; otherwise you wouldn't be reading this now. Eddie was more annoyed than nervous about my late arrival at the bottom. He had a date and now he'd be late, and it was all my fault for dawdling around so much and holding him up. I told him I had to come down carefully for fear of scratching the camera. He believed me, really, because he felt the same way about his Pierce. He could drive that car around sharp turns on two wheels or speed across the front of an onrushing locomotive, missing it by inches, and never turn a hair. But if anybody made so much as a smudge or a scratch on its mirror-bright surface, he'd bathe his hands in the culprit's heart's blood.

The time for me to go into the army was fast approaching. I had already received my notice, beginning with the familiar word, "Greetings." I had been notified as to where and when to undergo my physical examination, which I passed without comment. There was nothing to do now but wait for orders as to where to report for basic training.

Somebody on the set asked me, "Aren't you scared?"

Before I could think of a convincingly brave reply to the contrary, Griffith replied for me, "Of course he is. Everybody is. Oh, a lot of them say they're not, but that's only bravado, because any man who isn't afraid of going into this mess is a damn fool. Not that Karl has much to worry about. They'll probably send him to some quiet sector, such as the Vosges. I'll speak to General Crowder about it. Now, Billy, the next shot is of Miss Dempster at the doorway . . ."

Miss Dempster. She was a newcomer, but then Griffith was always bringing in newcomers, so that was no novelty. But Carol Dempster herself really was a novelty, at least to me. She was pretty enough, if you like them narrow-faced and with close-set eyes, and she behaved herself with what seemed to be overproper decorum on the set. She had but one defect that I could see and that was a little protruding bump at the tip end of her nose. Griffith used to bewail this bump during his characteristic monologues, delivered to himself through the small megaphone he now had the habit of carrying. "To think that perfect beauty can be marred by one little bit of misplaced flesh. What a shame, what a crying shame. Otherwise . . . perfection."

I thought to myself, "Perfection, my Aunt Aggie's aspidistra! Oh sure. she's fine if you like 'em slim-faced, but what ever happened to the lush Rubens-esque beauties of yesteryear, like Blanche Sweet or Seena Owen, who had curves enough for a roller coaster? And why play kindergarten teacher to this inexperienced snip who might be very good to her mother but who had no business being thought of in the same reverie with Lillian Gish, who could be as placid as a mirror lake in repose, but who could become heartbreakingly tragic under dramatic stress? Or for that matter, Dorothy, who could be any-thing from a dimpled angel to a volcano of hate at one word from Griffith?"

All I could think was that this was Griffith's way, as expressed in the popu-lar saying of that day, "Catch 'em young, treat 'em rough, tell 'em nothing." It had worked before. It would work again. He loved to find new talent, six-teen or under, and mold them into something new and strange. I couldn't fault him for this. Otherwise I'd have been out on my bumper long, long ago.

Thinking of Lillian brought to mind passport pictures. You know what they're like. All they lack is a conspicuous number under the full-face close-up. Tack them up in the post office under the Wanted list and they're indis-tinguishable from the other pictures displayed in this most public of show-ings kept on constant display by the police, who want very much to sit down and have a nice heart-to-heart talk with the subjects.

Lillian's was startlingly different. She was so astonishingly sweet in her pic-ture that it would have been nice to have in the home to put on toast in-stead of jam. Her eyes were alive with beaming life, her dimpled smile was so real and so rounded that you could reach right into the picture and touch it, while her lips were incomparably delicious just to look at. Her hair was in glowing tendrils, so alive that it was actually real, and not a picture at all. I stared at a copy of this picture, one of many that Griffith handed around to his other cameramen, including Bitzer, as a sort of mark for them to shoot at. Naturally enough, this burned Bitzer to a crisp, which was what Griffith wanted. It didn't burn me at all. It made me avidly eager to find out how this magic had been performed.

It had been performed by a man named Sartov, Henrik Sartov, who had been employed as a portraitist by the Hoover Art Company, photographers, up near Hollywood and Gower. It goes without saying that Griffith grabbed him and had him hog-tied by one of Banzhaf's celebrated leak-proof contracts. All Sartov ever had to do was make close-ups, nothing but close-ups. Which was just as well, because the magic lens that performed his miracles was quite long of focus, six or eight inches, and in order to make a full-head close-up he had to back away over almost to the other end of the stage, while his lens-shade* seemed eighteen inches long. Specially made, of course, and specially mounted. Not that it mattered to Griffith. Sartov's close-ups were worth whatever they cost in the way of special equipment and special high-intensity lights, and lots and lots of time fussing and fooling around to make sure everything was just right.

Sartov was a strange little man, balding in front and fuzzy at the back. He seemed to be—how shall I say it?—frightened and futile, perhaps because he lived in constant fear that someone might discover his secret and put him out of business by doing the same thing the same way with the same results, only faster and more professionally. Especially Bitzer, or Landers, or anyone else. But not me. I didn't count. And besides, I was going into the army pretty soon, so I was of no possible threat to his specialized gimmickry.

Yes, gimmickry. Every stage magician—and I had known many, from Kellar through Thurston to Houdini—had his gimmicks, his tricks that he had invented himself and that he guarded as though they were the crown jewels, which they really were as far as his professional life was concerned. I made it my business to find out what his gimmick was. Not out of any idea of exposing him and ruining his livelihood, but from a normal, kidlike urge to find out what makes the wheels go around. I had some knowledge of lenses, thanks to my insatiable curiosity, and I had studied every book on optics I could find in our library.

Lenses had been in use for a long time, dating back to I couldn't find out how far. Nero is supposed to have had a single eyeglass made of emerald, but I never believed the yarn because the emerald, a form of beryllium, is too hard to be ground into lenticular shape. The Phoenicians discovered glass in the form of sand melted by their campfires. Early scientists scorned this idea, saying that no bonfire could get hot enough to melt sand. But then these old alchemists had been somewhat like modern scientists who live in labs and who believe firmly that if they can't do any given thing in a lab, it can't be done at all by anybody, anywhere.

From glass came lenses. From lenses came prisms, and from prisms came the spectrum and the spectroscope. Put them all together and you get optics,

---

* Lens-shade-*cum*-matte box. KEVIN BROWNLOW

and optics proves that light spreads out and disperses to some degree, one color more than another. But not all kinds of glass are alike. Glass does not live by sand alone. Other minerals can be added, notably lead, in one or more of its various salts, along with other minerals that change the dispersal qualities to a marked degree. Shape means a lot, too. Rounded glasses make things look larger. Curved-in glasses make them seem smaller. Idea! Cement a pair of these glasses together so that the dispersal of one will be canceled by the opposite dispersal of the other. And lo! the doublet was born, and there were no color fringes and no fuzzy edges. From this, over the centuries, came the ultra-fast lenses that cost a lot of money but that are, in truth, nothing but a collection of spectacle lenses with a post-graduate college education, complete with Phi Beta Kappa keys.

By the use of ways that are dark and tricks that are vain, I got a good look at Sartov's miracle lens, which was nothing in the world but a yellowed old spectacle lens with all its imperfections on its head. It wasn't much more than the bottom of a beer bottle, and its great virtue was that it was full of all the bad faults that optical scientists had been working for decades to eliminate. It could form an image, yes, but only in the middle part. From that one inch or so of recognizable image, the rest splayed out like a raw egg dropped on the kitchen floor. And this image part was all loused up with chromatic and spherical aberration. However, if you'd stop it down far enough, these defects would diminish, and that was the gimmick, the whole gimmick, and nothing but the gimmick.

Adjust the stop until the two aberrations can be just barely sensed but not actually seen, make your exposure, and what you get is pure peaches and cream. So Sartov was indeed a genius in that he could get results, no matter how, and it is axiomatic that they pay off on results.

I felt terribly sorry for Bitzer. I really did. Not because he was ever a friend of mine. Quite the opposite. He hated my guts, because I had such an unbeatable advantage over him. I was young and ignorant and I had no reputation to maintain or protect; I could fail repeatedly and it didn't matter because nobody expected me to do anything else *but* fail. But if I should just happen accidentally to make something good enough to go into a Griffith picture, I was a genius, no less, at least for that one brief moment. But if Bitzer ever failed at all to produce his incomparable best, such as one scene out of a thousand that was not quite superlatively fine, then the old man was slipping and it would be well to look around for a replacement to have handy just in case.

And now Griffith had brought in Sartov to make a fool of Bitzer at his own specialty, the big beautiful close-ups of Lillian Gish. This must have been a real crusher for Bitzer, who had taken Griffith under his wing back in the old Biograph days, when Griffith had been a bad actor fighting a prop eagle,* and had patiently taught Griffith which end of a camera took the pictures.

But this was Griffith's way. Keep everybody in hot competition with any and all possible rivals. Let anyone, anyone at all, in any department, fail to give his or her most wonderful best and they were sidelined. Those who could not live and work under this highest of high tension begged to be released to work elsewhere under less demanding conditions. No harm ever came to such people. Contracts were not only voided by mutual consent and with what seemed to be an alarming frequency but Griffith himself would go to great lengths to make sure that whoever had sought and obtained a release was hired instantly by other companies at substantial increases of salary.

On the other hand, some were simply demoted. Billy Fildew, who had done well as a cameraman, must have become oversure of himself or careless—both being cardinal sins in Griffith's eyes—and so he found himself replacing Lippin in the title room, a terrible comedown. Woodbury disappeared, I don't know when or why, to be replaced by his assistant, a thin little man with the unusual name of Tycho. A new young man named Tom Buckingham was brought in to work with me in the experiment room, unquestionably to pose a threat over me if I ever faltered or failed to produce results. Another man by the strange name of Schreckengost took over the cutting room. Monte Blue abandoned flag waving and pistol shooting to turn up elsewhere as a star with his name on the marquee. Working with Griffith during those hectic days was like living in a corn popper. Nobody knew from hour to hour who would be in and who out. It was unnerving to say the least, but if you want to reach the top and stay at the top you have to be prepared to fend off all the slings and arrows outrageous fortune can throw at you.

During all this Griffith remained more happily content than I had ever known him to be. No more grand opera for his vocal exercises. Instead, he sang all the verses of "Casey Jones," and he told a strange story about a steamboat with seven decks and no bottom. His direction changed, too. Instead of impressing some actress with the intensity of the scene she was to play, he slouched carelessly back in his chair and told her to look like a dying duck in a thunderstorm.

Underneath all this seeming indifference, Griffith was going through his

---

* The film referred to here is *Rescued from an Eagle's Nest,* made for Edison early in 1908, before Griffith went to Biograph. GEORGE PRATT

own private hell. He was getting money, yes, from *The Birth of a Nation* and *Hearts of the World*. But there were a dozen hands grabbing for every dollar he took in. The moneymen were always hounding him for his unwritten promised repayment of their investment in *Intolerance*. Linda Griffith, the wife he hadn't lived with for years, was always after him for money, money, and more money.

The Griffith studio was just the same as it had always been, and yet it was entirely different. New people had replaced old, as new water replaces that which has gone by. The Russian Revolution had forced the nobility to flee the Romanov-murdering machine guns of the Bolsheviks, and now we had counts and princes sousing film in the lab. They were all over Hollywood, too, invading every studio as a sort of Russian take-over of the business.

All transitions are painful, but it seemed to me at the time that the turmoil in Hollywood was all but unbearably severe. Shortages, rationing, casualty lists from the front, the inevitable instinct to eat, drink, and be merry because tomorrow you die were tearing everybody apart.

Some of it seemed to be so unreasonable and so undeserved that it could be attributed to nothing but the workings of a malignant fate determined to punish the human race within an inch of its life. Weren't things bad enough without having that flu epidemic killing innocent people by the millions all around the world, even in the remote islands of the South Seas? Why did pestilence always have to tread on the heels of war?

My little family was no more safe from world disaster than any other. My father had lost his job in the Griffith stock company at the time Griffith himself seemed to be down and out. He was never rehired, so he had to take day work whenever and wherever he could find it. My mother, always as healthy as a weed, was stricken with a grave infection that called for major surgery. It was touch and go for a while, but she pulled through. I paid for it all and wound up broke.

The studio where I had lived and breathed and had my being for the past five years was now full of strangers and I'd go to work each morning feeling that strange lost sensation of a new boy in a new school.

Only Griffith remained unchanged. He was still the same White Knight of *Alice,* forever noble, forever gallant, forever dreaming, and forever falling off his horse. Needing money, he was practical-minded enough to make the little pictures that make money—obvious pictures that anyone could understand. No art. Melodrama in the Al Woods manner. There was one, appropriately mistitled *Scarlet Days,* in which an Eastern girl goes all the way to early San Francisco during the gold rush to be with her rich mother, who has been sending her lots and lots of money, only to discover that Mamma is making all this money through owning and operating the fanciest fancy house in all the West.*

I don't know how he ever got a happy ending out of that situation, because before it was finished I was ordered to report to the Arcade station to board a troop train to take me to Camp Kearny for basic training.

This was one scene I knew perfectly well how to play because I had seen it often enough in movie after movie. The tearful embraces, the tearing away from loved ones, hands reaching out of windows to touch hands, with people outside running along as the train gathers speed, and the final close-up of the Girl smiling bravely through her tears.

However, it didn't work out that way with me. Sure, I was sorry enough to leave my family, which by now practically included Edna. But there were compensations.

Civilian life in general and Hollywood life in particular had become one vast dog fight, with double-crossing and character assassination the normal routine. Much as I hated to leave my family destitute, for I had been the only one earning real money, all of which was now gone, I could not help feeling a sense of reprieve and relief. As each click of the rails carried me farther and farther away from hate-poisoned Hollywood, and closer and closer to the war, I could at last feel the hungered-for luxury of a little peace.

* The majority of *Scarlet Days* was shot in the summer of 1919. KEVIN BROWNLOW

❧ 15 ❧

Hun! Tuh! Three! Fahrrr!

You're in the Army now,
*   You're not behind the plow*
You'll never get rich,
*   You son of a gun,*
You're in the Army now ...
    WORLD WAR I MARCHING SONG,
        SLIGHTLY EDITED

I DON'T suppose there is anyone alive who does not know what basic training is like. It's like having yourself set back to zero and beginning all over again at the job of learning how to live; only this is a different life where everything is done by numbers and in alphabetical order, with plenty of copies for everybody to file and forget.

It was no different with me. The first three weeks were the toughest because they were weeks of adjustment to new ways of doing everything according to army regulations. They were also weeks of getting more and more physical examinations, and dental treatments, and Alpha tests to determine your I.Q., and of course the shots against every sort of disease known at that time, because there was no way of knowing where you might be shipped, whether to France or to Siberia or wherever.

But why bother to tell about something that everybody has been through for himself? Suffice it to say that I survived those three weeks of being at the bottom of the pecking order, the same as any other raw recruit, and that through some mysterious process we were all sorted out and assigned to this unit or that, in groups of six or eight or a dozen. As far as I could understand, the guiding principle was to find out, through elaborate tests, including psychological, what any given individual is best fitted to do by training and temperament, and then put him to work at something as nearly the exact opposite as possible.

The reason? Simple enough. You can train a man to do almost anything, but you can't *un*train him from his lifelong habits of doing any given thing. That's why our cowboys, all but born on horseback, wound up as foot-sloggers in the infantry, while the ribbon clerks and errand boys were turned into cavalrymen.

For that same reason I was assigned to a machine-gun company of the 32nd Infantry. The fact that I was a highly trained cameraman with aerial experience (one flight) ruled me out as a military photographer, even though experienced cameramen were in short supply and badly needed. I would know too much and I would be too much inclined to disagree with my superior officers, whose photographic experience had been a few Brownie Kodak snapshots of the family out on a picnic somewhere. No photography for this man. Send him over to the 32nd and put him to work grooming mules.

So that's where I landed, and that's what I did. Groomed mules—correction: groomed one particular mule, the one assigned to me, a gentle little mouse-colored lady mule, whom I promptly named Hortense and with whom I tried to establish a relationship of trust and affection. She responded in her own mule-headed way as best she could. Hortense never kicked me and she never even threatened to bite, which, although negative virtues, were valued nevertheless.

There were two duties that had to be performed each day when "Stable Call" was sounded by our bugler. The first was to clean out the stalls, particularly around the after part of the mules. This brought out the alleviating humor that seems to be characteristic of military men, especially privates. We referred to ourselves as pilots, because we worked with rakes and shovels to pilot here and pilot there, anywhere well away from the mules, so it wouldn't make their rear running gear sore and develop a condition known as thrush. Then came the delicate operation of lifting each rear hoof, one at a time, and of using a special tool to clean the hoofs of whatever had accumulated between the shoe and the frog, holding each hoof between your legs and digging in quite hard to make everything sweet and clean. Considering that each mule carried a dynamite kick in each rear hoof made this operation not without a certain degree of suspense, especially to one who had never had anything at all to do with mules before. But then, these mules had never had anything to do with raw recruits before, so that made everything even.

Hortense behaved herself as well if not better than any of the other mules. After all, she was a lady of dignity and reserve, the thoughtful kind who would not demean herself by bucking and snorting and striking but who tried the more intelligent and more dignified method of rolling over on her back and trying to scrape off that damned pack of ammunition cases and/or machine guns.

When the tumult and the shouting died, and the mules and their valets—meaning us—took off in a column of twos, we were like the animals going into Noah's ark. Our drill sergeant marched along with us, a little to one side and with a sharp eye for alignment as he sounded the cadence, "Hun, Tuh, Three, Fahrrr! Hup, hup, hup, hup—close up, you bastids, whaddaya think this is, a shirttail parade? Hup, hup, hup, hup! Keep them head and eyes off the ground!" But you know how drill sergeants are. Everybody does, from bitter personal experience.

We were supposed to click off the old cadence in perfect step and at the prescribed intervals. We had to hold the headstalls of our mules at just one certain point, not a fraction of an inch higher or lower. Naturally, we had to keep in step, and we were supposed to all move in a compact unit. The mules, being privileged characters, did not have to keep step, but they waggled their long ears more or less in time with whatever step they chose to take, so it was not too bad a show of military discipline, considering that we were all more or less scared of our mules and that the mules knew it.

My own dear Hortense was the best-behaved mule of the lot. She had only one defect. She had a mischievous sense of humor, which she expressed by reaching out wide with the front hoof nearest to me and bringing it down with all her weight on my foot.

This caused me to yell a little and to break military formation as I hopped along on my remaining good foot. It also caused the drill sergeant to give me what was spoken of as a chewing-out, all couched in the vigorous special language of non-coms the world over, using words that would lead to a fight to the death in civilian life but that were taken as part of being in the army by those in uniform.

Throughout all this, Hortense would stand simpering, with eyes modestly downcast, looking more angelic than a Sartov close-up of Lillian Gish. A dozen or so more steps and she'd do it again. More chewing-out, together with mention of a solid week of K.P. if I let it happen again.

It happened again and I got the K.P., which was always spoken of as cook's police, although the initials mean kitchen police. I didn't mind. They let you sit down—a rare privilege—to peel vegetables, while washing up after two hundred men's meals three times a day isn't so awfully bad, not after being walked on by a mule with a twisted sense of humor.

My final adventure with Hortense was nothing if not spectacular. We were turned out for a grand review, with the entire division slated to pass in review before the stand holding all the Big Brass. In company front, of course, and in perfect alignment, which is the toughest formation of all to hold. Espe-

cially with mules. We all knew what we were supposed to do. Our drill sergeant had been quite firm in his instructions. "An' annother thing! When the
command comes, 'Eyes right!' I wanna hear them eyeballs *click*!"

The great day came, and I was astonished to see the immensity of the
massed manpower that had been assembled at Camp Kearny. There was one
entire division, a bit short of division strength of ten thousand men, with part
of another division whose advance elements had been shipped out. There
was everything known to warfare, only, in true American Army tradition, it
was all mustered in the style of our last big war, which had ended in 1865.

The actual fighting units in Europe had been motorized for two years. But
not our army. What was good enough for grandpa was good enough for us,
so we had horse-drawn artillery, horse-drawn ambulances, and even a brave
and dashing display of cavalry, fifty years outmoded and hopelessly futile for
trench warfare, where men burrowed in the mud like moles and where
anything that showed itself six inches above ground level was instantly
drilled by machine guns from concrete pillboxes not more than a hundred
yards away across the barbed-wire network of no-man's-land.

But outmoded or not, it was worth ten years of peaceful life to see that
brave array, as Walter Scott wrote. The units moved forward, flags flying
and bands playing. It took a long time. We were somewhere in the middle
of that show of strength, and when we finally did manage to move forward,
we didn't look so bad after all. Our company front was pretty ragged and not
at all like the precision formations of West Point graduates, but we did the
best we could, and at the command, "Eyes Right!" we all snapped our eyes
toward the reviewing stand, where all the Big Brass was assembled, along
with high-powered civilian-dressed members of Congress.

It was at that instant, when my eyes were turned away, that Hortense
reached out and came down on my foot with her customary dead-shot aim. I
yelled as usual and did my one-legged dance, also as usual. This made me
lose my balance and I fell against Hortense, who shied away and hit the mule
on her starboard beam, who shied away and hit the next mule, who— Well,
it was at that precise instant that the domino theory, so learnedly discussed by
military experts to this day, was established. I take no credit for this myself. It
was all Hortense's idea, and it worked to perfection.

Before you could say Ossip Gabrilowitsch, every mule in the 32nd Infantry
Machine-Gun Company was bucking and snorting and braying and rattling
machine-gun and ammunition packs like so many castanets. They bucked
and they kicked and they hee-hawed. They charged into A Company, B
Company, and all the rest of the following infantrymen, scattering them like

leaves. The mules ran in all directions, some of them charging the reviewing stand. One high-ranking officer wearing stars roared out the command, "Stop those mules!" but he neglected to say how.

The mules solved the question all by themselves by hightailing it for the nearest horizon. A lot of red-faced, loud-roaring sergeants managed to bully us back into line, and we finished passing in review, empty-handed, no mules, no guns, nothing.

It was a black day for the 32nd, but even the blackest of days has its moments of relief. For the mules were gone and there would be no more stable calls until they were found and brought back. Some of them never were found, among these Hortense. I missed her, but not very much. Hardly at all, as a matter of fact. I bore my loss bravely, as a soldier should.

By a strange oversight on the part of the army, I was given a job that I was already trained and used to doing, that of managing a machine gun. Machine guns have tripods just like cameras, only heavier. They also pan and tilt, just like cameras. They have to be focused, so to speak, on a certain objective, just like cameras. I never had the slightest difficulty handling a Browning machine gun because it was just like a camera working in reverse. Instead of bringing an image *in*, it throws a stream of bullets *out*. Same thing, only different.

So at long last, after being in bad with everybody ever since I arrived in camp, I found myself suddenly accepted as something almost human, with vague but conceded possibilities.

But there was more to come. Much more. I was ordered to our C.O.'s office, where Captain Thompson was staring at a telegram he had just received from Washington. It ordered him to release me for one week's furlough to D. W. Griffith for special duty. It was signed by General Crowder, who was in charge of whatever department does all the recruiting and training.

I remembered Griffith saying, that day on the set, "Karl has nothing to worry about. I'll speak to General Crowder . . ." But how was I to guess that he'd remember, now that I was gone and out of his life and of no use to him? And what on earth could he possibly want of me, anyway? I was also wondering how I was going to manage the trip to the studio, because my pay had dropped to thirty dollars a month, less insurance, and there was that little problem of transportation.

How silly of me to worry. I had hardly finished talking with Captain Thompson when my own car drove up to the company clerk's office, with one of my former assistants at the wheel. George Larsen gave the keys to me, along with a pay envelope of the type we always used. I opened it and drew out a $100 bill, a fine-looking piece of valuable paper with a picture of Mercury printed on it in green, with the other side yellow, proving it to be a note redeemable in gold.

Jaws dropped all around me. I had been a strange sort of private from the very first. My *dossier* told that I had been earning more money each week than my officers had ever earned in a month. My theatrical background decreed that I should have on me at all times the most expensive diamond that I could afford, because a good diamond will always get you back to New York, where the jobs are, no matter where you're stranded. So, in a flush moment I had bought for myself a fine blue-white 1-carat Wesselton diamond, brilliant cut and mounted in a heavy platinum ring. I had also learned to enjoy a fine Havana cigar, so after experimenting with the better-known brands, such as the Corona-corona, the Ramon Allones and the Hoyo de Monterey, I discovered that the needle-pointed, swelled body shape called the Partagas was exactly to my taste.

I must have been a puzzling sort of recruit, dressed in fatigue blues, smelling to high heaven of Hortense, with a flashing diamond squirting rays of brilliant colors from my grimy hands as I gave Hortense her daily pedicure, meanwhile perfuming the air with the aroma of a fine Havana. And now to have my own driver bringing me my own car, together with a $100 bill for incidental expense, plus a telegram from General Crowder, the biggest of the Big Brass, practically paralyzed all onlookers from Captain Thompson on down.

The stage is a wonderful background for anyone with an instinct for carrying things off in style. I suppressed a polite yawn as I took my place at the wheel and waited with well-bred annoyance while the company clerk made out an all-inclusive pass to be signed by Captain Thompson, after which I whipped the car around and headed for the northern exit gate, wondering what the hell this was all about.

The trip from Camp Kearny to Hollywood was anything but a pleasure jaunt, thanks to the terrible condition of the roads. Luckily, I was able to avoid the dreaded Torrey Pines grade, one of the worst in California. It was so crooked and so steep and the turns were so sharp that people used to say you had to be mighty careful going around them turns or you'd bust right into yourself head-on and ruin your radiator.

The next forty miles or so of my journey clung to the shoreline, in the mistaken belief that the shortest distance between two points is a straight line. You'd grind along the edge of the beach for a mile or so and then climb straight up over the next headland, very steep and very trying for any car. Once on top it dropped precipitously down to the shoreline again, for more grinding along through sand, until it was time to do the Jacob's ladder act with the next headland.

Eventually this game was played out, and with Dana Point well in view from a high, rising plateau, the road crossed yet another of the innumerable real-estate developments that were scattered all over California. This consisted of raw, vacant land, with cliffs on the ocean side and steeply rising ground to the inland mountains. Here, lost in all this vast expanse, was a little real-estate office with nobody in it and no customers, which was normal. This was the newest and potentially the greatest home site in all the West. They even had a name for it: San Clemente. Well, it was a nice name, anyway. But there were plenty of other nice names going to waste in impossible locations like Encino or Zelza or Azusa. I wished them luck and went on my way.

The toughest and most time-wasting part of the trip was the checkerboard road east of Los Angeles. Here the main highway followed the property lines of the farms, so that you had to drive as though sailing a schooner into the wind, tacking this way and that way to make any forward headway at all. Ninety degrees right, then ninety degrees left, forever making right-angle turns and seemingly getting nowhere at all, especially if you were in as much of a hurry as I was at that time.

The first town of any visible importance to be encountered was a little place called Santa Ana. It didn't amount to much, while its next-door neighbor, Anaheim, was hardly a town at all, being mostly farms settled by German immigrants.

But despite all these road difficulties I made very good time, covering the hundred miles in somewhere between four and five hours. I drove straight to the studio and jumped out to look for Griffith to find out what was up. I knew exactly where to look for him—the projection room. I went right on in, even though this was against the rules.

Griffith stopped whatever he was running and the houselight—a feeble bulb, unshaded and set in the ceiling of the black-painted room—went on. He was sitting in his usual chair, a broken-down, leatherette-covered lounge chair that years of use had caused to sag and yield into a form that exactly fitted his long, angular body.

He looked up at me and said, without preface or explanation, "I want a river . . . a misty . . . misty river . . ." His long, sensitive hands were molding the picture that he was seeing with his inner eye. "A river of dreams . . . the Thames as Whistler or perhaps Turner might have painted it, only it must be a real river, do you understand? A real river, flowing, endlessly flowing, carrying destiny, the never-ending destiny of life on its tide. I must see that flow, that silent flow of time and fortune, with all the mystery of unknowable future there to be seen and yet not to be seen . . ." The vision vanished and with it the poetic spell. He asked, in his sharp, penetrating, directorial voice, "Do you know what I mean?"

I had been standing stiffly at attention throughout all this lucid, yet verbally incomprehensible speech. I answered crisply, "Yes, sir!" I had been so much in the habit of calling everybody "sir" for so long that I didn't know any other way to answer.

"Very well. Do it. Mr. Baker will give you some sketches. That's all. All right, Jimmy. Let's get back to work on that sequence."

The light went out and the projector began to whir. I unwittingly did a smart about-face, digging my toe into the floor back of my heel and whirling around with an all but audible "One, two!" as I executed the turn and marched out of the room. I hadn't the slightest idea in the world of what he was driving at, but if Charlie Baker had made some sketches that had been approved by Griffith, maybe I could figure it out in the morning.

I dismissed Larsen and drove home to a hero's welcome. Not because I had done anything heroic but because it was the fashion of the day to treat any man in uniform as the savior of his country. Everybody—my father and mother, Ida Belle, and of course Edna, were all over me with about as warm a welcome as though I had just brought the Kaiser home with a ring in his nose. The only member of the family that did not greet me with overwhelming affection was Lily, who shied suspiciously away from me, growling faintly.

The questions of my family were even more of an eye-opener. My mother, anxiously, "Are you getting enough to eat?" My father, proudly, "Hear you're doing fine, son—just fine!" And from Edna, as an up-and-coming young actress working with C. B. De Mille, "Where on earth did you get those awful pants?"

I couldn't answer any of them, not really, not so they'd understand. I was beginning to realize why all soldiers are so monosyllabic about their war adventures. People who have been fed a romantic mishmash of martial glory simply cannot be told the real facts of army life, because it is not romantic, not glorious, not much of anything but a fixed routine of boredom.

I could understand why Edna thought my pants (breeches) were so awful. In her world of movie make-believe, all soldiers are supplied with smartly tailored uniforms supplied by Western Costume, while ours had been shoved to us in a pile by the supply sergeant, and when nothing fit, he simply said, "Trade around like you're supposed to. Don't you know *anything?*"

So we traded around and managed to outfit ourselves with uniform clothing that fit close enough so it would not be so small as to choke or bind us into immobility or so large as to fit us like a tent and to fall off at embarrassing moments. Anything between these rather wide limits was considered to be a good fit. My breeches *were* too large by civilian standards, but with the help of a few strategically placed safety pins, modesty was protected and I looked about as well dressed as anyone else in the 32nd, which is to say, awful. But this stuff was all factory produced on a crash basis, millions of garments turned out in the fastest possible time by newly recruited, half-experienced sewing-machine operators, so what could you expect—Jermyn Street tailoring?

When we sat down to eat the poor little meal that was the best they could provide under wartime restrictions of meatless days and only one slice of bread to a customer and no butter at all, only cheap margarine, I couldn't help contrasting their very best with what we at camp were getting every day—unlimited supplies of meat and butter and milk, all of the finest quality, all commandeered by the army at the source with the leftovers and rejects going to the civilian population.

My father was full of enthusiasm for the regiment I had been foisted upon. "Great regiment, that 32nd," he said. "Old line. Solid. Full of traditions. Live up to 'em, my boy, and you can't go wrong."

Live up to 'em, eh? Easier said than done, because these tough old-timers had a way of shoving every unpleasant or annoying duty onto the raw recruits, who not only couldn't defend themselves but who did not even know how to begin. That's why we were getting our tails worked off, doing three men's work, while the wise old soldiers stood around and thought up new things for us to do.

What these old-line experts in army loafing didn't know, an entirely new breed of very young officers could invent. The army had no lack of draftable manpower from the population at large, but it was desperately short of low-ranking line officers, especially lieutenants. So the powers that be in Washington gathered in every young man who had ever been to any military academy as a kid and ran them through a crash program of officer training. An essential part of this training was what the army called equitation, meaning how to ride a horse. After ninety days of this, they were given their single gold bars and turned loose on the recruits. These smartly uniformed young gentlemen were known as ninety-day wonders among the polite, although I never heard them called other than sore-assed lieutenants among the rank and file, the reference being to their tender parts, which were kept in a state of raw-chafed pain by their enforced drill in horsemanship. And they were really sore, too. You could tell it by their wide-spraddled walk and the extreme care with which they eased themselves down whenever they sat.

But these fresh-hatched Napoleons were hell on discipline. Let any private fail to come up with a fast salute and to hold it until the salute was answered, and he'd get his name and serial number taken down and be put on report for discipline. In a camp crawling with brand-new brass on all sides, it was hard to keep up with this saluting business. And yet it had to be done, somehow. Spot one of these ultrasensitive, brand-new second lieutenants three hundred yards away and practically out of eyesight, and you'd better salute or you'd be in trouble.

My patience with this sort of nonsense is not unlimited, and so I cooked up a vicious little scheme that I had learned from the movies. Whenever anyone was making a cowboy-Indian epic on the cheap, it was customary to hire about twenty of each, find a nice high rock somewhere in Chatsworth, and run these twenty around and around the rock, giving the impression of there being hundreds and hundreds of them.

One day when I spotted one of these smartly tailored, pink-cheeked young martinets waiting patiently outside a brigadier's door, I gathered some fellow conspirators, and after a whispered consultation and an eager agreement, I led the way by marching past, clicking off the old cadence, and snapping up to a brisk right-hand salute, and holding it until the salute was answered. I went on my way, while another conspirator came along and did the same thing. Then another. And another. Meanwhile, I had doubled around back and came through a second time. And a third. And a fourth, followed by more and more eager volunteers.

Brigadiers are never in any hurry to keep lesser ranks from waiting, so that poor victim of our fiendish plot was kept answering salutes, like one of these Japanese toys that keep nodding and nodding at the touch of a fingertip. He must have known that he was getting the runaround—a movie term that has been absorbed into the language—but there wasn't a thing he could do about it. He was furious, too, but he was also helpless. Privates must salute officers; officers must answer the salute: regulations. We were within the law, he was within the law, and even if he could have proved that we were running around and around to wear him out, his superiors would have leaned back in their chairs and laughed themselves sick.

How could I explain any of this to my father? I couldn't, so I meekly said, "Yes, sir," and left his illusions about the grand traditions, the *esprit de corps,* and all the rest of the romantic moonshine of the storybooks undamaged.

The meal was eventually finished, and it was time to take Edna home. Now it so happened that I knew all about what happens when a soldier returns home on leave and meets his dearly beloved, because I had seen it time and time again in I don't know how many movies.

It goes just one way. They are alone at last, generally on a moonlit beach, where there is nobody within miles. He enfolds her gently in his arms. She responds with a kiss so passionate that it all but sets the film afire. Her hands go around his neck and her fingers clutch hard. He bends her over, and over . . . and over . . . and . . . and then all hell breaks loose as the thunder rolls (that's from a thunder cart being dragged back and forth by the backstage sound-effects men)—the lightning flashes (the backstage electrician wearing rubber gloves does this with carbons touched together and then drawn apart)—the orchestra goes into a Wagnerian frenzy of sound and fury—the picture is of a tremendous storm raging in the sky—and all this symbolism means, as well understood by all the audience, that things have gotten out of hand with the young lovers and that they've gone and done what they shouldn't have ought to but did anyway, this being war. Then the storm fades away and we're back on a close-up of the lovers, lying back dazed with happiness, or perhaps merely physically exhausted, and the string section of the orchestra plays Grieg's Morning Theme from the Peer Gynt Suite, augmented by the Mighty Wurlitzer, and she says to him in a spoken title, "You won't ever leave me? Not . . . not *now?*" To which he replies with a tender kiss, which is the most he can muster after what's just happened, "No, my dearest, never. Not . . . not *now. . ."*

Boy, oh boy, oh boy! This made going to war worthwhile. I drove Edna home filled to the bursting point with what I'd better call anticipation. I'd have rubbed my hands together with glee if I could have spared them from the wheel. Anyway, I lost no time in pulling up in front of her house and waiting for the big sequence to begin.

Edna said very sympathetically, "Poor boy, I know you must be tired after all that driving and the excitement and all. You've got an early call on the set and so have I, so I'll just say good night. See you tomorrow after work. Good night."

And she was gone. I sat there for a moment, wondering where all these moviemakers ever got their ideas. Probably through dreaming up what people would like to have happen.

So I drove home and got ready for bed. As soon as I was under the covers, Lily came in and jumped up onto the bed and nosed my hand apologetically. She knew me now that I had my funny-smelling clothes off. She was very contrite, and it was a comfort to have her with me.

But the bed itself was no comfort at all. Too soft, too yielding after the firm support of the hard army bunks. I kept feeling that I was going to sink down into the bed and smother.

Somehow I managed to doze off, and my last thought was of deep pity for the poor civilians who had to stay home and subsist somehow on the scraps left over by the army. It must be hell, I thought, to be a civilian in time of war . . .

This feeling was sharpened to an unbearable degree at breakfast the next morning. My plate was piled with as much as it would hold: bacon, eggs, fried potatoes, coffee, toast. But the coffee was bad and bitter, the milk blue-tinged and watery-weak, while my father and mother were having practically nothing. She said coffee was all she ever had in the morning, while my father was eating a small bowl of corn flakes, saying that he needed to take off weight. They were going without. For me.

Of all the bad feelings the worst is to be treated as a guest in your own home. That isn't what home is for. Home is a place where you can strip down and walk around in your soul, hiding nothing, pretending nothing, fearing nothing. That doesn't mean that everything is always sweetness and light. If you feel lousy, *feel* lousy. If you're sore about something, say so and get it off your chest. That, too, is what home is for. No false fronts, no putting on of acts, and above all, no phoniness. For home is where you can be human, not perfect, and everybody understands because they're human too. Home, in short, is the last inner citadel of individual honesty, to be defended at all costs.

So I decided to set the pace by being as honest as I could manage on short notice. I told them about Hortense and old man Rouse, our stable sergeant who was a grizzled old veteran so old that whenever we were whistled into formation, and our first sergeant, or top-kicker as we called him, waved old white-headed Rouse away and said, "No, not you," we knew we were going for that certain inspection during which the medical officers look us over to see if we had been loving not wisely but too well with the wrong sort of lady.

I told them about our long wooden mess hall, where the company offices were at the parade-ground end, the long tables for the men in the mid-section, the kitchen at the other end, with its enormous ranges and its huge, heavily tinned cooking vessels big enough to hold all the stew—invariably called "slum"—that our company of two hundred or so men could eat.

I told them how these mess halls were always the scene of these strictly masculine inspections, and how, on one memorable day when we were all lined up in the mess hall with the parts to be inspected open and ready, the door opened and one of our ninety-day wonders, a gold-bar lieutenant, stepped in with his mother and sister and sweetheart, and said, "This, my dears, is where the enlisted men eat . . ."

That's as far as he got. The ladies, unlike the fabled Peeping Tom, did not peek through their fingers but took a *good* look, memorizing the variations for future guidance, until our fine young officer, blushing a deep purple, hustled them from the room, followed by gales of ribald laughter from all our men.

There was something about this cutting up of old touches, as we called loose and carefree gossip, that broke the false spell of strangeness engendered by my uniform and that restored me to my true place as a member of the family and not as much a stranger to them as I had been to Lily. They began to talk, easily and eagerly, to bring me up to date with their own misadventures. The worst thing that had happened was the deadly epidemic of what was called the Spanish influenza, or "flu" in common speech.

This was a very old disease, dating back to the days when astrologers said it was caused by the malignant influence of evil stars—hence the term, influenza, or influence. It had come and gone for centuries under various names, one of them being the French term, *la Grippe*. But this one was different. Its deadliness came from its ability to render the victim so weak that he became easy prey to almost any other disease, with pneumonia leading the list of final killers.

This had played hell with show business from top to bottom. Crowds and gatherings were forbidden. The theaters went dark, so there was no work for legitimate actors on the legitimate stage. Movie houses closed their doors for the same reason. The studios, however, remained active, turning out products to be shown after the epidemic had passed.

Flu masks, consisting of oblongs of white gauze worn across the nose and mouth, were worn by everyone. The only medicine that was thought to have any effect was aspirin, which was in very short supply for the same reason that everything was in short supply: the armed forces had commandeered it.

Nothing seemed to afford much protection. A sort of fatalism followed the explosive building of the epidemic. You either got it or you didn't, and you either lived or you died. And that was that. Meanwhile, scratch for a living as best you could.

My father was not too badly situated, nor was my mother. Both were well known all over town. They did not have to stand around outside studios. But they *were* telephone-prisoners, hardly daring to leave the house for a moment for fear that might be the time a studio would call with the offer of a small part or bit at ten dollars a day.

They had both been working, off and on, enough to pay the rent and grocery bills and to keep Ida Belle on to take care of the house (and Lily) when they were both out working.

Time flew. I glanced at the silver wristwatch the studio had given me as a going-away present and noticed that it was high time for me to get to the studio and find out from Charlie Baker exactly what it was I had to put on the screen. I reached into my pocket for my car keys, and as I drew them out, that small manila pay envelope came out with them and fell to the floor.

I picked up the envelope, reflected for one chilling moment about how tragically easy it would be for me to lose that $100 bill. So I handed it over to my mother, asking her to take charge of it, since I had no possible use for money in the army, where absolutely everything is furnished, up to and including an enemy to fight.

They both stared at that $100 bill with reverential awe. My father began to weave marvelous plans of all the things they could buy with it. My mother pulled her grouch bag up from the front of her dress by the little chain that locked it around her neck, took the bill, gazed at it fondly, gave it a small but meaningful kiss, folded it carefully, tucked it into the bag, which she dropped down into no-man's-land with an air of complete and absolute possession. My father's plans dissolved into silence. That grouch bag was the deep dark depth from whence no money ever returneth, except in the hour of absolute need. I felt warm and good all over. They'd be able to eat for quite a while on that.

I drove around to the studio, not because the few steps it would have taken meant anything but mostly to make a grand entrance. Some are born hammy, some acquire hamminess, others have hamminess thrust upon them. I was endowed with all three. But I could have saved myself the trouble, because nobody so much as noticed me.

All attention was upon something you won't believe—a young and handsome Chinese, pigtail and all, in black silk with a frogged coat, apparently recruited from Hung Far Low's famous emporium in San Francisco. He was holding court, so to speak, smiling and chatting with his admirers in what I thought was remarkably good English for an Oriental.

I moved along the boardwalk leading to the big stage, where I encountered Lillian Gish. She was dressed very plainly, even poorly, evidently made up as a household slavey of some sort. But she was her own radiant self that defied costumery, and when she offered her hand and beamed one of her marvelous dimpled smiles upon me, and told me how glad Mr. Griffith was to borrow me from the army, I knew beyond question that this was my day.

And it was, too. Huck Wortman told me where to find Charlie Baker. He had been housed under the big rehearsal hall, in a low-ceilinged room where we used to hang all our costumes for *Intolerance,* thousands of them.

Charlie Baker was the same red-mustached, twinkly-eyed, slightly stooped master of the Cockney dialect he had always been. The costumes were gone, sold probably, to be made over into something else, because cloth, too, was in short supply. So Charlie had this whole big expanse of area for his studio. He had been putting it to good use, too, because the place was practically papered with his wonderful ink-and-watercolor creations, all in the proportion of four to five, which was the area of our camera frame lines. Apparently he had been drawing every scene of every picture Griffith had been working on since *Intolerance.**

The scene Griffith wanted me to do was of almost childish simplicity. Charlie showed me a picture of the Thames, shooting from Limehouse across the stream to a far-distant misty shore, with a few of the characteristically rigged Thames luggers, so unique as to be recognizable at a glance. It was a beautiful picture, perfectly composed and good enough to glorify anyone's wall.

The thing that impressed me most was Baker's superb handling of planes. In the right foreground was the black silhouette of a Chinese shop with a glowing lantern outside inscribed with Chinese characters. This did not merely *say* Limehouse, it shouted it. You didn't have to be a Londoner with a taste for slumming to recognize the locale at a glance. Thomas Burke's stories of Limehouse were enjoying a great vogue; these stories had been collected in two volumes, *Limehouse Nights* and *More Limehouse Nights*. I'd read all of them. So had everyone else. You might as well confess at once that you were utterly behind the times if you were not intimately acquainted with Burke's stories of Limehouse. The whole English-reading world knew every dark and dangerous alley of Limehouse as well as they knew the way to the corner grocery. And this was Limehouse and no mistake, all because of a single glimpse of a storefront, plus that Chinese-inscribed lantern.

The planes receded into dimness as the distances became greater and greater. In the extreme distance was the opposite shore, all but lost in the night mist. I may have been unusually impressionable, but at the moment I couldn't see why anybody would bother with Whistler when there was such a man as Charlie Baker around. But then grim realism took over and I remembered that Whistler was of the elite, while as for Charlie, this was his own, his native land, and he proved it with every word he spoke.

What was the problem? Nothing. Merely to make this painting move. And it really was nothing to me because I had been doing it for five years, surely long enough for anyone to master a technique so simple, once you get the hang of it.

The first step was to break the picture down into planes, exactly the same

---

* I cannot be sure, but this may have been another of Griffith's unsung innovations: designing a production setup by setup, long shots, cross shots, close-ups, everything. (Author)

as stage designers do with their wings and drops, teasers and sky borders. Charlie knew all about this because he had grown up backstage.

This, too, he had proved by his speech, because he spoke of a slot as a slote, and of the horizon as the horrizon. Anything that holds anything else, from a prop rock to an iron rod that holds a full-stage curtain, is a batten. These things can't be faked, and a person has to be very unwise to try it.

So when I spoke of breaking the picture down into ground rows, he knew exactly what I meant. Nothing could be easier for Charlie, who wanted to know only the size of the finished product. This made me think for a moment. There had to be water, because the water had to move. So did the luggers.

The more I had worked with these things, the more I was convinced that a fine small picture is better than a large bad one, a lesson I had learned back in the New York Metropolitan Museum by comparing such circus posters as "Washington Crossing the Delaware" and Rosa Bonheur's "Horse Fair" with the smaller but much more finely executed non-masterpieces of Meissonier, not the famous one of the French cavalry sweeping around in the foreground, while Napoleon sits on his white horse on a little hillock, but the smaller, almost postcard-size picture hidden over near the entrance wall and called "The Conscripts," a simple little tribute to earthy human dignity and not the flamboyant exhibitionism of the professionally great.

I had long ago given up carpenter-shop-produced miniatures of toy houses and toy everything else as an impossibly bad job. I had turned to photographs of the real thing, suitably profiled and sprayed with an airbrush for aerial perspective. I had worked this system with Charlie Baker on a scene of London being bombed by Zeps for *The Great Love*. Our working model had been from the *Illustrated London News*. It showed one of the two universally recognized landmarks of London, St. Paul's (the other being the Tower Bridge), looming in the distance like a captive balloon ready to be released, with a forest of chimney pots in the foreground.

We had cut this up into ground rows, added depth by spraying the intervening rows with an airbrush, and a simple double exposure had added moving clouds and Zeps of varying size, the nearer Zeps moving faster than those in the distance, to give what might be called motion perspective. The sweeping searchlights were simple spots mounted below and cut down to size by handmade diaphragms, while a hand-sprayed fog, also moving, picked up the beams and made them visible. Easy enough; ridiculously so, when you know how.

But easy or not, it had taken me five years, and I can't even guess how many artists, to teach me this simple technique. I was like the ignorant boy, described by Mark Twain, who admitted that he didn't know very much but that what he did know he knew like hell.

The secret of making any moving picture is to have something move. In the present instance it had to be the river. Very well. We had duplicated the flow of the Tigris–Euphrates in *Intolerance* by shooting a still lagoon over which a breeze was blowing, rippling the surface so it *looked* like a river.

There seemed to be no reason why this couldn't be duplicated on a small scale, so I had Huck build a small shallow trough, four feet wide and eight feet long. No problem about making it watertight. Simply paint it inside with a good thick coat of asphalt and the job is done.

Now the ground rows were mounted inside the trough at what would be water level when it was filled. These profiled sections of the original picture, airbrushed to provide the visual sense of a mile of distance to a faraway shore not two feet from the nearest profile building, gave great depth to the picture. Plumbers ran hose connections to supply water and to drain the trough, which had been placed on carefully leveled sawhorses. Electricians wheeled in a variety of spots for lighting, with plenty of frosted gelatin for diffusion. A tiny flashlight bulb was placed behind the Chinese-lettered sign. The cutout profile luggers were mounted on wooden floats, with lumps of lead on wires from underneath to keep them upright. A large electric office-type fan was provided to make the ripples and to cause the luggers to move ever so slightly.

Everything was ready, so I lit and shot the scene. I developed a test strip in the still room and blew up an eleven-by-fourteen enlargement. There was something wrong with it. It was not a river at all but a pool of black ink. Bright idea. Drop a tiny pinch of flash powder, which is mostly aluminum, on the surface. These little silvery grains shied away from one another as though they hated to be crowded. The surface was now that of a dull mirror. Careful, minute adjustment of the spots made the foreground water dark, shading off to a misty union with the distant shoreline. And—glory be —those luggers showed an ever-so-faint reflection in the water, which, under the impetus of the fan, flowed steadily out toward the estuary, as though Sunwise Turn were just out of the picture a little farther on.

This time everything was really right. I gave the film to Abe Scholtz, who lavished his tenderest attention upon it. Joe Aller did the printing himself, personally. It was good but not good enough. Not to suit him. So he toned the image to a luminous, translucent blue, stained the highlights a fine light orange, and there it was, Charlie Baker's painting reproduced in terms of a living, moving picture.

Griffith watched it through with leaning-forward attention, his eyes sharpened to detect any flaw. There was no "That is very fine" from him this time. Instead he said, "Run that scene again." It was done. He sat back in his broken-down chair with an air of almost surfeited satisfaction. He delivered his judgment slowly. "It's a painting—a *painting!—that moves!* Worth many telegrams to General Crowder. Thank you very much. That's all. See you after the war."

So that was the end of that. And all for only one scene. I left the projection room and wandered around, empty-handed and out of a job. A few questions here and there revealed that the picture this was for was called *Broken Blossoms,* a title so sickly sweet that the working crew, a godless bunch by definition, never called it anything but *Busted Posies.* That young Chinese turned out to be a new actor named Richard Barthelmess, while Donald Crisp, who had played every sort of character part known to the theater, was now swaggering ominously around looking exactly like the stage appearance of Bill Sikes on his way to beat poor Nancy to death, a scene that I had seen as a child and that had scared the living daylights out of me. I had read Burke's story, "The Chink and the Child," as who hadn't, and I knew that the Oriental got his revenge for the little girl's death by hiding a snake in the brutal murderer's bed. A weak and limping climax if I ever heard of one—revenge by proxy. Why not a face-to-face confrontation with Battling Burroughs getting his comeuppance by being beaned by a hot flat-iron, or a hatchet, or whatever else would be normally available in a Chinese laundry?

But this was no problem of mine. I had a war to fight, so away I went, this time alone and this time driving right up to the head of the company street. I had had plenty of time to cook up a deep-dyed Machiavellian scheme during the long drive to camp, and when Captain Thompson stepped out of the company office to wonder, in his mild-mannered way, what the hell I meant by driving a private car into government property and who the hell did I think I was, anyway, to expect to maintain my own car in camp and me nothing but a high private in the rear rank and nothing to brag about even at that?

My answer was all set and ready. I suggested most respectfully, sir, that I could leave the car at the main gate, outside the confines of the camp, and that the keys could be left in the company office, thus making the car available to any officers of our company who might want to use it for . . . well, for whatever reasons any young officer might want to visit nearby San Diego. Sir. But only for our own company officers, sir, and if they weren't used to driving this model, I was always right there within sound of the top-kicker's whistle, sir, and I'd be most happy to oblige at any time. Sir.

Hm. I could see his mind working. He'd have the only company in the entire division with its own car. "Suppose somebody busts it up, what then?" he asked, with true military appraisal of the entire situation.

"I have all the insurance on it I can get, sir. Auto Club. See the insignia? The car's protected. And it needs to be used, sir. It really does. Keeps the battery up. And it's a good car, too. Brand-new Paige, 1918 model. Just bought it this summer. Perfect condition. How about it, sir?"

I may have used one or two extra sirs, but the idea sold. He smiled as he thought of the possibilities. For life in the barracks, as Kipling has observed, does not turn men into plaster saints.

"Why, yes, I think that would be satisfactory," he said, trying to conceal his anticipation. "Only one drawback. I don't drive."

"No problem, sir," I reassured him. "I can. And of course I can always be assigned to special duty, can't I, sir? And I'm an excellent driver, sir. Taught by professionals. *Griffith* professionals. May I leave it here, sir? For *company* use?"

I could. And I did. And I never had another hour of K.P., and from that moment I spent more time in San Diego than I did in Camp Kearny, and not wasting it in cheap honky-tonks or slinking up dark alleys the way others of my lowly rank had to do. No, sir. My passengers were officers and gentlemen, and they wouldn't let me spend a cent when I spent my time in town at the U. S. Grant Hotel, the best in town, while the officers were paying their respects, as I guess you'd call it, to an inordinate number of sisters and cousins and aunts, mostly cousins of the gentler sex who had nice apartments .and understanding landladies.

Then came one fateful evening after retreat, when it was quite dark, and when Captain Thompson came to my squad tent, which I shared with seven others. Somebody caught the glint of those two silver bars and barked, " 'Ten-*shun!*"

We all sprang to our feet, including me, even though I had been feeling horribly bad for the past two days. The trouble was that I couldn't keep my feet under me and that I swayed forward and fell into the arms of Captain Thompson, who eased me to the floor of the tent. He felt my forehead briefly and then commanded, "Get an ambulance for this man. On the double!"

I must have fallen into a deep sleep, because I kept dreaming that I was hearing the Chopin Funeral March being played over and over again. Then, when I finally managed to achieve some semblance of awareness, I discovered that I was in a hospital bed along with ranks and ranks of other men, all in bed and all on a very long screened-in porch facing a roadway. It was daylight, and I was at least partially awake, because that Funeral March was being played by a military brass band as it moved slowly along the road, followed by a caisson carrying a flag-draped coffin.

It was hardly out of sight before another cortege came hard on the heels of the first, groaning out that same funeral march. And then another. And another. And this was to go on day after day for the unknowably long time I was destined to stay in that base hospital.

It was the flu, of course, killing without mercy and much more efficiently than the armies on the fighting front.

Battle-front casualties were far outstripped by the wholesale killing of this most deadly of epidemics. Nobody knew what to do about it, except to keep the victims quiet and in the virtual open air of these screened porches. And in the meantime those funeral processions kept streaming past, in plain sight, all alike down to the last detail. Washington had decreed that every soldier, high or low, must have a military funeral: band playing the Funeral March, followed by a flag and color guard, and a casket draped in the colors carried on an artillery caisson.

I was given nothing to eat. I didn't want anything anyway. I got a bunch of badly mauled and faded flowers from my father and mother, delayed I don't know how long in the flood of mail to the sick and dying. I tried to write a note to Edna, but I made a miserable mess of it. A nurse mailed it anyway, perhaps on the theory that hearing something from me was less ominous than hearing nothing.

The first sign that I was going to pull through was when they brought me my first food. It was a single baked potato, drowned in butter. I have searched high and low for the mate of that potato, hoping to taste once again something of its indescribable deliciousness. Perhaps that was the only one of its kind ever grown. If so, I was the one chosen to savor its delights, and there was that certain something about the idea of having been returned to a shattered world that made me feel that the tide had turned and that there was hope for the race of man yet. For if I could do it, anyone could do as well or better.

They released me from that base hospital the instant they thought I could make it on my own and not because I was anywhere near recovery. For the hospital was not only crowded but jammed, with cots and even pallets on the floor crowding every square inch of space. The doctors, commandeered from their civilian practices, had to step over these very sick young men, who were tossing in delirium on mattress pads on the floor. They didn't release me because I was well; they released me because they needed that bed. Desperately.

I was helped into my uniform. Two orderlies supported me to where a crowded ambulance was waiting. I had never seen such a miserable-looking lot in my life. Unshaven for many days, haggard and weak, limp rag dolls with hollow eyes and blistered lips. I ran my hand over my face and realized that I was probably the same as the rest.

They stopped at the head of my company street. I managed to crawl out. The driver asked, "Think you can make it?"

"Aw, sure," I answered, reeling forward and grabbing at the doorway of our company office for support. "Thanks for the ride."

The company clerk saw me holding on to the doorpost. He hurried out and grabbed me by one arm. One of our lieutenants grabbed the other. Between them I was supported into the presence of Captain Thompson, who was seated at his deskload of forms. A crazy thought crossed my befuddled mind. Napoleon was wrong. An army does not march on its belly, it marches on its paper work.

I was eased down into a chair, a lieutenant holding me by one arm, a corporal by the other. I should have saluted, but my arms were being held. Thompson didn't mind. He looked me over and said crisply, "Send this man to convalescent camp."

It was an order. Orders are not to be questioned. But I wasn't thinking straight, so I said, "If the captain will permit, I'd like very much to stay with my own outfit."

Thompson considered this silently. I added impulsively, "I want to stay where I belong. Here. Right here."

That did it. He ordered a tent to be rigged for me at the far end of the company street, well away from anyone else, and there I was placed, with orders to stay put, not to mingle with the others, to take my meals separately, and to rest (repeat, rest) for ten days, more if needed but certainly no less.

So I rested in lonely grandeur, listening to all the bugle calls, from first call in the dark of the winter morning to taps at night, and standing none of them. I took my meals between times, when the mess hall was empty, because I was considered something of a leper, a carrier of a deadly disease, and lacking only a bell to ring as I called, "Unclean! Unclean!" to round out the picture.

Those ten days of rest worked wonders. I was fit for duty and back at the unending job of finding out how to kill people without being killed in the process. The training program now was how to manage hand grenades. This called for a complete re-education in the art of throwing, especially for American boys who had grown up using the wrist-snap of baseball. We had to learn to bowl, as in cricket. But it was all safe enough, although a bit noisy. No danger at all. If anyone chanced to miss his throw and hit the edge of the parapet, causing a live grenade to roll back down, or if he fumbled or dropped the grenade, we were all under strict orders for the nearest man to fall on the grenade and smother it with his body, so that nobody would be hurt.

During all this we were under a constant barrage of rumors, guesses, and suppositions about the state of the war overseas. Most of these flying rumors came from the latrines, where many of our opinions were formed and molded into beliefs. This was no more than natural, because the latrines were the only places we were allowed to sit down.

According to latrine gossip (the army has a more fundamental term for this), the war was just about over. That the Allies had broken through and had the enemy on the run seemed to be well founded in fact, as supported by the maps published in all the newspapers. Then came the celebrated goof-up (there is an army term for this, too) that was called the false armistice, only to be followed two days later by the confirmed news of a real armistice, actually signed and sealed, and a cease-fire ordered for eleven in the morning of November 11, 1918.

And so, Othello's occupation was gone—*poof!*—like that, leaving our whole division all dressed up with no place to go. Oh well; sailor gare, as we were learning to say. The next order of business in everyone's mind was how to get the hell out of there and hightail it for home as soon as possible. Not so much to rejoin our families. There was that, of course. There is always that, as in coming home from a business trip. No, we were not trained economists, but it doesn't take a trained economist to realize that you can't release the five million men we had under arms at the close of the war and have nice fat cushy jobs ready and waiting for each and every one of them. Our places in the business world had been taken by civilians unfit for military duty, or by those of draft age whose number had not been called. The idea was to get back early and avoid the rush for our old jobs.

Now time began *really* to drag. The army as a whole, from here to Washington and points east, was flooded with tons of paper forms requesting discharges. These had to be processed, the claims verified, and everything cleaned up nice and tidy before any honorable discharges could be issued. This took time. You can't possibly imagine how much time this took.

Well, the time had to be put in somehow, so we were all put to work. There were muskets to be cleaned and recleaned to spotless, speckless perfection, after which they were packed away in Cosmoline to sleep in their greasy beds waiting for the next war. We cleaned and packed away everything we had ever used, all to be shipped to some storehouse. When we ran out of things to clean and pack, we were put to work at the sort of job I had heard of but that I had never really believed. I thought it was a gag, a joke. It wasn't.

It seems that back in the bad old days of slavery, when the Old Massa ran into an idle spell between picking and planting cotton, the idea was to divide the slave force into two equal bands: send one bunch out to dig postholes, with the second bunch assigned to follow close after and fill them up again. The reason: the old saw that Satan finds some mischief still for idle hands to do. And so, believe it or not, the army put all ten thousand of us to work with picks and shovels to tear down a hill and to fill up the adjoining valley. And we did it, too. Not with anything you'd call enthusiasm. But we did it. Slowly. Very slowly indeed. We were in no hurry. Nor were our non-coms in charge of the operation, for they were as bored and as sick of this brainless make-work treadmill as we were.

In the fullness of time, after what seemed to be several eternities of waiting, I was called to the company clerk's office to receive my discharge and to sign the various papers required to make the deal stick. I didn't really care *what* I signed. All I could see was that discharge, a piece of paper more precious to me than the original Magna Carta.

I was to travel home by rail. My car had been picked up long since by Larsen, as soon as it had been confirmed that I was in the army base hospital for a long, and perhaps an eternal tour of duty in the adjoining burial ground.

I was on the train early. Not that it mattered. I could wait there as well as I could anywhere else. And besides, it was at the terminal of a branch line built to supply the camp, so I could board it as early as I liked. I was so very early that I had the whole empty train of red-plush day-coach seats to choose from.

The train crew arrived and went about its business of getting up steam. This took quite a while, but I figured that it was better to be three hours early than half a second too late.

We pulled out. I looked out of the rear of the end coach, watching Camp Kearny recede from my sight and my life. There, on the right, stood the stables where my own dear Hortense used to live. I wondered what had ever become of her. After all, she had been guilty of at least two very serious crimes: deserting in time of war, and absconding with government property. I wondered if she'd ever been caught, and if so, if they'd bandaged her eyes and given her a final cigarette before standing her up before the firing squad.

The train gathered speed. There, also on my right, was the big, long, screened-in building of the base hospital, which was still crowded with flu victims, and there was not one but two military funerals passing that porch, groaning out that everlasting Chopin Funeral March, as laid down in the army rules and regulations. It was at that moment that I decided never, never to have a funeral for myself. There was an easy way around all that distressing ceremonial nonsense. Be lost at sea. Simple, easy, direct, and free of cost to anyone.

Camp Kearny passed out of sight, and at my last glimpse of that enormous layout, I made a wish in my heart that had all the fervency of a deeply felt prayer: that I might never see that place again.

It must have been a real prayer because it was granted, absolutely. I had occasion, a few years later, to visit the site of Camp Kearny in the line of business, and there was nothing there, nothing at all. The land was as free and open as it had been before the idea of using it as a camp had ever been thought of. Oh, there were a few little pieces of concrete foundation here and there, and I could locate the parade ground by its mile-square flatness, but everything else was gone. I drove to where we had watered the ground with our sweat, while tearing down a hill to fill up an adjoining valley. I couldn't quite precisely locate the spot. The winter rains had smoothed everything over, and both hill and dale were covered with a lush growth of wild oats and wild radish.

Thus does time cushion the pain of the past with the soothing philosophy of a more mature reflection. "While ye can yet say, *this is the worst*, the worst is not yet," as my favorite poet phrased it. The worst had not happened—yet.

I thought that nonsense of digging down a hill just to keep us busy and out of mischief was pretty silly. But we had it easy: just think of what those poor bastards overseas had to go through, rolling up all that barbed wire ...

∽ 16 ∽

And So, As the Sun Fades
Slowly into the West . . .

*And now, in conclusion, let
me say very briefly . . .*
MOST WELCOME WORDS
OF TONGUE OR PEN

GRIFFITH had said, "See you after the war." So I saw him, immediately upon arriving in Hollywood, as the first order of procedure, even before my family knew I was back in town. Our conversation was nothing if not brief.

"I suppose you want your old job back?"

"Yes, sir."

"You've got it."

End of interview. I marched immediately to my old experiment room, where I had an almost equally brief exchange of words with Bitzer.

"Well, I'm back," I said, tossing my army hat aside.

"You're *what?*"

"Back on the job."

I've never seen anyone quite so infuriated. "We'll just *see* about that!" And he was out of the room, heading at his fastest pace straight for where Griffith was always to be found, the projection room. I was not worried or disturbed. No suspense. For I'd had Griffith's word, which for his kind of gentleman was a matter of honor and thus much more binding than even the shrewdest of Banzhaf's contracts.

Bitzer was back in a very few moments. His naturally dark face was almost purple with rage. He didn't look at me, say anything, or do anything except head for the locked closet where we kept our lenses, hard-to-get chemicals, and film canned for future multiple exposures. He unlocked the closet with a key, found a bottle, and took a good long therapeutic drink. He closed and locked the closet, then grabbed his hat and coat, and made for the gate as fast as he could. I would see no more of him that day, or the next, or the next. Not that it made any difference. Griffith was between pictures, spending all his time cutting his last and preparing for his next, whatever it might chance to be. He had nothing for Bitzer to do, or for me, because he soon left town, probably for New York, where all the financial business was centered.

Then came a period of waiting, with absolutely nothing for me to do. I was paid regularly every payday, in cash, in the familiar small yellow manila pay envelopes. Checks were not used, because the banks didn't trust picture people and the picture people didn't trust banks. The business was all on a strictly cash basis.

The longer I waited and the less I had to do, the less chance I had of doing anything at all. Production was swirling all around me, but I could not be used for so much as one shot as an extra cameraman. They'd hire an outside cameraman for a single day's work, even though I was there on salary and idle.

It took me a long time to find out how or why this could be. The answer, when I finally managed to get to the bottom of it, was clear enough. Anyone using me for any reason at all had to pay my accumulated salary up to date, which came to a considerable sum of money over the weeks. It was cheaper by far to hire outside help. So I was in effect barred from working at all until Griffith returned and found something for me to do. The accumulation meant nothing to him, because he had already paid it. Anything I did for him that turned out to be of value was simply a matter of getting a bit of his own back.

I was now beginning to sympathize most deeply with the plight of those whom I had always considered to be sitting pretty, as we phrased it. Wonderful people at the very top of their profession and world-famous to boot. Lillian Gish, who had performed magnificently in *The Clansman,* cut down to a single scene in *Intolerance,* that of a mystic woman rocking a cradle, while others got all the big fat juicy parts. Seena Owen, whose lush beauty had made earlier pictures the success upon which Griffith's reputation rested, side-tracked indefinitely in favor of whatever newcomer had caught his eye and his imagination. And how about Bobby Harron, and Hank Walthall, and Donald Crisp, to name only a few who had contributed so much to Griffith's fame but who now found themselves hung up on a rack, like so many costumes in the wardrobe room, waiting until it would be time to take them down, dust them off, and use them again?

Most of all I sympathized with the plight of poor old Bitzer, who had started Griffith in the business and who was now being shunted aside by any newcomer who might have a new gimmick, like Sartov with his trick lens, or for that matter, by me—a mere kid with no more brains than to try any-thing and who sometimes—not often, but sometimes—accidentally happened to make something work.

I could understand full well why Bitzer hated my guts, because on the rare occasions when I did manage to come up with something new and strange—once out of fifty or a hundred tries—it showed him up as an old stick-in-the-mud whose best days were over and who was afraid to take the bold chance that was at the heart of every Griffith production. Which was untrue and un-fair. Bitzer had forgotten more about camera work than any other camera-man I had ever heard of. Lillian Gish and Dorothy Gish and Mae Marsh were far and away the finest actresses on the screen, dependably so at any and all times, because they had mastered the great art of making Griffith's dreams come true. And yet they too were sidelined, waiting indefinitely while Grif-fith was spending all his time and energy trying to do what was even for him the impossible: making a silk purse out of a—but no, I'd better not say that. He was trying to make the hopelessly inept Carol Dempster, with her bump-tipped nose, into a superb actress of the quality people were in the habit of seeing in Griffith pictures.

Maybe it was this on-again, off-again policy of his that was making us lose so many good people to other companies, chiefly Famous Players–Lasky, or simply the Lasky studio, as everyone called it. The Lasky studio was a sort of meat-and-potatoes outfit that turned out products for the general market, good run-of-the-mill stuff that satisfied everyone, especially the stockholders. They had their star director in Cecil B. De Mille, who could do whatever he pleased without let or hindrance from the front office because he *was* the front office.

Most of my information about the inner workings of the Lasky studio came from Edna. She was a solidly entrenched member of their stock company, acting under the name of Edna Mae Cooper. She worked mostly for and with De Mille, who was at that time involved in a series of pictures with peculiar titles such as *Old Wives for New, Don't Change Your Husband,* and the like. All strictly high class, dealing with the very rich in rich homes, giving the housewives of the world a good long look at how the upper classes lived and had their troubles the same as everyone else.

According to Edna, the superpower, known as the New York office (mean-ing Adolph Zukor), was busily engaged in trying this and trying that, with the aim of securing famous players in famous plays. There were not enough of either to keep a studio busy turning out product week after week all year long, so it became necessary to create both. This meant taking a chance on whatever talented players or playwrights were hanging around trying to break into pictures. Sometimes they made good, sometimes they didn't. They saved the good ones and built them sky-high through the crafty art of publicity. Florence "Flossy" Vidor was cast for the lead in *Old Wives for New*. The picture was a success, but the New York office (Zukor again) thought she was good but not outstanding. So they took a chance on a relatively unknown member of Sennett's comedy troupe, Gloria Swanson,* to do the lead in *Don't Change Your Husband,* and lo!—another winner.

The one and only surefire money-maker on the lot was Mary Pickford, who had only to shake her curls and look cute to make audiences around the world swoon for joy. Her favorite director was Marshall "Mickey" Neilan, who worked poor Edna all day long and all night long in heavily emotional scenes, twenty-six hours in all. I knew nothing about it until the morning after the ordeal, when Edna called me from the studio and asked if I'd mind coming out to drive her home because she was afraid she couldn't make it up to Hollywood Boulevard to wait for a streetcar.

So I drove out, got her, and delivered her to her mother, who had been up all night waiting and worrying about her. Mrs. Cooper put her girl tenderly to bed, while I drove back home, wondering about the strange ways of people and things.

Others, both men and women, roiled up from the most unlikely places to become directors and stars. Wallace Beery started as a female impersonator, playing burlesque Swedish maids, and became a top-ranking character man. Two of our cameramen, George Hill and Vic Fleming, became top directors. One of our stunt women, Julia Faye, who specialized in jumping out of burning buildings into a fire net, became a permanent fixture with the De Mille organization.

What goes up must come down. The reverse was also true. Bobby Harron had no time to resent being replaced by Dick Barthelmess, because poor Bobby was killed in an accident.**

But either way, the pot was boiling furiously and almost anybody could make good. One of our low-ranking assistants, George Beranger, was happy to earn eating money by carrying Griffith's thermos bottle of ice water so it would be close at hand whenever wanted, and Griffith's stagey voice crying,

---

* Between Sennett and De Mille, Miss Swanson starred in several pictures for Triangle, with such directors as Jack Conway, Albert Parker, and Frank Borzage. DEWITT BODEEN

** Harron died on September 5, 1920. Griffith had already supervised his departure to the Goldwyn company. KEVIN BROWNLOW

"Berangeh! Me thermos flahsk!" was a familiar sound on every hot day of shooting. But Beranger was caught in a sudden updraft, and he became André de Beranger overnight, much valued as a unique type of comedian.

During all this I was sidelined, idle, and as much out of pictures as though I had never been in the business at all. Not that I was immobilized. I was working and working hard on the steep uphill job of trying to educate myself, especially in the field of photography, with special emphasis on color, sound, and some sort of practical anybody-can-run-it, color-sound positive print that could be shown as effectively in little towns like Boiled Egg or Pillgarlic as in the Capitol Theater in New York.

It was a hopeless quest so far as any practical results were concerned, because I lacked the money, the influence, and, most of all, any possible demand for a color-sound system, even if one could have been developed. Nobody wanted anything that might upset the fantastically prosperous applecart of movies as they were. But it gave me something to do; my home laboratory was so filled to overflowing with experiments in progress that there was little room for anything else. This was aptly illustrated one evening when Edna was having dinner with us and she wanted to wash her hands; my mother had to tell her apologetically, "I'm sorry, but you'll have to use the kitchen sink, because Karl has the bathroom full of things drying, the tub full of things washing, and the washbasin crowded with funny-looking prints in all different colors. I *do* hope he finds what he's looking for pretty soon, because I'm getting awfully tired of taking sponge baths here in the kitchen."

I know I was a dreadful nuisance, but there were things I had to find out. Not new things, but old, like the Lippmann process, developed way back sometime in the eighties, which reproduced color, not through the use of dyes but through delivering the exact color in the form of wave lengths. It was a wonderful process, but it had one crippling defect. The negative had to be reversed to positive, and this reversed negative could be viewed only by light reflected by a bath of mercury. Too bad. There were other existing color processes actually on the market and available at our largest photo-supply shop, Howland and Dewey, on Broadway near Fifth. They carried the Dufay Dioptochrome plates and filters, these being plates ruled with very fine lines of the primary colors. Expose through these filters, print the negative on a lantern plate, then view against a light box with another ruled filter of red, green, and violet, adjusting until everything came into line and the right colors came through, and there you were. Seal it with gummed black paper tape called passe-partout, and you have one—count 'em—one positive plate in approximate color which could be projected or viewed by transmitted light.

Far and away the most popular of all the commercial color processes was the

Lumière Autochrome, in which grains of starch, dyed in the three primary colors and mixed in the proper proportion, were dusted on a sticky plate, flattened into a lot of very small filters scattered hit or miss, and then flowed with a panchromatic emulsion. Expose through the glass side, develop as usual, but instead of using a fixing bath, use a sulphuric acid-potassium permanganate solution to destroy the silver image, after which the unexposed emulsion is brought into white light, then developed into a positive that—with luck—produced an image that looked almost as if it were in color. It could be used for reproduction through three-color printing processes in publications or projected, but that's all.

I wasn't getting any further, but I was at least catching up with the past.

Griffith returned! That exclamation point expresses about how we all felt. Life could begin again, we thought. Instead, he had returned for the purpose of opening his long-delayed *Broken Blossoms* at Clune's Auditorium.

I had never seen the picture, except for that one scene I had been borrowed from the army to do, but I had heard all about it from those who seemed to know. It was that most hopeless of all hopeless things to offer to an amusement-crazy audience, a tragedy. No run to the rescue, nobody saved in the nick of time, nothing but a grim recital of a brute who beats his child to death because the only one who had ever shown the slightest admiration for her was this contemptible, pigtailed Chinese. What a dish to set before people out for a lighthearted evening of entertainment.

But people were eager to see it all the same. Tickets for the opening were grabbed, with no more to be had, even from speculators. However, I knew everyone in the publicity department and I managed to wheedle enough of the spares that they always held back for very important people to get seats for my family, which included Edna and her mother, plus two more which I was determined to send to Al Wyckoff, the man who had given me my second job in pictures, Leezer being the first.

This was not an entirely disinterested generosity. Al Wyckoff had known me almost from the first; Al Wyckoff had the hire-and-fire of cameramen at the Lasky studio, and although I had but one scene in *Broken Blossoms,* I wanted him to see that one scene, just in—well, just in case, for my contract had run out.

The great night came. The place was crowded to the rafters with everybody who was anybody in Hollywood, plus not a few from New York, newspaper people and magazine reviewers. The hour came for the lights to dim and the curtain to rise.

But no lights dimmed and no curtains rose. For some reason Griffith had become entranced by the music of a balalaika orchestra he had heard in New

York, and nothing would do but that particular orchestra to play *his* idea of the only music for *Broken Blossoms*. The train bringing this orchestra to Los Angeles was late, delayed by some trifling accident or other. Our company cars were waiting at the Arcade station to rush them to the theater, but there was no train, no Russians, no balalaikas, nothing but a chalked notice on the bulletin board stating that the train was one hour and fourteen minutes late at Barstow.

And so we waited, and waited, with those of us from the Griffith studio sweating blood, while the others sat glued grimly to their seats, determined to see this picture for better or worse, if it took all night. I couldn't help wondering what in the hell he wanted a Russian balalaika orchestra for in a story dealing with Limehouse.

Finally the Russians, beards and all, dressed in their shabby traveling clothes and not in the proper black ties of any decent orchestra, began to poke their heads up through the little doorway that led into the orchestra pit. A sigh of relief swept through the audience. The Russians spread out, taking whatever seats were handy. There was no score. They were going to play their own music, learned by heart, under the direction of a leader I had never seen before. The houselights dimmed, but not entirely so. Instead of darkness, the entire auditorium was suffused with a strange, unearthly blue that seemed to come from everywhere—from the chandelier, from spots ranged along the balconies, from the footlights. There was something eerily supernatural about it.

The balalaikas began to whimper a strange, haunting, shimmering melody. I could not place it, although I knew Russian music quite well. It must have been some traditional folk tune not yet committed to paper and to the improvements of Western-trained arrangers and instrumentalists. The big curtain whispered upward, revealing the screen, which was not at all white but bathed in that strange, all-suffusing blue coming from spots arranged around the inside of the proscenium arch.

Then the picture came on in a slow fade that revealed the scene I had been released from the army to make—but with *what* a difference. I had seen it in a black-painted little projection room on a white screen with black edges and in silence broken only by the whirring of the projection machine.

This was a vision of gold swimming in misty blue, a vision that seemed to reach on and on and on, far and away, as far as the mind could reach. The shimmering music echoed the shimmering of the water. The slow movement of the river was the endless motion of time itself. You could hear a gasp from the audience at the impact of pure beauty.

My mother, seated next to me, reached over and gripped my arm strongly. Pride and warmth and exultation were in that grip. It was praise beyond praise.

And yet I could feel no pride, no personal anything. For it was not my scene at all. I tried to think of how many men had been responsible. The men on the beach who had known how to set up the ground rows of the battleships. Cash Shockey, who knew how to paint them with the exact gray that would match the foggy horizon. Fireworks Wilson, who knew how to find and give me the right kind of squibs to duplicate the effect of distant gunfire. Of Hall, who had shown me all about perspective and how to use it. Of Charlie Baker, who knew exactly how to paint Limehouse so it would *be* Limehouse and no mistake. Of Abe Scholtz, who had produced a perfect negative, and of Joe Aller, whose idea of using a blue tone and a golden highlight must surely have given Griffith the inspiration of making his opening sequence a mystical vision of blue and gold. What had I done? What had I really done? I had turned the handle. Nothing else? Oh yes, I had sprinkled a little flash powder on the water, to get the reflections. That was *my* contribution. Nothing more. Unless you count time. That scene had not been made in one week. It had taken five years, beginning with the moment when Perley Poore Sheehan had shown me how to make a painted title card look real by the simple application of a smooth coat of fine varnish to what would otherwise have been a dull-gray wash drawing. Five years. A long time to learn how to make one simple little scene, made glorious by Griffith's inspired stagecraft.

The picture itself unfolded as an example of how close a film can come to perfection. Every note rang true. And what's more, every person in that audience knew it. They knew through something as mysterious as instinct itself. For the abysmal brute has always existed, and Battling Burrows was not Donald Crisp but an archetype of ignorant power exulting in cruelty for cruelty's sake. Lillian Gish was not a poor cringing slavey after all but a creature of exquisite beauty thrown by some unknowable fate into the grip of a monster. Dick Barthelmess was not a Chinese laundryman but a gentle, sensitive, poetic soul who could ignore the slime and stench of his surroundings to become lost in adoration of a single blossom, rapt in the mystery of so lovely a thing coming into being all by itself, out of nothing but dirt and water and a little sun.

The performances were fantastically wonderful. For it *was* a fantasy, a dream, a vision of archetypical beings out of the long inherited memory of the human race. No such people as we saw on the screen were ever alive in the workaday world of today or of any other day. They were, as Griffith had explained to me in that dark projection room, misty, misty . . . They were the creatures of a poetic imagination that had at very long last found its outlet in its own way in its own terms. It was a parable in poetry, timeless and eternally true, because it touched the deepest recesses of all who were there.

It was all very well for Keats to announce that truth was beauty and beauty truth. People knew that truth is brutality and violent death, and they were seeing it as they knew it to be. Truth is also adoration of the beautiful, and they knew that, too, if only in the childhood memory of some precious fleeting moment of purest delight.

The story itself was not a tragedy, no matter what the Hollywood wiseacres had said. The girl died, yes; but she died to become an object of profoundest worship in a cheap dive with but a single worshipper, a lowly Chinese kneeling in adoration before her flower-embowered bier.

The picture closed as it had begun, with that blue vision of the mysterious river of time, forever flowing yet forever the same, with the shimmering of the balalaikas dying away to silence.

The reaction of that crowded house was the ultimate in applause—a stunned silence of the deeply moved. This lasted a moment, and then came a spontaneous roar of sound, people on their feet shattering the air, hands smiting hands, voices crying "Bravo, bravo," and the walls loud with the echoed uproar.

This went on and on, until finally Griffith appeared, a small, frail figure all in black and seeming to be very tiny at the edge of that big proscenium. He said nothing. He let the waves sweep over him for a moment and then he was gone; the houselights came on and the audience began to leave, full of overflowing talk about the miracle they had witnessed.

Outside, they seemed to be reluctant to leave. They all had so much to say to one another that they crowded the sidewalk and overflowed into the street, reliving each moment of the picture in their own terms, ranging from the professional verdict of the case-hardened producers, "Well, the Old Man has got himself another knockout," to a dear old lady dabbing her eyes and declaring to a young woman, evidently her granddaughter, "I've never cried so much in all my life, not even when Willie died!"

The reviews were all but unbelievably exultant. Our publicity department collected them with the greediness of a miser adding to his gold. The reviews from London were especially wonderful, and to my somewhat embarrassed surprise, they picked on the single scene I had made as being the "exquisite vignette" that opened and closed the picture as the supreme example of Bitzer at his unapproachable best. They could find no words of praise fine enough to compliment Griffith on his meticulously accurate reproduction of Limehouse down to its tiniest detail. This was something no American should be capable of doing, because one must live in such a place for a lifetime to capture its inner spirit and not merely its outward appearance. And yet he had done it. They knew because London was their city. They even located the exact spot where the camera had been placed to take that opening "exquisite vignette." It was taken from Wapping Old Stairs.

No mention of Charlie Baker, who had made all of this mint-perfect accuracy possible through his drawings. And of course no mention of me, because I had not really been on the picture at all, except for that one scene. But Bitzer got—and deserved—the highest possible praise for the finest photography ever placed upon any screen. Perhaps that bad experience of having been sidelined while Sartov took his place had spurred him to surpass himself. As for Sartov, I never saw the picture he had made for Griffith,* but I did see the press books with their all but hopeless efforts to sell what they called the misty magic of the screen. It was misty, all right. I had examined a few of the cutouts and they looked as though they had been shot through a lantern plate smeared with Vaseline.

Broken Blossoms was no longer derided as *Busted Posies*. Instead, having been any part of that masterpiece was an honor to be worn with pride. Then a disquieting rumor swept the studio. It began as a vague guess, firmed into common knowledge, and finally crystallized into a grim certainty. Griffith was going to move his organization, bag and baggage, back East to a place called Mamaroneck, not far from Whitestone, where I had happened to blunder into the picture business.

It put me in a very difficult position. That I was slated to go with him was a certainty, because Banzhaf had mailed me a new contract, drawn up in his own puncture-proof style. Griffith had already signed it. It required only my signature to make it binding. One little scratch of the pen and I was sure of a job for another stretch of years. And it would be my hand and my pen this time, because I was over twenty-one and no mother could make up my mind for me.

It was that hardest of all possible struggles, the struggle one has to fight with oneself. There were powerful influences in opposition: security and money if I signed, freedom and home if I did not. Not my old home with Father and Mother and Lily and Ida Belle but a brand-new home of my own, or, more accurately, *our* home, because Edna had finally, after two years of hard trying on my part, consented to marry me.

Now this contract, if signed, would change all that. Edna had worked long and hard to gain a firm foothold in the Lasky studio. I could not in conscience ask her to give this up for the vague chance of perhaps doing something for Griffith. So I would have to go alone, and to what? Money instead of happiness, security instead of freedom. I had seen quite enough of what security does to people. It's a sort of slavery, a surrender of individual initiative to the whim

* Sartov worked on several pictures for Griffith; I cannot agree with Karl Brown's judgment of him. KEVIN BROWNLOW

of whoever is the Big Boss. And if that Big Boss happens to be a genius, as Griffith most assuredly was, it becomes a matter of confusion thrice confounded. It has been said that genius is hard to live with. *I* say it's impossible.

This contract was much more than a small sheaf of typewritten pages stapled together with a blue backing. It was Griffith's hand, offered in good faith and firm friendship. How could I bring myself to slap it away, or even worse, insultingly ignore it? I had come to him as an awkward kid with two left feet, three whiskers, and a pimple; eager, inept, and forever bumping into people in my headlong rush to get from here to there. He had taken me under his wing, so to speak, and he had *paid* me to make the mistakes through which everyone has to learn, for there is no other way. If I had given him five years of my life, he had evened the score by giving me five equal years of his patient, wise, inspiring training, not by words but by example. He had made me from nothing into something.

I knew absolutely that I had become something because Al Wyckoff had written me a letter of such extravagant praise for that one scene in *Broken Blossoms* that my mother had claimed it and had hidden it away among her most precious private treasures. She, too, had had more than a small hand in the matter, giving me life and molding my character into whatever it now was and would continue to be. Yes, continue—or she'd break my damned neck. Nobody could let *her* down. That letter from Wyckoff had become her diploma, her proof of a job well done or, to change the figure, her White Plume, to be worn as proudly as any of Cyrano's.

I had lived for five years in the shadow of that rarest of human beings, a dedicated gentleman whose simple word, witnessed or not, was to him a matter of honor, never to be broken. Some of this had seeped into me through the familiar process of like master, like man. How could I bring myself to refuse an offer so generously meant? If I had been half a man I would have gone to him, explained my predicament, made my position clear, and had it out with him. But I had been a man in the eyes of the law for only six or eight months, so I was only a beginner, an untried apprentice, unsure of myself and bewildered in the face of a crucial decision.

I took the coward's way out. Instead of facing up to the decision boldly, I simply mailed the contract, unsigned, back to Banzhaf. *Jacta est alea:* the die had been cast. How it would turn out nobody could foresee. Again to change the figure, maybe I had taken the wrong crossroad. There was no telling. But I was able to dredge up one small crumb of comfort. I had braved myself to the point of doing something unprecedented: I had refused a Griffith contract. Probably nobody had ever done that before. It made me feel a little better, but not much.

I stood on the same old steps to see them leave. It was as it had been way back on the fateful day in 1913, only in reverse. The same people, the same parade of cars, only this time headed in the other direction. The same swarming crowd, only this time to see them go, not arrive. The little string of cars pulled away, headed by Griffith in his big blue Fiat, driven by frozen-faced Mac. They disappeared around the curve of Sunset Boulevard, gone perhaps forever.

The studio, now grown to giant proportions, was like a great dead sprawling monster. The body was there, but the heart was still and the soul departed. I couldn't stand it. I went home and tried to forget. It was no go. Nobody could forget Griffith. Nobody ever has.

My marriage to Edna took place soon after. She was surpassingly lovely in her pure white, girlishly informal wedding dress, a gift from Geraldine Farrar. Like all divas, La Farrar was a stickler for propriety. White satin is all very well for a young woman's formal church wedding but not for a young girl in her own home. So it was white chiffon with a pleated skirt. I was so proud of her that there was no room left in me for nervousness. I didn't even forget the ring, which was of platinum paved with diamonds, not half good enough for her but the best our leading jeweler, Brock's, could supply. So it would have to do.

Lois Wilson was there as bridesmaid, with Wanda Hawley as matron of honor. Hawley, her husband, served as best man, a matter that momentarily bothered me, because I had heard a story in which the bride suddenly changed her mind and married the Best Man.* But he was already married, so I was safe on that score at least.

Everything went without a hitch, even though there had been no rehearsal. I wondered, halfway through the wedding breakfast, how everybody could have been so letter-perfect in their parts, so free and easy and confident, until it came to me, belatedly as usual, that we had all seen weddings played before the cameras so often that this was just another retake of a familiar routine. The only departure from the cut-and-dried procedure was that my father kept pinching the minister's wine, downing it at a gulp, and then calling loudly for more wine for His Reverence.

The breakfast was soon over, and we left our respective old homesteads to found one of our own. Securely armed with the blithe ignorance of youth and filled with the bright fallacy of boundless hope, we ventured forth together toward fresh woods and pastures new.

* This was at a nudist wedding. (Author)

Index

Index

Index

D.W. Griffith

Billy Bitzer

Lillian Gish

Fred B. Hamer

George Fawcett

Joseph Henabery

G.W. Bitzer

Dorothy Gish

Josephine Crowell

G.E. Bidwell

Donald Crisp

Carl Brown

Bobby Harron

Air Smith

Clyde

R.S. Smith

James E. Smith

Robert Harron

Freda Loeffler

John Pfahlerm

Allen A. Fernandez

Frank Wortman

J.C. Epperman

Chas Thomen

Holmes

Max Davidson

Minnie Frey

Holmes

J.Q. Jorey

Jack Lloyd

G. [illegible] W.F. + J.E.E. Taylor